Indigenous Passages to Cuba, 1515–1900

UNIVERSITY PRESS OF FLORIDA

Florida A&M University, Tallahassee
Florida Atlantic University, Boca Raton
Florida Gulf Coast University, Ft. Myers
Florida International University, Miami
Florida State University, Tallahassee
New College of Florida, Sarasota
University of Central Florida, Orlando
University of Florida, Gainesville
University of North Florida, Jacksonville
University of South Florida, Tampa
University of West Florida, Pensacola

INDIGENOUS PASSAGES TO CUBA, 1515–1900

JASON M. YAREMKO

University Press of Florida

Gainesville · Tallahassee · Tampa · Boca Raton

Pensacola · Orlando · Miami · Jacksonville · Ft. Myers · Sarasota

First cloth printing, 2016
First paperback printing, 2020

25 24 23 22 21 20   6 5 4 3 2 1

Library of Congress Cataloging-in-Publication Data
Names: Yaremko, Jason M., 1961- author.
Title: Indigenous passages to Cuba, 1515-1900 / Jason M. Yaremko.
Description: Gainesville : University Press of Florida, [2016] | 2016. |
Includes bibliographical references and index.
Identifiers: LCCN 2016004175 | ISBN 9780813062808 (cloth : alk. paper)
ISBN 9780813068435 (pbk.)
Subjects: LCSH: Indigenous peoples—Cuba—History. |
Immigrants—Cuba—History. | Cuba—Emigration and immigration—History. |
North America—Emigration and immigration—History. |
Cubans—Migrations—History. | Cuba—Colonization—History.
Classification: LCC F1769 .Y37 2016 | DDC 305.897/07291—dc23
LC record available at http://lccn.loc.gov/2016004175

The University Press of Florida is the scholarly publishing agency for the State
University System of Florida, comprising Florida A&M University, Florida Atlantic
University, Florida Gulf Coast University, Florida International University, Florida
State University, New College of Florida, University of Central Florida, University of
Florida, University of North Florida, University of South Florida, and University of
West Florida.

University Press of Florida
2046 NE Waldo Road
Suite 2100
Gainesville, FL 32609
http://upress.ufl.edu

For Cheryl, always.

CONTENTS

ACKNOWLEDGMENTS

I would like to acknowledge the support of the Social Sciences and Humanities Research Council of Canada, which provided the funding that enabled me to conduct the research for this study. At the same time, as important as funding undeniably is, it is incomplete without a network of human support to augment it, to make it work, in this case, over a number of borders, in several countries. This complex exists at various levels, from the institutional to the emotional and/or personal, and although there are too many people to name here, it does not lessen my gratitude toward them. It includes those people working in archives and other repositories in Cuba, among them the Archivo Nacional de Cuba, the Archivo del Museo de la Ciudad de La Habana, the Archivo Histórico Provincial de Matanzas, the Biblioteca Nacional José Martí, and the Instituto de Literatura y Lingüística. I am very grateful to the directors and staffs of these repositories. I also want to give thanks to the Archivo General de la Nación in Mexico City and for the research support that facilitated the work there. In Spain, many thanks go to the director and staff of the Archivo General de Indias in Seville as well as to the Archivo Histórico Nacional and the Biblioteca Nacional de España in Madrid. In the United States, my thanks go to the good people of the William Clements Library in Ann Arbor, Michigan, who enabled me to gather and cite from documents in the Thomas Gage Papers. Thanks also to Daniel Schafer, coordinator of the University of North Florida's *Florida History Online*, and James Hill, translator of selected documents from the Archivo General de Indias made available on the FHO web page "The Indian Frontier in British East Florida: Spanish Correspondence Concerning the Uchiz Indians, 1771–1783," for permission to cite from some of these translations included in chapter 2.

In Cuba I benefited immensely from the support and guidance of colleagues and friends at the University of Havana. I am particularly grateful to Francisca "Paquita" López Civeira, Edelberto Leiva, and Sergio Guerra Vilaboy of the Faculty of Philosophy and History. Professors Guerra and, in Mexico, Carlos Bojórquez Urzaiz of the Universidad de Oriente, Yucatan shared their knowledge, insight, and support for publication of some of this research (*Chacmool*). Closer to home, the manuscript benefited greatly from the scrutiny of the reviewers: thanks go to Maximilian C. Forte and Cynthia Radding. Other *colegas*, like my mentor Timothy Anna, along with Mark Meuwese, Roland Bohr, Jennifer Brown, and John Worth, reviewed individual chapters in various forms and gave generously of their knowledge. Still other friends and colleagues have played significant roles in the evolution of this work; these include David Burley, Jorge Nallim, Nolan Reilly, Cristina Díaz, Carlos Alzugaray, Gustavo Velasco, Eliakim Sibanda, and Hal Klepak.

I also wish to thank the people at the University Press of Florida for their interest and support in the various stages of this project. I wish to thank former senior editor Amy Gorelick for beginning this journey with me and Erika Stevens, who has proven more than capable in providing guidance the rest of the way. Thanks also go to project editor Eleanor Deumens.

Limited portions of my essay "'Frontier Indians': 'Indios Mansos,' 'Indios Bravos,' and the Layers of Indigenous Existence in the Caribbean Borderlands," in *Borderlands in World History: 1700–1914*, edited by Paul Readman, Cynthia Radding, and Chad Bryant (London: Palgrave Macmillan, 2014), are reproduced with permission of Palgrave Macmillan. I wish to thank the Canadian Association for Latin American and Caribbean Studies for permission to reprint portions from my article "Colonial Wars and Indigenous Geopolitics: Aboriginal Agency, the Cuba-Florida-Mexico Nexus, and the Other Diaspora," in the *Canadian Journal of Latin American and Caribbean Studies* 35, no. 70 (2011): 165–96. Parts of chapters 4 and 5 of the present work appear in "'Los Indios de Campeche': The Maya Diaspora and the Mesoamerican Presence in Colonial Cuba," in *Cuban Archaeology in the Caribbean*, edited by Ivan Roksandic (Gainesville: University Press of Florida, 2016).

Of course, neither I nor this work would exist if not for my family. Many thanks go to my parents, Mike and Sylvia (who actually do read my stuff), and to my extended family, especially to Marlene, the soulful survivor and family matriarch. Finally, to my daughter, Erin, and son, Jeffrey, two of my biggest supporters and sources of hope, thank you. And most of all, to the heart and soul of this human network, *mi vida*, Cheryl, for whom I am eternally grateful and can never give thanks enough, but will keep trying.

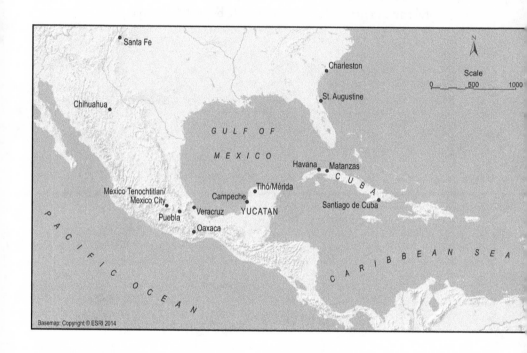

INTRODUCTION

David J. Robinson observes in his introduction to the important volume *found everywhere* *Migration in Colonial Spanish America* that migration was a "ubiquitous phenomenon." It was "one important way in which the very colonial world of Spanish America was created. The diffusion of Spanish immigrants throughout the continent . . . triggered a migrational response on the part of the aboriginal Indians. . . . Invasion and immigration for whites often meant retreat, and emigration for Indians."[1] While migration was ubiquitous and seminal, it was also highly differentiated, as "each and every individual migrant moved for specific and, for us, still obscure reasons."[2] Only those migrants "who left a trail of evidence, or crossed boundaries important enough to be noted in the documentation of the time, or created serious problems for those charged with maintaining colonial rule, are recoverable. The many millions of migrants thus have to be represented by the few thousands that we can extract from the opaque colonial records."[3] The geographical focus for Robinson's statement is the American continents, the foci of indigenous migrations overwhelmingly within the continents and, to a considerably lesser extent, from the mainland to the Caribbean basin.

One of my core objectives in this book is also to examine the dynamic of migrations in Spanish America during the colonial period, with a difference. I follow a series of movements and migrations from their origins in several regions of North America into the Caribbean basin and to the largest island in the Caribbean, Cuba. The central agents of this story are the indigenous peoples of New Spain and its northern provinces (the present-day southeastern and southwestern United States as well as Mexico), thousands of whom traveled independently as traders, diplomats, missionary candidates, and as immigrants and refugees; some journeyed to Cuba, forcibly transported as captives—as slaves, indentured laborers, and prisoners of war. It is noteworthy that many of those who migrated involuntarily remained in Cuba. As immigration history, this study engages a unique and understudied perspective, that of an Amerindian diaspora from the North American continent to the Caribbean region.

Homeland to the descendants of the indigenous Arawak Taíno peoples, Cuba also served, over the half millennia after contact, as the principal destination and residence of indigenous peoples as diverse as the Yucatec Maya of Mexico, the Calusa, Timucua, Creek, and Seminole of Florida, and those of the Apache and Puebloan cultures of the northern provinces of New Spain. Many settled in pueblos or villages in Cuba that endured and evolved into the nineteenth century as autonomous municipalities and other urban centers later populated by indigenous and immigrant Amerindian descendants and their mestizo (mixed-blood) progeny. In many cases, these were journeys begun long before the arrival of the colonizers. In the present volume, however, I focus on the postcontact period and on a history that remains largely off the historiographical radar: that of the journeys of numerous indigenous individuals, groups, and communities to the largest island in the Caribbean and their multifaceted and dynamic experiences of survival, adaptation, resistance, and negotiation within Cuban colonial society.

With the establishment of the first permanent European settlement in the Western Hemisphere in 1496 at Santo Domingo (present-day Dominican Republic) and the conquest of Cuba more than a decade later, the Caribbean became the first theater of sustained European-indigenous encounters in what became known as the Americas. After the conquest of Mexico in 1521, the Caribbean colonial towns and settlements that had been until that time multiplying and growing underwent a considerable drain and decline as thousands of Spanish colonists embarked on an exodus to the continents. This provided a considerable respite for exploited indigenous peoples like the Arawak Taíno, who came to represent a majority in a number of these towns, especially in Cuba. At the same time, the imperial shift from the Caribbean to the continents meant that many indigenous peoples encountered by Europeans in Mexico and North America struggled under the impact of conquest and colonization. As European empires penetrated and imperial competition intensified, indigenous peoples adapted economically, politically, and culturally to the changes in defense of their own interests. During an ensuing era of colonial wars, mass European migrations, and continuing colonization, migrations in the opposite direction were increasingly undertaken by the continent's indigenous peoples. In this context, Cuba was viewed historically as a frontier outpost, gateway into the Americas, and key to the defense of the Spanish American empire. The island colony played a crucial role in the lives of increasing numbers of the hemisphere's indigenous peoples. This entailed a range of needs and interests that encompassed labor, trade, diplomacy, education, refuge, settlement, war, and even religion or faith. By the late eighteenth century, as a result of disease and colonial wars, the overwhelming majority of the indigenous peoples of Florida had fled to Cuba. Likewise, by the late nineteenth and early twentieth centuries, indigenous peoples from various regions of the southern United States and Mexico were (and still are) to be found in Cuba. This is the broader scope of a study that encompasses, chronologically, the early sixteenth to late nineteenth centuries while at the same time focusing on specifically identified and defined groups in overlapping colonial, geopolitical or imperial, and national contexts.

This book, therefore, addresses the various movements and migrations including the "other," Amerindian, diaspora (as opposed to the west Indian, African, or Chinese), that have also played important roles in identity formation in Cuban and Caribbean history. By no means definitive, it is an historical survey with all the attendant strengths and weaknesses. In addition to Amerindian journeys for trade, diplomatic, and other missions, I endeavor to examine what James Clifford described as "tribal predicaments," that is, specific historical processes in which indigenous peoples become diasporic: dispersed communities of peoples who share common experiences of dispossession, displacement, alienation, adaptation, and so on.[4]

First Nations peoples do, as Clifford puts it, "occupy the autochthonous end of a spectrum of indigenous attachments": peoples who "deeply belong" and have a sense of rootedness in the land—"precisely what diasporic peoples have lost."[5] Yet, although indigenous claims to aboriginality and First Nationhood may appear to be based on stationary or immobile bonds to the land since time immemorial, this is a simplistic understanding that ignores the fact that Amerindian peoples have never been merely "local": they have always been "rooted and routed in particular landscapes, regional and interregional networks."[6] Furthermore, as a result of the sustained assault on indigenous sovereignty by colonialism and later by emerging nation-states and transnational capital, many indigenous cultures were forced to survive under extreme conditions of displacement, dispossession, dispersal, relocation, and adaptation.[7] Indigenous communities, therefore, have long possessed a diasporic dimension as part of an array of adaptive responses to threats to their existence.

Although the Amerindian diasporic dynamic has undergone increasingly intensive study, particular focus has concentrated on a broad range of indigenous peoples under colonialism in the American continents. The problem, then, is a matter of focus. Until recently, Cuba and the Caribbean played no significant part in this history, save for their role as a launching base for Spanish expeditions into the continents. Nor, until recently, was Cuba considered to have what might be termed an indigenous history, at least not one that reached substantively beyond the first century of the early colonial period, and in which more archaeologists than historians were active (Felipe Pichardo Moya being perhaps the lone Cuban exception). And while historians and other scholars have established that human migration is a significant part of Cuban history, the overriding historical emphasis has remained on European, Cuban, African, and even Chinese in- and outmigration. In the present study I attempt to fill a significant gap in the historical record: to demonstrate the substantial potential not only for a study of Amerindian peoples in Cuba but also of another, to-date understudied dimension of diaspora history: that of the movement and migration of Amerindian peoples from the continental Americas to the largest island in the Caribbean.

The history of this aboriginal migratory process is in fact extensive, reaching from the sixteenth through the nineteenth centuries, and involves a range of conditions under and responses to growing European influences, from diplomacy to voluntary immigration to forced migration. While European colonialism, expansionism, and nationalism represent fundamental factors behind these migrations, as does indigenous adaptability, the end results of these journeys were as varied as the specific circumstances that generated them. That is to say that Amerindian individuals, families, and communities came to Cuba under various conditions. Notably, the evidence strongly suggests that, whether voluntarily or involuntarily, many Amerindians remained in Cuba as part of a diasporic process that endured well into the late nineteenth century but one that had its beginnings, under colonialism in the Americas, very shortly after Spanish landings in the Caribbean.

As a history of transculturation, this study also traces the movements and migrations of indigenous peoples to Cuba, homeland to the first indigenous culture to meet Columbus, imperial Spain's second colony in the "New World," and middle ground for European and Amerindian—indigenous and regional—encounters. This research relies to a considerable extent for its framework on a revised and expanded version of the Bolton school of borderland studies pioneered by Herbert E. Bolton, designating borderlands as the contested boundaries between colonial and cultural domains. As noted, this research draws on the scholarly consensus concerning borderlands and diasporic and/or migration studies but expands on these to include understudied regions, peoples, and processes. Current conventional borderlands studies continue to emphasize continental populations to the effective exclusion of other peoples and regions. While the middle ground conceived by Richard White is being studied in the context of Great Lakes interculturation, this is decidedly not the case for areas like the very palpable middle ground that encompasses the peoples of the continents in relation to the Caribbean.

With respect to the more complex question of transculturation, Matthew Restall has pointed out that both the "persistent myth . . . shared by imperialists and many (Western) critics of imperialism of a single decisive conquest, occupation, or establishment of colonial power" and the more binary-oriented perspective on cultural history that romanticizes indigenous resistance and cultural persistence in absolute form have only very recently begun to be transcended by research based on a more nuanced understanding of "the interculturation process." This approach incorporates the new understanding of the middle ground as "that fascinating grey zone of ethnic interaction" and "gradual spectrum of mixed-up differences."[8] Restall's research has been reinforced by Stephen Aron, Susan Kellogg, Steve Stern, David J. Weber, John Kicza, Cynthia Radding, Marie-Areti Hers, and Cecilia Sheridan Prieto, among other scholars. At the same time, the focus of these more recent studies has been and continues to be on the Mesoamerican and Andean regions and their indigenous inhabitants in a manner that thus far has tended to overlook other groups, movements, and/or migrations beyond the interior, over a broader geographical area, and their impacts on the interculturation process.

Within these middle-ground spaces, imperial European governments sent their diplomatic and Christian missions, but so too did the *indígenas*.

Indigenous peoples responded to imperial European geopolitics, but empires also had to take into account the geopolitics of Amerindian rivalries and relationships. If European imperial politics eventually prevailed over those of indigenous peoples, this did not occur without influencing to some degree the imperial government and colonial membership while also affecting interculturation among Amerindians at the microcosmic level, ultimately contributing to questions of global events and local effects and outcomes. If this now appears as a truism for histories of the continents, it remains a question in serious need of study in the indigenous Caribbean.

To the extent that the prevailing "borderlands" literature centers on indigenous migration, it has been overwhelmingly limited to studies of the dynamic of movements of indigenous peoples within constituted national boundaries, while a few others transcend those boundaries yet remain landlocked, that is, in regions within the continents. With too few exceptions, extracontinental studies, for the most part, continue to be limited to the precolonial period, the domain of archaeology. My focus in this study is the dynamic of Amerindian movements and migrations from the continents and into the Caribbean after 1492, journeys undertaken in the wake of European invasion, imperial geopolitics, and colonialism; it also encompasses a context in which by the nineteenth century, waning imperial powers like Spain confronted newly independent republics like the United States and Mexico. Whether in the context of colonialism, imperialism, incipient republicanism, or nationalism or under circumstances when all converged simultaneously, and whether indigenous peoples were forcibly relocated and transported as slaves, prisoners, or indentured laborers or freely embarked on their own journeys, missions, and diasporas, they were never passive objects merely acted upon but cognizant agents exercising some means or degree of power or influence and acting in their own interests and those of their families and communities. In the foundational and important but landlocked borderlands historiography of the continents, this argument has been well documented and is well established. The same cannot be said for the borderland spaces in between *tierra firme* and the Caribbean.

In the case of histories of indigenous migrations to Cuba and the Caribbean, this remains fertile ground the surface of which, to date, has been merely scratched and in great need of cultivation. Beyond Christon Archer's 1973 article on Apache deportation and Moisés González Navarro's earlier brief explorations of Maya traffic, precious little research has been conducted; most studies make only passing reference to such passages, connections, and the possible outcomes. James Brooks's monumental work *Captives and Cousins: Slavery, Kinship, and Community in the Southwest Borderlands*, for example, refers briefly to the presence of indigenous Plains women in Cuba. Other substantial studies by Amy Turner Bushnell, John Hann, Jerald Milanich, Emilio Roig de Leuchsenring, and John Worth on the southeastern United States likewise note in passing the movements and migrations of various diverse indigenous peoples to Spain's insular colony. Pieces of a larger puzzle, these substantial events, their outcomes, and the larger and long-term implications remain unstudied.[9]

With too few exceptions, the tendency of scholars of the Americas to overlook indigenous peoples within the Caribbean—and Amerindian passages between that region and the continents—has facilitated an historical and historiographical trend that has tended to parallel the patterns of movements of the conquistadors: moving from the initial staging area of the Caribbean toward various El Dorados in Mexico and elsewhere in the continental Americas, never looking back. Notably, although a small number of studies have been conducted by Cuban scholars, few of these extend beyond the conquest period, and those few that have begun to study later periods, like the work of Marcos A. Rodríguez Villamil, while important, do not address issues of identity or intercultural relations.[10] Subsequently, particularly large gaps persist in our knowledge of the Caribbean region's indigenous inhabitants, generating new questions not only about the original autochthons but also of Amerindian peoples from the continents and their modern-day descendants.

In this study I examine the multidimensional dynamics of a multifaceted indigenous diaspora, the many outcomes of which, while not always clear or evident, reveal much about human capacities for adaptation, initiative, ingenuity, innovation, resourcefulness, and resistance. The case studies explored in the following chapters underscore indigenous peoples' great propensity for struggle and adaptation based on both their own ancient traditions and those of the foreign colonizers. Furthermore, this ongoing adaptation and change occurred, somewhat ironically and paradoxically, at the same time that European colonial powers like the Spanish insisted on the stasis of indigenous cultures, on the perpetuity of their own cultures and traditions, and on increasingly outmoded and obsolete ways such as slavery. Indigenous adaptations in the face of journeys undertaken freely for trade or diplomacy, or in bondage as prisoners or slaves, followed no set pattern of action save for the generalized need for independence and freedom. As will be seen, in the case of enslaved or indentured indigenous captives forcibly transported to Cuba from the sixteenth through nineteenth centuries, the responses ranged the spectrum from the violent physical resistance by Apaches, to the legal claims and political negotiations undertaken by Yucatec Mayas.

For obvious reasons, the African slave trade has dominated the study of diaspora and colonial intercultural relations in Cuba. In my examination of the indigenous diaspora in Cuba, I attempt to illustrate the experiences and responses of the indigenous immigrants en route to and in Spain's largest Caribbean colony. The theoretical foundations for such historiography are therefore well established and based on the foundational works of a broad-ranging, interdisciplinary, and rich scholarship, from Manuel Moreno Fraginals and Rebecca Scott to James Scott and Manuel Barcia.[11] I am indebted to these scholars. For its own theoretical framework, this work relies on several paradigms, ideas that have come to inform relations between colonizers and subject peoples, albeit in a history heretofore unexamined.

James C. Scott's seminal work on everyday or "quieter" forms of resistance remains of great value to subaltern studies, including some of the works noted above. As such, it is highly relevant to the present investigation of diasporic indigenous peoples in colonial Cuba. With the possible exception of deported Apache prisoners, indigenous immigrants practiced a complex range of subtler forms of resistance, from foot-dragging, deception, and flight to somewhat less subtle forms like arson, sabotage, and theft.[12] As the works of Charles Cutter, María de los Angeles Romero Frizzi, Yanna Yannakakis, and others have demonstrated, indigenous peoples also practiced an ancient resourcefulness in colonial relations and conflict that included adaptation and negotiation: through political maneuvering and the use and manipulation of military and political alliances in times of colonial wars or by protest, petition, and the invocation and application of Spanish laws to defend themselves and their families against unscrupulous colonists and government officials.[13] Finally, I consider the perspectives of colonial elites, many of whom rationalized and profited, literally and figuratively, from these migrations and diasporas. Here, Scott's later work on domination, resistance, and hidden transcripts comes into play along with that of José Cuello, Susan Deeds, and Brooke Larson, as indigenous immigrants encountered elites—colonial in Cuba and national in Mexico—whose public and private agendas not infrequently conflicted, especially for indentured Maya workers, where "free" labor often differed little if at all from forced or slave labor.[14]

The story that follows is an effort at piecing together a larger puzzle, albeit an uneven one, toward a synthesis of histories that have existed only in fragments, some smaller, some larger, many concealed or at best only partially revealed. One central focus throughout the chapters is the duality of diversity and commonality of the dynamic roles and pathways of indigenous peoples in their journeys to colonial Cuba—from smaller, short-term movements to relatively larger-scale migrations and diasporas—and, where the evidence allows, examination of the role of Amerindians within colonial society in Cuba.

The chronological period encompassing these Amerindian passages is necessarily expansive—from the sixteenth through nineteenth centuries—traversing colonialism but also eventually crossing into eras of entangled history such that, by the late eighteenth and early nineteenth centuries, colonialism and imperialism meet and sometimes collide with fledgling or incipient nationalism or republicanism. The sixteenth century is possessed of a certain duality in that it represents two seminal beginnings: the first is that of the encounters, relations, and relationships between indigenous peoples and European newcomers; the second is that of European colonization and colonialism in the Americas spearheaded by the Spanish, whose hemispheric hegemony was then challenged by the entrance of other imperial powers like Portugal, England, and France. In the context of both, this century was also marked by some of the earliest instances of indigenous movement and migration under colonialism, occasionally voluntary, as with the Calusa and Tequesta missions from the Florida peninsula, and other times, most often, in fact, quite involuntary, as with the Yucatec Mayas enslaved by the Spanish to replace the diminished indigenous labor in their Caribbean colonies—both destined for the largest island colony, Cuba. As the centuries progressed, so too did the dynamic of indigenous mobility, voluntary and involuntary, and as a result, the multicultural indigenous presence in Cuba, the product of Spanish and imperial rivals' expansion through the continents. Throughout the eighteenth century, Spanish colonization of the northern provinces of New Spain and English penetration of Spain's La Florida contributed to the perpetuation of the migratory indigenous dynamic that forced each region's indigenous inhabitants to resist, adapt, negotiate, or employ any combination of these responses. Again, migration, principally to Cuba, was the ultimate outcome, albeit in substantively different modes: forced deportation for the resistant Apaches and voluntary migration for the last remaining indigenous peoples of the Florida peninsula.

Next to indigenous initiative, Amerindian passages to Cuba are further distinguished by being the products of important turning points in the history of the region. The British invasion of Cuba and the Spanish cession of Florida in 1762–63, while significant to European colonizers and indigenous peoples (as discussed in chapter 1), also marked the end of one epoch and the beginning of a new one for Amerindian passages to Cuba, as new indigenous groups made the trek to the island colony. Likewise, Mexico's and other colonies' independence from Spain in the early nineteenth century may have ended the forced relocation of Apaches but, barely two decades later in the throes of the Caste War of Yucatan and the aggressive indigenous rejection of the persistence of ancient and colonial burdens in republican guise, initiated new waves of human traffic. These were the Yucatec Mayas shipped to Cuba as slaves in the sixteenth century, as convicted rebels in the eighteenth century, or as captives forcibly relocated to Cuba as indentured labor in the nineteenth century. Such labor was, in turn, sorely needed by an island plantation economy fast becoming the world's foremost producer of sugar, one whose rapidly developing and labor-hungry sugar industry further sought to reinforce and complement if not counterbalance a less stable supply of African slave and Chinese labor. A study of Amerindian journeys to colonial Cuba therefore entails both continuity and change, while it also is ensconced in the broader dynamic of the hemisphere's history of struggles, especially, in this case, in the Cuba–Florida–Mexico nexus.

The chapters are structured accordingly. Of the indigenous peoples whose journeys are considered in this volume, the first chapter introduces those who represent the one case study in which passage to Cuba was the most consistently, though not exclusively, voluntary. Chapter 1 sets the stage with a discussion of early Spanish attempts at colonization of La Florida and proceeds with an examination of the earliest and most active exchanges between the various indigenous peoples of the Florida peninsula and surrounding regions that included Cuba in an historical moment that encompassed an initial period of encounters with the Spanish on the peninsula that then gradually and eventually intensified into a pattern of indigenous journeys to the island colony. These initial indigenous forays were undertaken for a range of reasons and varied in duration from a few days to many months. Once there, indigenous delegations like those of the Calusa and Tekesta and their leaders often met with colonial government and church officials and otherwise interacted with the insular colonial population at several levels, demonstrating a complex interplay with Spanish interests in the region in a process that eventually also included the facilitation of settlement for increasing numbers of indigenous refugees fleeing the epidemic devastation of colonial wars.

The second chapter extends the story of indigenous passages and the Florida-Cuba nexus into the late eighteenth and early nineteenth centuries. As the imperial geopolitics of the region were altered by the more aggressive entry of the British after 1762, the English occupation of Cuba, and then the recovery of the Pearl of the Antilles by the Spanish, indigenous peoples continued to adapt in myriad ways in their responses to the alternating waves of colonizers penetrating the continent and surrounding region. Mobility remained key as hundreds again took flight to and refuge in Cuba. Others, especially Amerindian newcomers to Florida like the Lower Creeks, journeyed to the island, like their predecessors, using it to promote their own geopolitical interests, a story that, as far as we know, is marked by the eventual end of this phase of indigenous migration to Cuba with the territorial takeover and "Indian removal" by the United States.

We then turn, in chapter 3, to the next case study in indigenous diasporas to Cuba, one that sets the tone for the rest of the book in its examination of indigenous passages based largely on involuntary or forced migrations to the island. In another region of the continent to the west of Florida but during the same period, the Apache peoples of the southwestern region or northern New Spain also struggled with Spanish colonization. Unlike their southeastern counterparts, Apache and Puebloan peoples, deemed "bárbaros" in their aggressive resistance to Spanish attempts to colonize the northern provinces, were almost invariably taken to Cuba involuntarily, as hundreds of captives were forcibly deported and relocated, banished to insular exile and slavery. Many were welcomed by their colonial hosts for their servitude; their compliance in colonial Cuban society, however, is another question.

The fourth chapter and third case study center on the history of indigenous peoples no less dynamic in their will to adapt, negotiate, and/

or resist in colonial-era Cuba. Like the indigenous peoples of Florida and the Southwest or northern New Spain, their journeys from ancestral homelands began early on as the consequence of protracted martial resistance to Spanish conquest and colonization. In their passages to Cuba, the Mayas of Yucatan shared elements with their northern neighbors to the east and west—the first to come and the many who followed came as slaves and then indentured laborers, but Mayas also came of their own volition. In either case, they adapted in degrees through journeys involuntary and voluntary. The Mayas of Yucatan came as slaves, helped build, in this new era, what became one of the greatest cities in the Americas, and played various roles through the centuries as they continued to come collectively and as individuals, often against their will and in servitude but occasionally freely. However, as will be seen, Yucatec Mayas were not the only indigenous Mesoamerican peoples to arrive in Cuba. The Mesoamerican presence in late colonial Cuba contributed its own diversity, as indígenas from central and southern Mexico, transported as *forzados* (forced laborers), arrived in Havana, destined for hard labor in the fortifications of the colony. While Mesoamerican peoples like the Nahuas and others may have accompanied Mayas in Cuba at different points during this period, Maya longevity appears to have prevailed. Maya passages to the island predominated in continuity and duration over a half millennium; Mayas represented the most enduring Mesoamerican presence in Cuba. Finally, if most Mayas who came to Cuba were *macehualob* (commoners, peasants) transported as slaves or forzados, this was by no means absolute and was qualified by the presence of a small but significant population of diverse Maya immigrants who came of their own accord and stayed.

Chapter 5 picks up the Yucatecan thread with an examination of the continuation of the Maya diaspora in the nineteenth century, focusing on one of the largest single waves of Mayas to come to Cuba during the late colonial period. The prolonged Caste War of Yucatan, a Maya rebellion, initiated another in a series of conflagrations in that peninsula, the repercussions of which soon became felt in Cuba as several thousand Mayas were, like the Apaches merely a few decades earlier, forcibly transported to the island colony to remove the indigenous threat for both the Mexican and state governments and to provide badly needed labor for Cuban planters. Notably, some Mayas also fled to Cuba in search of safety from the *insurrectos*, those rebelling against colonial government and labor conditions. In any case, as petitions and police and court documents attest, whether as prisoners of war, indentured labor, or voluntary immigrants, Mayas in Cuba were neither passive nor invariably subservient, making active use, for example, of Spanish labor laws for the protection of themselves and their families. Meanwhile, thousands more were anticipated by the Mexican state, Spanish imperial rule, and enterprising individuals under both regimes.

In chapter 6 I examine more closely the contradictions of the evolving labor system and society in which, by the mid- to late nineteenth century, indigenous immigrant workers found themselves immersed: the paradox of a transitional labor system caught ambiguously between slavery and free labor; the concomitant *mentalité* of *patrones* and members of the state; and the attempt by those in power to prolong an ostensibly obsolete system of *repartimiento* labor through extensive efforts and campaigns to bring many more *colonos indios* into Cuba. In this chapter I examine the dynamic of indigenous diaspora in a Cuba at the apex of the island's existence as a plantation society grounded in slavery and colonialism, in the throes of repeated and intensifying struggles for independence from Spain, along with the broader implications for studies of both labor and indigenous immigrant workers in Cuba. Like the other chapters, this one raises the question of a revisionist, holistic history of Cuba inclusive of peoples who played significant roles in its rise as a colony and nation—even as participants in the independence movement—but who, in no small part due to a specific kind of Cuban and North American historiography rooted in the past, found themselves to be largely a people without history.

Finally, the conclusion gives brief and further consideration to the question of transculturation as well as to the legacy of indigenous diasporas to Cuba, particularly with respect to the question of surviving descendants and communities of indigenous immigrants in the country by the twentieth century. By logical extension, the conclusion also considers the larger question of indigenous history and legacy in Cuba writ large, that is, with respect to the indigenous Arawak Taíno peoples and indigenous newcomers, some of whom intermarried and created mixed, culturally rich indigenous-descendant communities in the western regions and other areas of the country as living symbols of a multicultural indigenous presence in Cuba with deep roots.

1

IMPERIAL GEOPOLITICS, THE FLORIDA-CUBA NEXUS, AND AMERINDIAN PASSAGES

By the late 1520s, while Spain had long begun building colonies on the ruins of the Mexica-Aztec empire and its conquest of Central America progressed, the Spanish Empire had failed to establish a settlement in La Florida. Yet much in the way of reconnaissance had been gained about the North American coasts. Like Cuba, La Florida occupied a strategic position relative to Mexico, Central America, the Caribbean, and the shipping lanes that linked Spain to those regions. The protection of the shipping lanes and growing Spanish American empire dictated that Spain control La Florida.[1] A logical step toward that end, Jerald Milanich observes, "was to extend Spanish hegemony northward from the new gulf settlements on the east coast of Mexico, tying La Florida to Spain."[2]

From the 1520s to the mid-sixteenth century, the crown contracted a number of conquistadors from Mexico and Cuba who, each in his turn, undertook expeditions to secure the peninsula and surrounding regions for conquest and colonization under Spain. As it was for Mexico, Cuba likewise was the launching point and regional administrative center for the conquest of La Florida.

Several decades later, however, stable European settlements in La Florida were conspicuously absent. Juan Ponce de León's second campaign ended in failure; he returned to Cuba only to die from a Calusa arrow wound. The 1528 expedition of veteran conquistador Pánfilo de Narváez, infamous for his cruelty toward the Arawak Taíno people in the conquest of Cuba, also met with a catastrophic end. Only four members of the expedition survived as captives among the Indians of coastal Texas until they escaped and were found by Spanish slavers in northern Mexico in 1536, among them Alvar Cabeza de Vaca, who related the story of his ordeal to the Spanish court a year later. Cabeza de Vaca's descriptions of La Florida as a veritable Eden impressed other conquistadors like Hernando de Soto, who departed Cuba with his own fleet in 1539. Four years later, in the autumn of 1543, only about half of that expedition's members had survived and returned. De Soto died the previous year of an illness.

Characteristic of all of these early attempts by Spain to take La Florida were the European presumption of success through "efficient exploitation" (coercion and conquest) and the persistent resistance by the region's indigenous inhabitants. Both Narváez and de Soto began their expeditions on the southwest coast of Florida near present-day Tampa Bay. Both, as their respective campaigns moved northward, also planned to coerce the Indians they encountered into supplying food and bearing the expeditions' supplies. Perhaps hundreds of men and women were exploited. Resistance was often quickly answered with force, including captivity and torture, with hostages a common bargaining tool. In spite of their contracts' clauses insisting on the humane treatment of Indians, the two men had lamentable records of cruelty toward indigenous people.

Yet, contrary to the presumptions of the conquistadors, La Florida was not Mexico. Numerous indigenous communities did indeed persist in various forms of resistance. The Spaniards were simultaneously dominant over and dependent upon their captives, needing them as carriers and as guides, and were not infrequently outmaneuvered by those they sought to conquer. Narváez's expedition was manipulated by the Timucua and then by the Apalachee, who steered them away from populous villages, through unforgiving terrain, and sometimes into traps exploited by raiding parties.[3] Indigenous hostages proved of little insurance to the conquistadors. De Soto also was misled by the Timucua, attacked by the Apalachee, and otherwise variously and aggressively resisted. Succeeding expeditions, like that of Tristan de Luna y Arellano in the 1550s, fared no better, thwarted by La Florida's terrain and, Milanich notes, "outwitted by the Indians, who allowed them nothing."[4] That this period coincided with a dramatic rise in the frequency of slave raids along the Gulf and Atlantic coasts likely contributed significantly to the resistance of aboriginal peoples encountered in Florida by the expeditions from Cuba. Yet the Spanish, too, persisted. Motivated by the Chicora legend of rich and boundless lands and by intelligence regarding the imperial machinations of France in the region, the Spanish crown was determined to secure La Florida for the empire.

In 1565, Pedro Menéndez de Avilés led the largest expedition to La Florida to that point, defeated the French, and established the first successful settlement at St. Augustine on the peninsula's northeast coast. If the hold was ultimately tenuous in the short and long run, St. Augustine provided the precedent for the spread of Spanish influence into North America. At the same time, the ensuing indigenous-Spanish exchanges provided the framework for the evolution of a complex and substantial relationship, much of which would be wrought through the impetus of indigenous mobility and some of the earliest movements and migrations of indigenous peoples during the colonial period, passages that would transpire between the continent and the Spanish Caribbean, with Cuba as the principal destination.

In La Florida, after a string of failed conquest attempts and with competition from Britain and France closing in on the region, the Spanish were forced to adopt other forms of "pacification"—more cooperative and less violent (though never abandoning the latter)—in order to succeed there. Likewise, indigenous groups adapted in order to take advantage of the offerings of the Spanish and use them as allies against traditional enemies like the Uchise and others who received backing from the British. Each group was forced to establish alliances and modes of exchange that would enable them to continue to coexist and live under the evolving new order of things.

Importantly, the Calusa and Tequesta, like many coastal Florida groups, with varying success retained their indigenous belief systems, sociopolitical structures, settlement patterns, and subsistence practices (primarily fishing), in other words, their autonomy, until the end of the seventeenth century, some even later.[5] The relative isolation and independence of the Calusa became sources for the attraction and frustration of Spanish missionaries. Other peoples, like the Timucua and Guale, generally experienced intensive European interaction as Spanish colonization and concomitant evangelization took hold early on; although evidence suggests a persistence in political organization of hereditary chiefdoms, in the course of the late sixteenth century and the seventeenth century, Victor Thompson and John Worth report, "demography, settlement systems, subsistence strategies and diet (traditionally fishing but, over time, increasingly maize agriculture and livestock), belief systems, sociopolitical organization, and many other facets of life were all affected to some extent in the context of missionization."[6]

The Spanish policy of pacification by gifts, first implemented on the frontiers of northern New Spain and aided by the Franciscans, was initiated in Florida later, the conditions and qualifications of which are aptly summarized by Amy Turner Bushnell:

[T]he policy of "peace by purchase" appropriate to a nonsedentary native society with a low level of social stratification was overlaid by the policy of "conquest by contract" suitable to a more sedentary and stratified native society. Gifts from the king were means by which civil and religious authorities attracted, attached, and empowered the "lords of the land" and through them exercised control over commoners. . . . [S]uborned by gifts, the Florida caciques induced their followers to be baptized, to restrict their trade to españoles, and to function as a labor reserve. In the Spanish model of European-Native relations, they were the enablers.[7]

Spanish colonization led to various levels of exchange between La Florida and Cuba. Hann has argued that the initial failure of military conquest in La Florida necessitated the institution in practice of what was supposed to have been, for Catholic Spain, the cardinal colonizing institution: the Church. Implicit in Menéndez de Avilés's broader plan to extend trade routes, develop alliances with the Indians, and expand Spanish colonization generally, the new governor sought to convert the Indians of La Florida and subject them to the rule of Catholic Spain. Menéndez de Avilés's initial negotiations with the Tequesta and Calusa led to friendly relations with the principal Calusa chief, Carlos, and acceptance of the cacique's sister as his wife.[8] The governor also encouraged his indigenous allies to make peace with their traditional enemies, a nagging bone of contention especially as the Spanish asserted and inserted themselves in these relations.

For Spain, the establishment of Christian missions among the indigenous peoples of La Florida was as much a moral imperative as an imperial one.[9] Historically, this imperative dictated the relocation to and *reducción* (concentration) of prospective indigenous converts in areas that were, in the words of the Laws of the Indies, away from their homes "in the mountains and wildernesses, where they are deprived of all spiritual and temporal comforts, the aid of our ministers, and those other things which human necessities oblige men to give to one another."[10] As Spain demonstrated in the forced migration and relocation of so many indigenous peoples throughout the American colonies, migration possessed a very direct relation to Christianity and evangelization and played an essential role in the Christianization and assimilation of indigenous peoples under Spanish colonization.

In the Floridian possessions, the Spanish naturally relied on the missions to follow suit. Whether in the initial attempts at conquest by arms or the concomitant spiritual conquest, however, La Florida, again, was not Mexico. At the same time, the relation between Christian missions and indigenous mobility still held, though in a somewhat ironic subversion of that anticipated by the Spanish. During the early colonial period, mobility, migration, and relocation were instead adapted by the peninsula's indigenous peoples as vehicles, even if not always entirely in their control, but means nonetheless for their own ends in relation to their encounters with Christian missions and the Spanish Empire. Whether among the horticulturalists of the north or the more mobile communities of the south, mobility and migration became substantive vehicles for resistance to and negotiation with a hegemonic Spanish juggernaut whose imperial vision insisted on the organization of space and control of population movement.[11]

With the establishment of the St. Augustine settlement in the spring of 1565, Menéndez de Avilés soon wrote to General Francisco Borgia, head of the Jesuit order, to invite the newly formed Society of Jesus to start a mission in La Florida.[12] Motivated by several factors—the legal and moral responsibility to ensure the conversion of the Indians, the need for a labor force, and the protection of colonists—the governor sponsored the Jesuit missions among the Calusa and Tequesta. Menéndez de Avilés petitioned the Jesuits to supplement the diocesan priests as missionaries to the Indians. In early 1567, two Jesuits left the Spanish Caribbean headquarters in Havana for South Florida. Father Juan Rogel went to a military outpost near present-day Charlotte Harbor to minister to the Calusa, while Fray Francisco Villareal went to Biscayne Bay to work with the Tequesta and began a somewhat strategic mission, the nearest in Florida to the military and mission headquarters of Havana.[13] Consistent with the tradition of the setting up such mission garrisons, Menéndez de Avilés himself formally established the Biscayne Bay (Miami) outpost by remaining there for some four days in 1567 and erecting a cross, a sure sign of the initiation of Catholicism in the region.[14]

Menéndez de Avilés conceived a plan to help establish a Jesuit school in Cuba for the religious education of Amerindian children, particularly the heirs of principal chiefs.[15] The governor encouraged and exhorted the Jesuits to set up the school in Havana. There, he asserted, the sons of the principal chiefs, particularly those who were to inherit the respective *cacicazgos* (chiefdoms), would learn Spanish and Christianity, and after a few years, return to their provinces, converted and transformed into Spain's Hispanicized allies.[16] Menéndez de Avilés and the Jesuits envisioned a virtually steady stream of candidates commuting between Havana and La Florida.[17] The Jesuit schools in Cuba were to serve as means of more concretely establishing Spanish influence among the Amerindians through their elites.

The groundwork had been laid for the Jesuit program in Havana but not solely at Spanish initiative. In order to cement their respective alliances with the newcomers, an indigenous delegation representing the Calusa and Tequesta went to Cuba to meet with the governor. Eighteen Indians, twelve Calusa and six Tequesta, including the second son of the principal chief of the Tequesta, arrived in Havana in early December 1566. According to Rogel, the Calusa and Tequesta made overtures to the Spanish, promoting the forging of an alliance, and asked the Jesuit to communicate to Menéndez de Avilés their interest in becoming Christians.[18] The indigenous delegates were very pleased with their treatment while in Havana, the Jesuit observed, and reiterated their desire to become Christians. He wasted no time in grasping the opportunity to teach and convert, holding classes in his church.[19] Rogel further pointed out that some members of the La Florida delegation also knew Spanish and acted as interpreters on their own group's behalf. Importantly, in Hann's view, this was clearly a sign "that the Tequesta as well as the Calusa had had considerable contact with the Spaniards."[20]

If the most significant basis for this contact was the incipient garrison and mission system in Florida, it is also true that another substantive source of exchange was to be found in the mobility of indigenous peoples like the Calusa and Tequesta as they traversed the straits between the peninsula and its keys and the largest island colony in the Caribbean to meet, treat, and trade with the Spanish. Religion and geopolitics played no less significant (if not necessarily parallel) roles in the launching and increasing frequency of indigenous expeditions to colonial Cuba, journeys whose purposes spanned the range from missions to junkets, and through the eventual, inevitable, widespread devastation of war, to exile.

Over the next several years, as the evangelization process proceeded, its uneven and halting pace made the Jesuits increasingly wonder about the sincerity and motivations of that delegation of prospective indigenous converts whom they had welcomed earlier in Havana. In La Florida, the missionaries reported progress but not without a number of difficulties encountered in working with their catechists. Rogel reported a considerable difference between the delegations of Calusa and Tequesta who had come to Havana; he considered the Tequesta delegates to be genuine, humble, and receptive to evangelization.[21] The Calusa envoys Rogel found to be agitated and restive.[22]

The missionary Francisco Villareal appeared pleased with his young Tequesta catechists in La Florida and observed that his classes were being attended by boys and girls as old as fifteen years of age; most reportedly made significant progress often under less than ideal conditions, with Villareal citing illness and a shortage of food as examples.[23] Notably, these were problems that would also later plague the Jesuit school for indigenous children in Havana. Villareal further noted a contrast in the attitudes of Tequesta adults toward the Tequesta mission school compared to the children. Unlike the children and the delegates' apparent evangelical enthusiasm when in Havana, when back at the mission in La Florida, Tequesta adults demonstrated considerably less interest in the teachings of Catholic doctrine. Villareal lamented that these Indians came only a few times to lessons, gave little or no indication of a desire to be proselytized, and by the spring of 1568, when they (if not the missionaries) appeared satisfied that they and their children knew the teachings, insisted that the missionaries go away.[24] Among the Calusa, Rogel fared no better.

Between the struggles of the missionaries with their resistant indigenous flocks and the political meddling of the Spanish military among the Calusa and Tequesta in an aggressive, Machiavellian, and failed attempt to influence indigenous leadership, the Spanish Jesuit missions fared poorly.[25] This, along with the missionaries' continued insistence that the caciques renounce their faith, idols, and custom of marrying female siblings, practices intimately woven into Calusa political culture, made the situation untenable for the Calusa.[26] Rogel reports that the cacique Felipe upbraided him for attempting to change the established ways and worldview of the adults and elders, and pointed him instead to the children, whose potential for change was greater.[27] To accentuate the point, the Calusa defiantly attempted to turn the tables by sending a procession of idols to the mission garrison, an effort that was aggressively turned away by the Spanish.[28]

Back in Cuba, Rogel reflected on the Jesuits' failed mission in La Florida. He became convinced that the Calusa mission to Cuba had been a ruse and that they were more interested in the Spaniards as politico-military allies and suppliers of materiel like maize. The Calusa overture in Havana, he concluded, had merely been an opportunity for duping the Jesuits into thinking that they were dedicated to becoming Christians.[29] By the end of 1568, the Jesuits had failed to convert more than a tiny minority of individuals, and the authenticity of those conversions remained unclear.

Significantly, one of Rogel's few successful Amerindian conversions took place in Havana, where he encountered an indigenous woman from the peninsula brought to the island by the Adelantado.[30] After a period of catechetical instruction and then repeated exhortations by the woman and others of her readiness for conversion, the Jesuit eventually agreed to baptize the woman.[31]

The baptism took place at Mass on January 6, the day of the Three Kings, before most if not all of the residents of Havana, including the governor, who had agreed to be the godfather. Rogel then entrusted the new Christian to the household of a local affluent and well-regarded family, hopeful that, eventually, she would marry a Spaniard and pursue the missionizing quest.[32]

Rogel's experiences are indicative of several important points, all related directly or indirectly to the dynamic of indigenous mobility and migration to Cuba. Downcast by the audacity of the Calusa and Tequesta in coming to Cuba to promote their interests by using the missions as a subterfuge, the missionary no doubt wondered at the utility and wisdom of allowing any further meetings with such indigenous delegations in the island colony. At the same time, there were those Indians who came to Cuba and remained, souls apparently genuinely desirous of salvation, as demonstrated by the indigenous women in Havana whom he himself baptized. The combination of failure in La Florida and this early indigenous presence in colonial Cuba must have played no small part in the next step taken by church and government officials on the island: bringing the Indians to Cuba.

Rogel's reflections on the apparent success in converting La Florida Indians in Cuba were shared by colonial officials in Havana. Governor Menéndez de Avilés and the Jesuits hoped that conflicts like that encountered in La Florida missions would be vitiated by transporting the children of La Florida's caciques—particularly the sons—to Cuba and educating and indoctrinating them in the Jesuit school in Havana. Work began among three of the first candidates—two boys from the Calusa and one from the Tequesta—at least as early as 1568.[33] Encouraged by these beginnings, Jesuit Juan Bautista de Segura, in a letter to General Borgia in November 1568, stressed the importance of founding a formal institution in Havana to continue this process for the Indians of La Florida and eventually the West Indies as well.[34] Bautista de Segura added that such an enterprise had the support not only of the governor but of the citizens of Cuba and Hispaniola as well.[35] By late 1569, at a time when Jesuit missionaries in La Florida were either dying violently or from disease or taking flight back to Cuba, the school in Havana gained ascendancy with the approval of secular and ecclesiastical interests. Most returning missionaries went to work in the school, increasingly viewed as perhaps the last chance for Jesuit success in La Florida. Any substantial success with bringing indigenous children to be schooled in Cuba, however, proved relatively short-lived, as events on the island paralleled those in the peninsula.

While church and government officials appear to have succeeded in convincing indigenous families to allow some of their young to be brought to the island colony for schooling, the results, at least in the short term, were far from encouraging. Two of the three children under the Jesuits' care, the first students in the first class in the Havana Jesuit school for caciques' sons, died. At the same time, among those missionaries who returned to work in the school in Havana, some like Fathers Rogel and Antonia Sedeño did not come empty-handed, bringing indigenous children with them back to Cuba.[36]

Governor Menéndez de Avilés persevered in his support for the school at a time when there was some concern among the Jesuits about the potential for success.[37] In 1571, Menéndez de Avilés, Rogel, and other Jesuits remained somewhat optimistic about the potential of the Jesuit school in Havana for educating and indoctrinating the children of caciques and other principal leaders.[38] That year, in a letter to the Jesuit general, the governor reiterated his belief in the Havana school's long-term importance for the region and the Spanish Americas generally. He vowed to introduce as many of the male progeny of La Florida's caciques as he could to the institution for Christian instruction and indoctrination, confident that its indigenous graduates, when reinserted into settler society on the peninsula, would carry on the work of evangelization.[39] The extent to which, numerically speaking, the vision of Menéndez de Avilés was realized is less clear, but its enduring legacy is not. More than two centuries later, indigenous migration to Cuba for the purposes of education and/or indoctrination remained of significant interest to colonial ecclesiastical interests and, if to a lesser extent, indigenous visitors.[40]

Meanwhile, the establishment in 1566 of the first permanent Spanish settlement at St. Augustine in the northern region of the peninsula reinforced the regularity and frequency of indigenous visitation and immigration to Havana and environs. Cuba, where much of the indigenous Arawak Taíno population was being decimated by the multifarious and devastating effects of Spanish conquest and colonization, remained a regular destination for the indigenous peoples of La Florida and, subsequently, a field for missionary work. The Jesuits continued their spiritual campaign through the education and indoctrination of caciques' sons and daughters in the school in Havana, an enterprise that continued to have the support of Menéndez de Avilés and the colonial government after 1572. If the indigenous population was diminishing in Cuba, the multicultural Amerindian presence was otherwise very palpable in the various indigenous peoples of the peninsula who passed through the school halls and who visited or came to reside in the fledgling city, including some who, like Doña Antonia, a daughter of Calusa nobility, lived the life of a Castilian and remained in Havana the rest of their lives.[41]

The schooling or instruction of indigenous children and adults in Cuba remained a factor in the dynamic of indigenous immigration. Even amid the vicissitudes of the incipient diaspora from the region of La Florida, it continued to have the support of the church, imperial government, and colonial population in Cuba. In the mid-seventeenth century, the founding of a seminary or college in Havana, supported by a petition from the *cabildo* (town council), and the *ayuntamiento* (municipal government) of Havana, reinforced this dynamic.[42] In an atmosphere of rising regional imperial competition and war, indigenous migration to the island colony continued, influenced as much by Spanish motives and interests, from the religious to the geopolitical, as by indigenous material needs and sociopolitical objectives.

While the missions to its south courted failure, the mission at St. Augustine in the northern part of the peninsula became yet another point of departure for indigenous passage to Cuba. Moreover, in coming to the island colony, the Calusa, the largest of the southern Florida nations, had demonstrated agency and an assertive self-interest in their exchanges with the insular Spanish, whether as fishermen and traders or as political leaders and diplomats. They and other nations in transit would continue to test the Spanish, learning about Spanish culture and religion, for example, to the extent that it would benefit them in their fledgling alliances and then broader relations with the newcomers. Rogel and the other Jesuit missionaries discovered to their great chagrin that the Amerindians' hidden transcripts had concealed the fact, at least during this early period, that most were more interested in their children's absorption of Christian doctrine for strategic reasons than from conviction. Outside of a small minority, they demonstrated considerably less interest in Christianity as time progressed and eventually made their interests quite and, for the missionaries, painfully clear. Indigenous leaders and their delegations used Cuba as a gauge for measuring the nature, strength, and power of the Spanish in the Americas; Havana, for both the Spanish and the Indians, became a venue for conference and diplomacy but also for reconnaissance, political positioning, and gain.

In some respects, therefore, compared to their indigenous counterparts, and most dramatically in the case of the Jesuit missions, the Spanish certainly came off the worse for wear. By 1572, in spite of the great fanfare that had accompanied the visiting indigenous delegations to Havana, the conferences with senior colonial government and church officials, and the concomitant optimism and anticipation in no small part influenced by the indigenous delegations, the Jesuits ultimately fared poorly, Milanich asserts: "It was a terrible loss. By 1572 nine of the Jesuits who had gone to La Florida had been killed at the hands of the very people they had sought to convert to Christianity.... [T]he remaining Jesuits were withdrawn that year; some moved on to Mexico. The successes the Jesuits would enjoy in Brazil and elsewhere in the Americas would not be duplicated in La Florida."[43] Jesuit priests were, however, followed by the Franciscans, who established an extensive system of Indian missions in northern Florida. Beyond the Jesuit efforts of 1567 and 1743, no records indicate attempts to establish substantive Catholic missions in southern Florida.[44] Yet the missions would continue, and Cuba remained an important base of operations for Spanish colonization and evangelization in the continental Americas, as it did a destination for indigenous peoples from the eastern regions of the continent.

Notably, while Calusa and other indigenous visitations and migrations to Cuba were fundamentally voluntary in nature and their freedom while in Havana and environs unfettered, this was not always the case. During the seventeenth century there were incidents in which indigenous visitors or migrants from La Florida faced trial and even incarceration. In one such incident, two Timucuan Indians were incarcerated for seven years in the prison of El Morro for their role in a 1628 insurrection.[45]

Overwhelmingly, however, the patterns of movement and migration of indigenous peoples from La Florida to and in Cuba during the colonial period remained based on a voluntary mobility, whether facilitated by indigenous vessels, Spanish ships, or both.[46] Furthermore, these early journeys developed into a pattern that would endure for several centuries, rooted in Spanish attempts to Christianize and assimilate Amerindians, intensifying and increasingly devastating and displacing colonial wars, and the indigenous nations' own perceptions, needs, interests, and resourcefulness. During a period when Spanish and North American indigenous geopolitics were inseparable from religious or spiritual considerations, the latter understandably continued to play as much a role in repeated Spanish attempts to assimilate and control the Amerindians as it did in indigenous resistance to these campaigns. Paradoxically, Havana increasingly served as the forum or stage where this drama of domination versus resistance and/or negotiation played itself out, with Cuba the sanctuary for indigenous converts and refugees fleeing the escalating plagues of war and disease on the continent. Indigenous journeys to Cuba remained the means of conveying indigenous independence and of seeking refuge. The Spanish facilitated this process directly, indirectly, and sometimes inadvertently, as it persisted into the seventeenth and eighteenth centuries.

The resurrection of Spanish attempts to secure missions in south Florida during the seventeenth century is yet another example of inadvertent Spanish facilitation of indigenous interests through migration, and it received at least some impetus from the governor of Florida at that time, Pablo de Hita Salazar. The governor informed the crown in 1680 that there were "neighboring heathens" in the south, some inland and some on the coast facing Cuba, who had "been neglected" and were in need of conversion.[47] Due in large part to the support of the bishop of Santiago de Cuba, Juan Garcia de Palacios, the campaign to establish missions among the Ais and Calusa in south Florida was revived, though several years passed before the crown formally reordered the governor in Havana to recruit missionaries for the field. This later attempt at spiritual conquest, though also short-lived, is particularly significant in the introduction of an additional element into the dynamic of regional indigenous mobility, migration, and transculturation in Cuba.

In 1689 an opportunity presented itself when the chief of the Calusa of southwest Florida, "who," Worth notes, "had practiced an official policy of isolationism for practically the entire 175-year period previous to that time," conveyed a willingness to accept Spanish missionaries and Christianity.[48] The new bishop of Santiago de Cuba, Diego Ebelino de Compostela, responded accordingly, contacting a fisherman, "resident in this city," who "left from its port headed for the bay of the said cacique with whom he said he held communication and correspondence so that he might bring to his notice these dispositions on the part of his Majesty looking to the promotion of their greater welfare. . . . And likewise we charged him that he should greatly encourage him so that he might be willing to come to this port in his company so that we might have the occasion for entertaining him and conferring [with him] about this matter."[49]

After meeting with the Cuban fisherman and then holding council with his own people, the cacique Carlos conveyed his ambivalence toward the offer of the crown's envoy. The cacique was wary, even suspecting "that the objective of converting them to our Holy Law was in order to hold them captive."[50] Nor did other Calusa make him any less ambivalent: "it being so that other Indians that had come to this city in other times and who have returned to that land to live, affirmed to him that they had received bad treatment in this [city] and that even the young boys persecuted them and threw stones at them.[51] Carlos apparently overcame some, if not all, of his doubts and fears and "trusted a poor fisherman who brought him in his vessel."[52]

The cacique was treated royally, feasted and entertained, while his presence at "divine services and at ecclesiastical and political functions" was ensured, "taking care so that the interpreters would explain to him, so that after making a comparison [of them] with the orderless manner with which they govern themselves, he might recognize the good order of our Holy Law and Christian Republic."[53] According to the bishop, a good time was had by all: "[T]hose who were with him assured me that he was approving of everything that he saw being carried out and that he characterized it as more consistent with reason."[54] Based on such happy tidings and, Hann observes, "moved by new pressures from authorities in Spain to launch the mission to the Calusa and impelled particularly by the Calusa Chief's acceptance of the bishop's invitation to visit him in Cuba," the bishop "appealed to his clergy anew for volunteers to evangelize the Calusa."[55] In his appeal, the bishop asserted the urgency of attending to the Christianization of the "heathen Indians" who "frequent this city of Havana."[56]

second attempt to evangelize the Calusa

The subsequent mission of five Franciscan friars sent to south Florida ended disastrously: barely two months in, the missionaries were thoroughly rejected and aggressively ejected by their indigenous flocks. According to the testimony of the friars, the Calusa behaved toward the Franciscans much as had earlier generations toward the Jesuits.[57] The friars characterized the Calusa as "rice Christians" whose initial welcome soon wore thin when cognizant that the food, clothing, and other largesse given to their representatives in Havana were not to be so distributed upon their conversion in their own land; one cacique demanded, "give me the clothing that the king gives."[58] In further testimony, lay witnesses contrasted the weak interest of adult Calusa in conversion to their interest in having their children attend catechism and be baptized.[59] In its investigation into the failed mission, the Council of the Indies concluded that the Calusa "were moved solely by self-interest."[60] The council neglected to mention other factors at work: the missionaries, as the old principal chief reminded them, had arrived seven years after Carlos's visit to Cuba, had behaved overzealously and aggressively in their proselytizing, and may have been the victims of misunderstanding and also of factionalism within the Calusa leadership.[61]

In spite of the abject failure and expulsion of the Franciscans, the pattern of increased Spanish-indigenous interaction through indigenous movements and migrations from Florida to Cuba had now been set, a process facilitated further by the use of Cuban fishermen who served as liaisons, escorts, and more.[62] By the beginning of the eighteenth century, conditions on the mainland reinforced this configuration of imperial geopolitics, indigenous mobility, and Cuba as the principal indigenous destination.

The Florida frontier, Robert Galgano notes, "became embroiled in the imperial pretentions of European crowns," and indigenous peoples and Spaniards "began to feel the shockwaves."[63] Missionized indigenous peoples like those among the various Timucua had long felt the shockwaves and adapted to intensive Spanish colonization and missions. A half century of integration into the colonial system centered at St. Augustine had proven a mixed blessing. Far from being passive victims of colonialism, the missionized peoples of La Florida played an active role in the developing colonial system, providing the labor and staple foods, for example, on which the residents of St. Augustine depended.[64] Paradoxically, indigenous groups' dependence and vulnerability became manifest in their growing dependence on maize agriculture and livestock as they moved away from coastal diets and toward more sedentary and relatively vulnerable lifestyles susceptible to foes both human and natural.

By the late seventeenth century, nutritional stress, burgeoning workloads, and the intensifying attacks of imperially abetted indigenous adversaries were taking their toll: disease, famine, death, and flight had devastated the communities of Timucua and other indigenous peoples.[65] The Timucua fought back; some mounted a rebellion against the Spanish in 1656 in a struggle over land, labor, and power that ended in indigenous defeat and even deeper integration into the colonial system.[66] In turn, as the Spanish system came under greater attack from its imperial rivals, the indigenous inhabitants of the region became increasingly entangled in those geopolitical conflicts. Whether as allies or as adversaries, the resource base for many of Florida's indigenous peoples shrank, coastal homelands were abandoned and then reoccupied by peoples from the interior, livelihoods were disrupted, and slave raids and other attacks on missions and settlements became an almost incessant plague.

In 1702, on the heels of the opening of the War of the Spanish Succession, English and Amerindian attacks into northeast Florida peaked in intensity. By 1708, English and indigenous raiders had penetrated the southern part of the peninsula and were attacking Calusa and other groups; population attrition among the Calusa had reached crisis proportions, as disease and attacks by Amerindian enemies allied with the British took their toll.[67] One such ally, the Yamasee, embroiled most indigenous communities in the South Carolina and Georgia region in warfare, conducting slave raids and driving southward, displacing many peoples, until they themselves were later replaced and displaced as refugees by the new allies of the British, the Uchisi. In response to these conditions, some groups, like the Mayaca, Jororo, and others from the peninsular southeast, migrated northward to settlements near the fortified St. Augustine mission for protection.[68] Others fled to sanctuary in Cuba.

As John Worth has pointed out, the existing connection between Havana and south Florida served as a catalyst for the events that followed. Probably in part due to the earlier and numerous exchanges in Havana and to indigenous experiences in the island colony, such as the eighteen-month residence of numerous Calusa families, indigenous refugees among the Calusa sought refuge in Cuba. In turn, the colonial government in Cuba granted permission for indigenous emigrants from Cayo de Huesos, or Key West, to settle permanently in La Cabaña, on a promontory opposite downtown Havana, the same place where other indigenous immigrants had earlier been settled and one that would become the primary site for the resettlement of indigenous refugees from southern Florida for the next half century.[69]

This was followed in 1711 by one of the largest migrations of Florida Amerindians to Cuba. Later Spanish reports traced this migration to a visit made by the Franciscan fray Alonso de San Jurgo to Key West during Holy Week in 1710. There, San Jurgo encountered the principal chief of the Calusa, who, having fallen gravely ill, requested baptism.[70] Importantly, before his death, he also gathered his people together and exhorted them to move to Havana and become Christians. In February 1711, an indigenous delegation arrived in Cuba by Spanish vessel. In Havana they made a desperate appeal to the bishop for assistance in arranging transportation to the island for a large number of indigenous migrants from south Florida so that they could escape the escalating attacks and enslavement by the British and their Yamasee allies.[71] According to the then bishop of Santiago de Cuba, Geronimo de Valdés, the appeal came from the chiefs Carlos and Coletos as well as leaders of other south Florida groups. From the perspective of these leaders, the solution to their ills was clear, Bishop Valdés attests in a letter to the king: "[T]hey gave an account to me of their very strong desire that I should assist in transporting them to this city with their families, wives, and children to receive the holy sacrament of baptism and to follow Christianity, thereby assuring their concentration and the welfare of their souls and security for their lives."[72]

In addition to petitioning the crown, on May 5 the bishop issued an *auto* (writ) reporting on his meeting with the chiefs and exhorting the governor and captain-general of Cuba as well as the general citizenry of Havana to support this cause. Their response: "[T]hey promised to provide the assistance that should be necessary concerning this matter and that they would contribute the resources for it that they could."[73] Valdés raised enough funds to dispatch two ships to the Keys under Captain Luis Perdomo. Upon arrival, Perdomo learned that many Calusa including the chief were away fighting the Yamasee. Rather than waiting for their return, Perdomo dispatched a message to the chief and returned to Cuba with some 280 Indians, including the brother of the Calusa chief, "the hereditary son" of the former, deceased Calusa chief, that chief's "Great Captain," and a number of other caciques of the "Jove, Maymi, Tamcha (or Cancha), Muspa, and Rioseco."[74]

Perdomo reported to the bishop that there were many more Indians prepared to leave than he could possibly accommodate with only two ships; the number of Indians who could be brought to Cuba was very limited. The captain "stated that he would have brought more than two thousand had he the vessels," adding that "those who were asking for the water of baptism surpass six thousand."[75] Accordingly, Valdés reported, "with a brother of the aforesaid cacique and other Indians of the first rank," the bishop, Perdomo, governors, and other colonial government officials met in Havana to plan the swiftest means for transporting the remaining indigenous refugees to Cuba.[76]

[margin handwriting: seeking refuge in Cuba from Britishtaly violence]

While colonial government officials in Cuba appeared initially receptive to accepting some Amerindian immigrants, Hann observes, "when informed of the potential for far larger migrations, they flatly refused to authorize the transport of any additional Florida Indians to Cuba without express orders to that effect from the Crown."[77] Explicit orders from the crown in support of the bishop's enterprise enforced the royal will, but only after several years of stonewalling by the colonial government. The crown decreed that "a strict order be given . . . to the governor and royal officials of that city to the effect that from whatsoever resources [there are] from the royal treasury, with your participation, they are to make from them all the expenditures necessary for the transport of the Indians who may wish to receive holy baptism and that, in accord as they proceed to arrive, they are to assign villages for them where they may live a civilized existence and Christianly under my vassalage and protection."[78]

The colonial government remained unmoved. Other letters from the crown conveyed the "great displeasure" incurred and included firm reprimands for Cuba's governor and colonial officials for not having reported on the enterprise, "the omission of which has been most remarkable and deserving of the most severe reprehension."[79] Consistent with the tradition of *obedezco pero no cumplo* (I obey but do not comply), the colonial government in Cuba continued to ignore orders from Spain. As church authorities in Cuba pressed the issue, the crown continued to send orders to the island colony for the transportation of the Amerindians for the next two decades.[80] In the summer of 1732, when the governor of Cuba, Dionisio Martínez de la Vega, finally did respond to the crown's orders and admonishments, he merely addressed the colonial government's unresponsiveness (purportedly the mail did not arrive) and the status of those same indigenous arrivals of 1711 and their condition in Cuba more than twenty years later.

The news was not good. According to the governor, of those approximately 280 indigenous immigrants who arrived in Havana that year, "few remained."[81] The governor provided no elaboration or explanation, concluding only that Indians were "inclined by their nature to negotiate in bad faith, [and] any kindly actions whatsoever that are expended on them are wasted as your Majesty will understand from the ones practiced lately."[82] Martínez could think of no other "suitable mission that would suffice for reducing them than that of arms, which is the ultimate among the measures that will be necessary for their conversion, in relation to which any other efforts will be illusory. The inveterate vice of the evil way of life of all those who are adults and even of the younger ones [assures this?], for there has been no lack of examples of ones who, after having been brought up here and after having spent thirty years in the Christian school have returned to the keys to follow their evil nature."[83]

A somewhat expanded accounting of the lives of the 280 Amerindians was given a decade later by one of Martínez's successors, Governor Juan Francisco de Güemes y Horcasitas, who reported that "of the two hundred and eighty who came during the year ten," death had taken four caciques and "up to two hundred of the Indians through violent illnesses that their poorly suited constitution left them open to," while the rest "were split up, with some seeking refuge in private houses and sixteen or eighteen of them returning to the keys according to the reports that have been dug up with careful inquiry."[84] The veracity of this account remains in question, especially since there is little or no detail of the status of the indigenous immigrants. Caution must be exercised, therefore, in taking this statement at face value, especially when a number of factors, are considered, among them clear indications of colonial government antipathy toward Indians, acts of misleading and ignoring the Spanish crown, and general self-interest toward discouraging Amerindian settlements in Cuba in the interest of keeping them in Florida as a strategic buffer. Ecclesiastical sources offer additional conflicting evidence. At least one document, a testimony by the protector of Indians and interpreter Christóbal de Sayas Bazán, indicates that more than two hundred of these Amerindians lived in a community close to Havana (probably Guanabacoa) during the 1720s.[85] Sayas Bazán was assigned by the bishop to missionize these indigenous immigrants and learn their language.[86]

In spite of "the indifference and opposition of the royal officials in Cuba," Hann observes, "successive bishops of Cuba had kept the issue alive."[87] The crown followed through by once again issuing orders, this time in 1730, authorizing expenditures for the transport of Amerindians from Florida to Cuba. In June 1732 yet another expedition was sent to Florida, accompanied by six Amerindians, indigenous immigrants resident in Havana who had been sent as envoys. They returned to Havana with an Amerindian delegation led by Diego, a principal cacique, and thirteen leading men. A junta, or meeting, was convened that included these delegates, colonial officials, and members of the church in Cuba. According to the record of that meeting, the cacique was told in considerable detail of the plan to move his community to the island colony and to assist them in the transition to becoming productive Christian subjects of the crown. The cacique Diego reportedly thoroughly understood the interpreter, "embraced the will of H.M. and promised to cross over to his villages in person and to transport all the Indians to this plaza, so that, having been instructed in the articles of the faith, they might receive holy baptism and live as Catholics under the protection of H.M." In turn, "the señor governor promised to give to him and to his [people] lands on the shores of this island where they might carry out their fisheries and plantings and that he would place a minister with them so that he might labor in the vineyard of the Lord, so that by this means H.M.'s desires would be served and carried out."[88]

Two ships were sent to the Keys, firing cannons upon their arrival to announce their presence. The principal chief Diego and his cohort then disembarked and supposedly proceeded to meet with other Amerindians about immigrating to Cuba. The expedition lasted some four days, during which Diego and others reportedly "were coming to and going from the said vessels to drink rum and eat the provisions."[89] By the fourth day, neither the cacique nor any other Amerindian remained but instead returned to the interior, "a certain sign that they did not want to come back."[90] The ships returned to Cuba, emptied of provisions and Indians.

Certain aspects of the circumstances surrounding the 1730 migration and others, however, appear marked by some vagueness along with contradictions or discrepancies that require clarification and, ultimately, more evidence. Regarding the six indigenous immigrants delegated to invite those from the Keys to Cuba, for example, Hann states that there were six Amerindians from the Keys in Cuba at that time.[91] Likewise, Milanich asserts that the Amerindians from Havana were "the only survivors" of the 280 indigenous people who migrated to Cuba in 1711.[92]

Other reports from the period convey little certainty of the whereabouts of the 1711 immigrants and state that these six were "among those who were to be found in that city," suggesting that they were only some of the Amerindians that crown officials were able to locate in Havana at that time.[93] Furthermore, as noted, at least some documentation offers conflicting evidence, arguing instead that more than two hundred of these indigenous immigrants lived in Havana and environs during the period.[94] According to research conducted by anthropologist John Worth in the parish records of Guanabacoa, though the mission's success was apparently limited during this period, there is record of at least one Calusa woman, baptized Leonor de Sayas (the name of the missionary's mother and sister), who also gave birth in Guanabacoa to two daughters, in 1729 and 1731, merely one indication of survivorship during this period.[95]

There were very palpable reasons for the apparently inconsistent responses of the Amerindians of Florida to Spanish overtures, some based in the inconsistent behavior of the Spanish themselves: indigenous communities in Florida were diminishing, the result of the twin plagues of war and disease. Refugees congregated at St. Augustine in the north, while others fled in various other directions.[96] Not to deny the ability of the Calusa, Ais, and others to exploit the Spanish for their own ends, as the Spanish did them, immigration to Cuba became a more crucial choice for indigenous peoples increasingly and violently displaced on the continent. At the same time, it is clear that in their dispute with the Church, the colonial government in Cuba contributed to the chaos by ignoring and otherwise deceiving the crown and delaying or denying transport for a number of years after the initial requests of the would-be immigrants. To the extent that nearly three hundred Amerindians made the journey to Cuba in 1711, attributing succeeding immigration failures to "Indian guile" appears as an inadequate and incomplete, if not ethnocentric, bit of reasoning. Certainly, even contemporaries who opposed the enterprise conceded some Spanish culpability. In his 1743 report, Governor Güemes y Horcasitas suggested that there were a number of times "when the migrations of these Indians have come to naught, with the result of making them mistrustful, as was manifested in the year of thirty-two, when they made another request [to be brought over]."[97]

Not incidentally, Hann concludes from this gambit the implication that no Amerindians migrated to Cuba in 1732. Yet in an earlier study, William Sturtevant concludes the opposite.[98] The testimonies of Captain Gomez and other participants in the 1732 attempt appear to suggest that no Amerindians returned with the Spanish to Cuba that year, though, again, this remains inconclusive. For its part, the crown, stung by the deceptions and subterfuge of earlier colonial governments in Cuba and suspicious of the motives of this one, remained allied with the Church in Cuba. Spain ordered that the colonial government in Cuba remain on the lookout for indigenous refugees in Florida.

Indigenous deputations continued their journeys to Havana throughout the 1730s, 1740s, and 1750s. In 1739 a delegation of eleven Amerindians from south Florida came to Cuba with yet another appeal for missionaries to come and work among the indigenous communities of the Keys; it is unclear, despite reassurances by the bishop of Cuba to the crown, that the colonial government responded at all. Some four years later, another delegation led by principal leaders of the Calusa presented a petition to the governor calling for the presence of missionaries in their lands.[99] Mindful of the crown's persistent predisposition toward bringing Amerindians to safe settlement and Christianization in Cuba, Güemes y Horcasitas sent a mission to the Keys and the Biscayne Bay area to assess the numbers and locations of the appellants. While he made clear his preference for a mission on the peninsula, asserting the mortality rates and mistrustful nature of the Indians, the governor's real concerns were likely more strategic: Spain needed a buffer in Florida to defend against the intruding English.[100] Meanwhile, a memorial was presented that year to the governor by "don Pablo Chichi, cacique of Carlos, don Domingo, great captain, and Sandino, sergeant-major," urging the Cuban colonial government to meet the request of the Indians for a mission.[101] Scholars suggest that the document was written by friends and/or acquaintances from Cuba, possibly Cuban fishermen who frequented the eastern coast and often worked with the Indians there.

The Jesuits arrived, as requested, near Boca Raton in July 1743. During their reconnaissance, they found several hundred prospective converts. Along the coast they noted that most of the men "understand and speak Castilian moderately well because of the frequent commerce with the boatmen from Havana."[102] Upon commencing their good works, the missionaries were soon disabused of whatever optimism they may have initially harbored. Once again, their treatment at the hands of their indigenous flocks was quite inconsistent with the tenor of the Amerindians' appeal in Havana. The Jesuits José María Monaco and José Javier Alaña reported, "The reception that they gave us was very rude. And once they had taken from us with intolerable importunity the provisions destined for them . . . they openly declared their displeasure over our coming, to the point of denying on repeated occasions, with evident falsity, that while in Havana they had asked for priests who would make Christians of them."[103] According to the missionaries, their indigenous hosts laid down the terms by which they and their children would suffer the priests: "that . . . the king our lord is to support and clothe them . . . ; that he was to furnish them with rum . . . ; the superstitions that they are full of are to be allowed to remain in place; and last, in the teaching of the children, no punishment at all is to be used."[104]

After centuries of contact and interaction with the Spanish, particularly with those in Cuba, the Amerindians of Florida had indeed become, Hann tells us, "keen observers of Spanish ways," and shrewd negotiators.[105] This latest indigenous overture may also have been a hoax, orchestrated, as the Jesuits concluded, merely to obtain needed provisions. Or, judging in part from the albeit qualified willingness to have their children Christianized, it may have been more. Indeed, the persistence of these indigenous passages to Cuba over both the short and long term throughout the early colonial period suggests that the Spanish were not rejected outright by their Amerindian counterparts. Regardless of all the problems, Governor Güemes y Horcasitas conceded to the crown, the south Florida Indians remained loyal allies of the Spaniards, having "contributed many times to the saving of shipwrecked Spaniards and as a scourge for the enemy."[106] Importantly, the governor added, "they have proved their friendship and good faith with the fact that for all the boats that go out to the coast from here [Cuba] for the fishery, they are the ones who do it [the work]."[107] Through the 1750s and early 1760s, at least two more substantial migrations of Amerindians from Florida to Cuba were undertaken to escape continued attacks from the British-allied Uchisi.[108] Even the Jesuit Francisco Javier Alegre agreed that, though "idolatrous," the Indians of south Florida, "migrating from one [key] to another to the seasons of the year, [and] the opportunity for fishing," remained allies of the Spanish and "enemies of the English."[109]

In the struggle to dominate, the Spanish interpreted indigenous efforts to make passage to Cuba as the response of peoples in desperate need of Spanish aid, tutelage, and guidance. They were all the more flabbergasted when their ostensible wards asserted their own interpretations and will. Conditions were being imposed, this time, from the other end, in a kind of reversal of the imperial role. Increasingly well versed in the advantages and disadvantages of association with the Spanish and perhaps and understandably even resentful of the wars and disease thrust upon them by the European invaders of whom the Spanish were one offending party, the Amerindians of south Florida determined to interact with them on their own terms. No longer merely a launching ground and center whereby diplomacy and political manipulation were the monopoly of the Spanish, Havana, Cuba, served Amerindian leaders on the continent as a destination, venue, and means for indigenous ends, whether for diplomatic conference and trade or refuge, settlement, and residence. In this context, both the Spanish and the indigenous peoples of Florida persisted in their attempts to influence and exercise their will toward one another.

Like their neighbors to the south, St. Augustine's Amerindian population continued to decrease, victim of the combined forces of disease, enemy raids, and social problems stemming from alcohol. Milanich argues that "rum from Cuba was too easily obtained by Indians whose lives had been turned inside out by colonialism and warfare."[110] As the Seven Years War raged, the numbers of indigenous casualties, displaced, and dispossessed escalated. By 1760, the five mission villages surrounding St. Augustine had dwindled to just two. These last two villages, Tolomato and Nombre de Dios, "represented all that remained of the La Florida Indians: Yamasee, Chiluque, and Casipuya Indians (probably Cusabo), all latecomers to the Spanish missions from the Carolinas; Timucua and Guale Indians ... and Costa and Chickasaw Indians, refugees who came to St. Augustine in the mid-eighteenth century."[111] Likewise, in the south, the unrelenting and pervasive attacks of English-allied Creeks forced the flight of even more of Spain's indigenous allies to Havana, dozens of Keys Indians who were resettled at La Cabaña. Ironically, during the invasion of Cuba by the British in 1762, La Cabaña became the site where the British set up their artillery for the bombardment of Havana, and in Guanabacoa, another indigenous settlement site, they established a siege camp.[112] While some indigenous residents were later relocated to Guanabacoa, British occupation likely contributed in no small degree to a dispersal of the indigenous immigrants at La Cabaña, especially as, after the war, it became the site of the largest stone fortress in the Caribbean.[113]

Following the end of the Seven Years War, more indigenous survivors made their way into exile, some to Veracruz, Mexico, for resettlement; others migrated to and resettled in Cuba. In any event, Amerindian missions and migrations between mainland America and Cuba remained integral vehicles for indigenous-Spanish alliances and relations in general. During the second half of the eighteenth century, this was perhaps most abundantly evident with the end of the Seven Years War and the cession of Florida to the British in 1763.

In 1763 the "fortunes of European war" and imperial geopolitics combined to yet again force the many indigenous inhabitants of the peninsula and surrounding region from their ancestral homelands.[114] Florida was ceded by Spain to Britain with the ratification of the Treaty of Paris. Spain traded its St. Augustine province in North America to the British for Cuba, which had been taken and occupied by the British during the last stages of the war. That the transfer process went relatively smoothly can be attributed in no small part to the dispatch with which the Spanish crown evacuated, relocated, and resettled the population of colonial Florida, including the indigenous members of that population.[115]

During the evacuation of St. Augustine in 1763–64, more than 3,000 people left Spanish Florida; among them some 150 Indians emigrated, the majority to Cuba. Apalachees from villages in the vicinity of St. Augustine accompanied Spanish soldiers to Havana; Christian Indians from the mission villages were also transported to Havana for resettlement. Some twenty Amerindian families migrated from St. Augustine to Cuba. These families had formerly resided in the last remaining mission villages near St. Augustine, where they grew maize and vegetables, and acted as guides, scouts, and couriers for the Spanish. According to Spanish reports, there were about twenty men, thirty-two women, and thirty-seven children (eighteen boys and nineteen girls). Destined for the pueblo of Guanabacoa, Cuba, the families received payments of one and one-half real per diem from September 1763 to April 1764, after which they received weekly payments of three and one-half reales.[116]

Another group of indigenous refugees who promised to convert to Catholicism made the journey to Havana with a Spanish officer and his troops.[117] Bernard Romans, an English surveyor, reported that in 1763 "about eighty families" of Calusa from the Keys "left this last possession of their native lands and went to Havannah [sic]."[118] In Guanabacoa they found "vestiges of familiar institutions," among these, indigenous municipal and church organizations and autonomous militias led by indigenous leaders.[119] At least for a time, these indigenous refugees also were able to maintain contact with their Spanish acquaintances. At the church in Guanabacoa, María Uriza had her daughter, María Francisca de los Dolores, baptized by a Padre Gines Sánchez, the same Franciscan friar who had ministered to them at one of the St. Augustine mission villages.[120]

Although most of the indigenous refugees appear to have migrated to Cuba, the length and location of residence, mortality rates, and other indicators remain unclear.[121] Some scholars suggest that Amerindian mortality in Cuba was considerable in the first years after 1763, and the survivors "scattered about in various points in Cuba."[122] Some of these same scholars, however, also concede that more substantial evidence is needed for corroboration regarding the whereabouts and fates of many of the Indians who settled in Cuba.[123] With the exception of a few "Lists of Indian Families of Florida" generated by the Spanish colonial government to monitor immigrants in Cuban pueblos like Guanabacoa, the record remains less clear, particularly when it comes to identification.[124]

Identity is another area in which there are more questions than answers. The available evidence suggests that Amerindian refugees from the mission villages at St. Augustine, most of whom appear to have been settled in Guanabacoa, consisted of Yamasee, Timucua, Costa, and other peoples who had resided at the mission and were accompanied by nearby Apalachee. The "Costa," a problematic term used by the Spanish to refer to coastal dwellers, probably included Calusa as well as some Ais and other Keys Indians and possibly a few others.[125] Nonetheless, these refugees joined the rest of the remaining indigenous community in Guanabacoa, "virtually the last refuge for the few surviving descendants of as many as perhaps two hundred thousand indigenous southeastern Indians from Florida and southeastern Georgia."[126] It is clear that at least some of the 1763 immigrants survived into the early nineteenth century, married, and had children. Some, like Josepha Dominguez, or Dominga, the Yamasee widow of Chief Juan Manuel Sánchez, were still drawing widow's pensions as late as 1800.[127]

The loss of Florida to Britain did not signal the end of Spain's or Cuba's relations with the region. Spain retained a "lively interest" in the former province and its eventual recovery.[128] This interest was kept alive in large part through evolving Spanish relations with the Creeks and descendant Seminoles who began to settle in the peninsula by 1763. Many established relations and passage to Cuba with some of the same Cuban fishermen who had so often traversed the straits to transport indigenous delegates from south Florida to Havana. Creek visitors were accommodated similarly in Guanabacoa and Regla, the latter also near central Havana and the base of the south Florida Cuban fishing fleet.[129] For the duration of the eighteenth century and later, the Creek Confederacy played a central part in the diplomatic struggles between the surrounding colonial powers, and Cuba continued to play a key role for Amerindians as a place of diplomatic conference, trade, and also settlement.[130]

2

THE "EVIL DESIGNS"
OF "FREQUENT INTERCOURSE"

Havana, Empire, and Indigenous Geopolitics

A year after the British invasion and occupation of Havana and a few months after Britain returned the principal Cuban city to the Spanish in exchange for Florida in 1763, the British secretary for Indian affairs in the Southern District, John Stuart, assembled his officers and readied them for their duties among the indigenous peoples of the peninsula. In a circular letter dated February 8, 1764, Stuart ordered his officers to report "everything" related to the "savages," especially any of their "evil designs" affecting British colonial policy.[1]

A couple of weeks later, Captain J. Harries reported on the assumption of control at Apalachee in Florida and made a number of observations on the local indigenous inhabitants. He urged the "absolute necessity of making the Indians presents, for they come hungry and ravenous, and expect to be supplied now with the provisions as they were by the Spaniards."[2] Harries added that some of the Indians had already become "greatly disaffected" with the British and were trading with the Spanish at "Havanna."[3] Like him, John Stuart was among those who blamed the Spanish for "tampering with our Indians" by "enticing the Creeks to the Havannah."[4] British officers characteristically attributed the "evil designs" of Creek and other indigenous traders to "the designs of the Spaniards" in meeting with Amerindian leaders in Havana.[5] A decade later, Stuart and the British in Florida still complained of the "constant" and "frequent intercourse" between "their" Indians and the Spanish in Cuba.[6]

The various movements and migrations of indigenous peoples continued from the Florida region across the straits to Cuba, passages that endured for the duration of the eighteenth century and into the nineteenth and possessed qualities both distinctive and consistent relative to the early colonial period. Indigenous peoples continued to come to Cuba, and contrary to the ethnocentric perceptions of the European colonials, they did so of their own volition. At the same time, if by the late eighteenth century many of the imperial European players remained more or less the same, the regional, imperial, and geopolitical context had most certainly shifted as an irrefutable result of the British "soundly defeating" Spain and France in the Seven Years War.[7] In the aftermath of the Paris negotiations that followed it, Britain took all of Spanish Florida and the eastern half of French Louisiana, securing colonies in South Carolina, Georgia, East Florida, and West Florida.

The British, however, were not the only new inhabitants of the region. Depopulated of the original denizens, many of whom, like the Calusa, Tequesta, and Ais, had died, dispersed, or fled to Cuba, the region became repopulated by new indigenous settlers. The indigenous peoples whom the British found in the southeastern tip of the continent and peninsula were no longer those first encountered by the Spanish. The expeditions, missions, and migrations to Havana that resumed did so, therefore, under the aegis of new indigenous protagonists. Chief among these were the Creeks.[8] Although victimized by the imperial and colonial machinations of their European counterparts, indigenous leaders among the Creeks and others also actively sought, not unlike their European counterparts, to protect their peoples' interests. They did not see themselves as the pawns or possessions of the European powers but as allies and adversaries—sometimes simultaneously, depending on the circumstances. Further, in the context of the European and indigenous geopolitics of the time, these indigenous leaders also saw and utilized Cuba as a venue for various purposes, as a forum for negotiation, trade, and eventually as a sanctuary. As British Indian Affairs agents and their Spanish counterparts in Cuba acknowledged, during the late eighteenth century Amerindians frequented the city of Havana and its environs, even while European imperialists, the British especially, tended to attribute agency to others for Amerindian journeys to and transactions in Cuba.

The tectonic shift in the hemisphere's international power relations therefore was not exclusive of the influence of its indigenous inhabitants. As the colonial wars approached a culmination in the eastern regions of the northern continent, Cuba assumed greater significance for many of the indigenous nations that had become entangled in European geopolitics. The island colony, long the Spanish "pearl" of the Antilles, gateway to the Caribbean, and launching pad for Spain's continental conquests, had also, by the mid-eighteenth century, increasingly come to serve Amerindians' purposes in their political battles and relations with European powers. Importantly, while these relations appeared to continue to serve the interests of indigenous allies, this was not necessarily the case for either old allies like the Spanish or new ones like the British. Havana, recently the acquisition of Britain until traded for Spanish Florida, became an important focus once again for both empires now, in the context of the dynamic of indigenous geopolitics, though the British, at least, did not necessarily see it this way.

"The year 1763," J. Leitch Wright Jr. has observed, "was decisive for the Indians."[9] The Treaty of Paris officially ended the presence of France in continental North America when, Olive Dickason notes, it "handed over the largest extent of territory ever covered by any treaty dealing with the American hemisphere before or since."[10] To the south, the royal proclamation of October 7 produced the two new colonies of East and West Florida, the proclamation line running from them north to Canada establishing a massive "Indian country" and separating Amerindians from whites (soldiers and traders excepted). Meanwhile, immigration was focused on the seaboard colonies and Florida. After 1763, "Britain controlled all the Southeast" and virtually monopolized trade with the region's indigenous inhabitants.[11]

The downfall of the French and rise of the British in North America did not bode well for many Amerindians, J. Wright observes: "British negotiators at Paris never inquired how Spain and France had obtained these lands from the Indians. In British eyes what the Indians conceded in the Florida treaties was their right of occupancy, and use of the soil or usufruct. George III, of course, already owned all the land in question."[12] Despite the British acknowledgment of indigenous territorial rights and the government's need for indigenous allies and trading partners, many Amerindian nations like the Creek experienced early on the actions of land-hungry, trespassing settlers and aggressive, unscrupulous traders, which tended to fuel their ambivalence about relations with the British.

As the British gradually assumed authority over the peninsula and its inhabitants, including the Amerindians by way of the royal proclamation, various Apalachee, Calusa, and other indigenous peoples of east and south Florida left with their Spanish allies and relations for Mexico and Cuba, most of them destined for the island colony. Effectively depopulating south Florida of its indigenous inhabitants, they were replaced largely by the diverse, mostly Muscogee-speaking peoples who had occupied and then migrated from lands encompassing present-day Alabama and Georgia and whose hunting territories extended from northern Florida to the Keys. These were the Creeks, a name the British used to describe the various indigenous communities that came to dominate north Florida and that the peoples themselves appropriated as their own, along with the Algonkian name "Muskogee," or "people of the swampy ground."[13] Tracing their lineage through matrilineal clans, these groups pervaded the Creek towns and villages established by the eighteenth century.

By the mid-1700s, as warfare, trade, and disease took their cumulative toll, groups of "wayward Creeks," many if not most of them young warriors dissatisfied with the Creek-Spanish alliance, broke away and moved farther south, down the peninsula, establishing themselves and their families in what the Spanish called "renegade" settlements. These became known as the Seminoles.[14] While Creek leaders later came to see their estranged relations as renegades, the relationship between the two remained more complex than either Spanish or British understandings suggest. The total indigenous population of the region figured as high as 16,000 by the end of the eighteenth century; the Spanish population between 2,500 and 3,500.[15] The Creeks farmed, hunted, and traded and when the Europeans arrived, incorporated them into long-standing patterns of exchange. Though the tension between Creek adaptation and European influence would reach a disruptive climax by the nineteenth century, indigenous influences on their British and Spanish counterparts remained palpable and even persistent throughout this period.[16]

Despite the efforts by the British to forge alliances with the province's indigenous nations through the proclamation's affirmation of the inviolability of Indian country, the response of the autochthons was, like that of the peoples themselves, not monolithic. Florida on its own was demonstrative of a variety of indigenous responses to the imposition of British hegemony on the peninsula. Several predominated but none absolutely or without qualification. Alliances were formed primarily through treaties; John Stuart cultivated alliances with and received the acquiescence of the Upper Creeks in the area of St. Marks in 1764 and with the Upper and Lower Creeks at Picolata in 1765. After 1763, Wright observes, indigenous leaders "might reminisce about prior visits to Saint Augustine or Havana, and Indians in Florida might still wear crucifixes and speak broken Spanish, but the Union Jack now waved over Saint Augustine, Apalachee, and Pensacola."[17]

Yet, if the British assumed that their new indigenous wards could, should, and would shift allegiances, many of the latter did not share such an understanding and begged to differ. Declarations to the contrary notwithstanding, relations with the former imperial hegemon were not easily discarded or old allegiances forgotten. A number of leaders among the Lower Creeks claimed continued loyalty to the Spanish. The responses of some to the assumption of British control and flight of the Spanish were quite hostile, especially as the "land-grabbing schemes" of colonists and abuses of traders persisted.[18] Regardless of treaties and promises of land rights, many Amerindians reacted violently to news of the imperial exchange; Gold asserts that "the skeptical Indians brutally assaulted outposts and plantations on the Anglo-Spanish frontier. Indian barbarities continued to occur in Georgia and South Carolina even after presents were distributed."[19]

Still others persisted in their relations with their Spanish allies irrespective of the knowledge or obvious preferences of the British. In his important work on Florida Indians, Charles Fairbanks has observed that the first report of "Creek relationships with the Spanish in Cuba" was in 1767.[20] However, these relations probably formed earlier, as suggested by Spanish reports dated several years earlier. The ink on the proclamation barely dry and British control of Florida newly taken, both before and after the treaties and the gift-giving, Amerindians in Florida went to the Spanish in Cuba. In January 1764 Spanish reports from Apalachee spoke of "Indians which went to that place [Havana]" and returned, greeted by dozens of others awaiting their reports of the "generous treatment" accorded them, noting further that the Amerindian delegation to Havana arrived expressing "a thousand exclamations for the courtesies" extended to them by the colonial government in Cuba.[21] The report's writer, Ventura Díaz, added, "They will later go from village to village discoursing on that place, and I have no doubt that if I have room, many will go with me."[22]

Chief Tunape (or Tonabe), an influential Lower Creek leader, was one of the first to direct his people to accept Spanish overtures. *openings* "Enticed by an independent source of trading goods that could help maintain their identity," they traveled to Havana by way of their own vessels or those of the Spanish, treating and trading in the capital city.[23] Numerous Amerindians registered their dissatisfaction with being labeled "inferiors, slaves or 'stinkards'" by relocating closer to the Spanish; among them was Tunape, who moved with his people from Coweta (near Columbus, Georgia) to what is now Tallahassee, Florida.[24] For some, the trail would eventually end in Cuba. Drawing the line between loyalty and self-interest was no less futile a task here than it was for the northern Cree of the Hudson Bay lowlands; after 1821, ostensibly loyal to the dominant Hudson's Bay Company, these Cree earned the ire of individual company factors through trekking great distances from one post to the next in search of the best values for their furs. So, too, thousands of miles to the south, Lower Creek leaders and their people persisted in journeys across the Florida Straits to treat and trade with the Spanish in Cuba as their interests dictated.

Accordingly, in March 1767 Stuart reported from Charles Town to General Thomas Gage that he had been told by various Creeks about their plans to travel to Havana.[25] The secretary notes from an interpreter's report that the Indians were quite explicit about their relations with the Spanish and their intentions. The Spanish, they informed Stuart, had "sent a talk to the Young Lieutenant of the Cowetas, and all of the Headmen of the Lower Creeks, and . . . the Young Lieutenant has sent his Spanish commission with a friendly talk by Thlawhulgee to the Spaniards. As the time appointed for Thlawhulgee to meet them was to be in January last, and this Thlawhulgee is gone to Tampa Bay, he is to go over to the Havannah and his sons to return to the Nation with his answer to the Young Lieutenant of the Cowetas, Escouchabe."[26] The secretary adds, "Nothing is more certain than the Spaniards have sent a talk into their Nation, by Thlawhulgee, this fellow is one of the Headmen of the Tomathlaws, Chauyauhiga a medal chief, brought down the Young Lieutenant of the Coweta Spanish commission, and the talk of this Thlawhulgee to give to the Spaniards. . . . [T]hey are all quiet about how they had the Spanish talk."[27]

Over the next several years, British reports continued to observe Creek Indians traveling to Cuba and back, as they would for the duration of the

British period in Florida. Indigenous travels to Havana, many extending from one to several months or more in duration, were frequent and persistent enough to concern and perplex the British and to provoke an imperial response; some officers urged their superiors to send in a British warship to intercept the Amerindians and/or their Spanish abettors.[28] This reaction came somewhat later due to the persistence of the indigenous journeys and was vehemently insisted upon by some British authorities; understandably, such responses appear to have been only half-heartedly enforced, if at all.

The other, more actively enforced strategy put into practice by the British was to gather intelligence on Creek and other Amerindian trips to Havana in order to determine Spanish "designs." To this end, Stuart recruited agents such as Pierce A. Sinnott and then David Taitt to monitor Spanish-Creek "intercourse" at Havana. Sinnott and Taitt were to earn the confidence of the Creeks to facilitate the intelligence gathering, and the two would report back to Stuart. This they did. Over the next two decades, the two spies generated a number of reports in their endeavors to monitor Amerindian comings from and goings to Cuba.

In one such account, dated March 1768, Sinnott reported that

> the Indians who went to the Havannah are returned home and look very gay in their Spanish cloaths. The Packhorseman who is come down says that they arrived about a week or ten days ago, and are dressed in rich laced cloaths. The Indian fellow who follows letters with this hath just told me that a great part of the Nation want the Spaniards to live near them as they should be better off than now and that they have offered them lands near the River Appallachecola; he further says that a great many Headmen are to meet next moon to deliberate upon some great affair.[29]

On the nature of the "great affair," however, Sinnott's reports fall short. This would become a well-worn and frustrating pattern for the British agents and their superiors: they became painfully aware of the many indigenous expeditions to Cuba through their informants and sundry espionage, but the specific details of the meetings in Havana remained as a fog to the British.

Four and then again ten months later Sinnott confirmed the continued travels of Creeks to Havana but, as Stuart concedes, "had not been able to penetrate any further into the designs of the Spaniards."[30] Two years later, in May 1770, Stuart lamented that with the help of fishing vessels from Cuba, the Creeks continued their visits to Havana, including a delegation of six men who had returned the previous February.[31] Later that same year, in December 1770, Stuart received reports from Emistisiguo "that the Young Lieutenant of the Cowetas is going to the Havannah this fall and has sent word through the whole Nation, he says he will be back in the Spring."[32] In December 1771 Stuart related, "Emistisiguo acquainted me that the Seminolies or east Florida Creeks had frequent intercourse with Spaniards at the Havannah by means of fishing vessels which frequent the bay on the western side of the peninsula; he lately seen some of them just returned at the Coweta town and expected to have heard some talk of consequence from persons who had travelled so far, but that they could [would?] tell him nothing."[33] In February 1772 General Gage agonized over the "East Florida Indians" who "go so frequently to the Havannah," and he ruminated over the design of the Spanish "in their invitations to those Indians."[34]

Over the next several years and for the duration of the decade, the accumulation of reports like these paralleled the persistence of Amerindian passages to Cuba. In December 1773 John Stuart, with some frustration, summarized for Gage the preceding twelve months' events: the Lower Creeks persisted in their frequent intercourse with the Spanish in Cuba, "which renders these savages more insolent and unruly than they would otherwise be."[35] In May 1774, British Indian agent Charles Stuart reported, "I am told that the Lower Creeks have a constant intercourse with the Spaniards who supply them with ammunition at a place near Cape Florida called Pea Creek in the province of East Florida, and that some of them have got Spanish commissions, especially one fellow called the Aligater [sic], who was at the Havannah and brought some papers to one Escootchabe who is said to be the principal concerned in the present disturbances."[36]

That same year, Charles Stuart reported further and with no little alarm that the Spanish were now "tampering with the Choctaws," with the implication that soon they and possibly other Amerindian nations would soon be following in the wake of the Creeks and making their way to Havana, if they had not already done so. Agonizing in a vein reminiscent of later theories of falling dominoes, Stuart concluded with an order to his agents and officers to pay out a "handsome reward" to the Creeks and Choctaws for the capture of any of the Spanish infiltrators.[37] It is not clear or perhaps likely that Charles Stuart's indigenous informants complied. A year later, John Stuart reported yet again with irritation on the Lower Creeks traveling to Havana in Spanish fishing vessels, an intercourse that "cannot be prevented while the Spaniards frequent that coast."[38] In fact, for the next several decades Cuban fishermen and Spanish agents continued to frequent the coast of the peninsula, just as the Creeks continued to return with the fishermen to Havana. Meanwhile, in 1775, British, Spanish, and indigenous nations found themselves embroiled in the American Revolution.

Geopolitics—imperial and indigenous—and persistent indigenous resistance to the directive of the hegemon account in good part for this state of affairs. First, Britain sought to maintain the peace with a Spain that, if in decline, still dominated much of the hemisphere. Furthermore, as much as they were able to exercise their hegemonic imperial mandate, the British also still needed the cooperation of their indigenous allies to carry out that mandate, a reality perhaps somewhat less evident in the context of Anglo-American land-grabbing but more vividly extant in the minds of colonial administrators when it came to indigenous intertribal or interregional diplomacy, infrapolitics,[39] and trade. In other words, the likelihood, even after years of defiant indigenous expeditions to Cuba and repeated calls by British agents, officers, and administrators, of sending one or more warships to prevent such frequent intercourse remained nil. But the English were not the only imperial power struggling to more absolutely impose their interests and restrict or sever the Creek-Havana nexus.

The proclivity of Spanish colonial administrators toward their Amerindian counterparts was to "conserve their correspondence and friendship."[40] Yet, the frequency of Creek and other indigenous visits and the rising costs of their accommodation were taking a considerable toll on colonial coffers and, by extension, the imperial treasury, as was especially noticeable at a time when Spain had embarked on a program to rationalize its imperial enterprise in the Americas. Friendship had its limits.

Were that not enough, amid the chaos of revolutionary war and in its aftermath, the British and Spanish commiserated over what the Spanish governor of Louisiana, Francois Luis Hector, the barón de Carondelet described as "the unmeasured ambition of a new and vigorous people, hostile to all subjection, advancing and multiplying . . . with a prodigious rapidity."[41] Kathleen DuVal has noted that neither Spaniards nor Indians who had fought in the independence war were consulted or invited to take part in this Treaty of Paris that ceded what would later be the states of Tennessee, Mississippi, and Alabama to the United States, the lands of which the new government wasted no time in surveying and selling. Indigenous peoples to the east, therefore, worried with good reason about this "new kind of European" who called themselves Americans, this "plague of locusts" that invaded "in unprecedented numbers" and "trampled Indian land rights."[42]

The Creeks, of course, were not the first to encounter the depredations of land colonization. Like those of their indigenous predecessors, Creek farmlands and hunting territories suffered extensive damage from cattle and settlers trespassing and trampling their birthright underfoot, damage that had as much impact on the ecological system as it did on Creek culture and identity.[43] Creek leaders, recognizing the threat, confronted their imperial allies. During the 1770s, Emistiseguo and other Creek leaders reminded British officials that "it was promised that no more Cattle should be drove through our Nation but that the Path should be always kept Green," and they protested when "Many Cattle" continued to be driven through Creek lands.[44] By the 1790s, Creek objections persisted in tandem with the trespasses of their lands by settlers and their roving livestock.[45]

As conditions worsened for the indigenous inhabitants of the newly surrendered territories and as the western neighbors of the Creeks contemplated invasions by the "new Europeans," the British and Spanish maintained, for a time, a rotational hegemony over the remaining southeastern seaboard for which even the new Americans retained a healthy respect.[46] Then and for the duration of the eighteenth century, the Creeks endured assaults as colonists and cattle encroached on their lands, as hunters became more burdened by debt, and as divisions worsened among the Creeks over alliances with the Europeans, slavery, and the accumulation of private property.[47] Creek journeys to Cuba, whether by Creek or Spanish vessel, were in no small way responses to the local and regional dynamics of imperialism.

In the context of war and its consequences, Amerindians of Florida continued to come to Cuba. For the next decade and in fact longer, various Creek and Seminole groups and individuals persisted in their passages to the island colony. Spanish reports confirm the frequency of southeastern Amerindians' earlier visits to and residence in Havana, including the countless visits they made for the duration of the 1770s; the reports furnish further evidence of the endurance of these visits through the 1780s and later.[48] Not only did the indigenous expeditions continue, but successive colonial governments in Cuba paid for the expense of these visitations. The evidence for this exists in the many lists of provisions gifted to the Amerindian individuals, families, and delegations for their stays and their return journeys; the lists, depending on the size of the delegation, length of stay, and sundry requests, were often very extensive.

Typical was the inventory noted in the report of the Spanish accountant and Indian agent Juan Josef Eligio de la Puente; he listed goods provided for three visitors from the village of Coweta—Chanillá, Chaquilayque, and Ynculeyche—who arrived in Havana on April 13, 1777, and stayed there about a month, until May 16. According to de la Puente, costs included "the gifts that have been made to them, maintenance during their residence here, food for the journey (home), and freight for the said schooner that returned to carry them."[49] He itemized a wide assortment of clothing, foodstuffs, textiles, sundry dry goods such as grooming products, and small tools, along with ammunition and other hunting and fishing supplies. The total cost for accommodating these three individuals alone amounted to more than 423 pesos.[50]

Several years earlier, de la Puente reported that another delegation, this one composed of fourteen individuals whose stay lasted nineteen days, had cost the crown more than 1,100 pesos.[51] In January 1781, in one of a number of such visits and subsequent reports, the Spanish responded to indigenous arrivals by supplying generous provisions for the delegations' journeys and for their accommodations while in Havana and environs—food, clothing, tobacco, ammunition, housing, and countless other sundry goods, usually with something for everyone, including the children.[52] Similar gifts and supplies continued to be provided to Amerindian groups well into the 1780s and later, at least until the United States acquired Florida in 1821.

At a time, therefore, when the British Empire in North America was either contemplating or acting on the desire to cut back on or eliminate the seminal tradition of gifting with their Amerindian allies, with this portentous break in custom reinforced by the aggressions of traders and the trespasses of land-hungry settlers, indigenous nations like the Creek turned to the Spanish and to Havana as a meeting place and a forum for negotiation and reaffirmation of mutual allegiance. To the Creeks and Spain's other indigenous allies, Cuba remained literally and figuratively an island in a sea of geopolitical and cultural change that too often seemed to bode ill for the independence and future of autochthonous peoples. Cuba proved useful to the region's indigenous peoples as a diplomatic venue, a place of trade, and a temporary refuge or permanent sanctuary. Despite the apparent mutual utility of such an arrangement, this pact was not infrequently also to the chagrin of the Spanish.

As for their adversaries, it is more likely that the gifting practices of the Spanish toward their aboriginal counterparts contributed to and reinforced the preconceived notions of the British about Spanish manipulation of the Creeks and other Amerindian allies for evil Spanish ends. In turn, this implied that the Amerindians were compliant dupes of the Spanish. A number of British military officials variously remarked that the Spanish were tampering with their Indians.[53] General Gage agreed and insisted that "the Spaniards must have some design in enticing the Creeks to the Havannah and dressing them out so fine."[54] In the early 1770s, convinced that Spanish interest had faded from "tampering" to "inattention," John Stuart appeared almost incredulous at reports describing the continued interaction of the Amerindians with the Spanish in Cuba: "I have heard it mentioned that the Spaniards from the Havannah have been tampering with the Lower Creeks; I now believe it is so and as soon as I can gain a more certain account of this matter shall write to the Governor of Havannah concerning it."[55] In late 1772, Stuart again reported on the situation: "There is certainly a constant intercourse carried on between the Lower Creeks and the Spaniards at the Havannah. . . . [T]his connection and intercourse may put it in their [Spanish] power to give trouble."[56] Aboriginal agency and initiative rarely figured as a decisive factor in the geopolitical dynamic of Anglo-Spanish diplomacy and positioning.

Yet one medium in which indigenous wayfarers and delegations initiated and persisted in their communications with the Spanish in Havana was by seagoing vessel, whether their own, that of Spanish sea merchants or Cuban fishermen or some combination of these. Although Cuban fishing vessels transported Amerindian delegates to Cuba, this was not always at the behest of the Spanish government. By the early 1770s, if not earlier, some colonial officials in Havana began to take stock of the costs versus the benefits of facilitating Creek and other groups' visitations to the island colony. Then governor and captain-general, the marquis de la Torre concluded in April 1774, "Desiring that these visits are not repeated due to the little fruit which has, in my opinion, been borne of them," Cuban fishing vessels would be prevented from going to the Florida coast, which was considered "the best possible way to prevent them from having to take Indians on board while finding a pretext with which to hide my true intentions."[57]

It is unclear just how many Spanish vessels the colonial government was able to prevent sailing to the coast of the Florida peninsula. It is clear, however, that neither he nor anyone else in the government would have desired to stop Cuban fishermen and impair the Spanish fisheries along the coast. Finally, it is also clear that neither the governor nor the captains of Spanish vessels could prevent the Creeks or other indigenous parties from journeying to Cuba by means of their vessels. The governor himself reported a year and a half later on yet another unsolicited delegation: "The Captain of the boat assured me that, although he wanted to deny them [permission] to board as commanded by his orders, he was pressured to receive him by the crowd of Natives that congregated of the reception of the cacique Escuchapé, who he carried to this post."[58] In April 1776 the marquis reiterated that "despite the repeated orders not to admit them on board . . . while on the beaches they are overwhelmed by large numbers of Indians who come in their canoes and oblige them to admit them [to their vessels] and transport them, always claiming that they have grave matters to discuss with the General of Havana."[59]

The incidence of such incidents increased as the decade progressed, while the size, frequency, and residence of Creek and Seminole delegations in Cuba expanded through the 1770s. Seminole delegations were in Havana every year from 1772 through 1778.[60] One such party consisted of "fourteen Indians of the Uchise nation who occupy the Province of Coweta in the vast extension from the Point of Tanche as far as Santa Rosa." The leaders of the delegation were the "Captain Estimalauche and cacique Lajaliqui," of whom the auditor Juan Josef Eligio de le Puente took charge. He met with them and discerned the object of their mission, "which in brief is their desire for the restitution of the Spanish dominion of the English establishments in that province, which they call theirs, for the attainment of which, with the Tallapoosa, Apizca, and Chataa nations [they desire to] wage pitiless war against them in this province if they are provided with arms and munitions."[61] In turn, the fortress of San Marcos would be delivered to the Spanish, Catholicism embraced, and the domination of the Spanish crown reaffirmed. Characteristically, the governor concluded, "Notwithstanding the misleading inconstancy of these people and the present harmony of Spain with England, it appears unwise to emphatically scorn their proposals, for the great convenience in any event to have these barbarians as friends."[62]

The Spanish certainly did have their own motives for continuing to promote, however unevenly, their relationship with their Amerindian allies in British Florida. De la Puente, as Spain's agent for Indian affairs in the region, felt strongly about Spanish cultivation of relations with the Creeks and other indigenous peoples in anticipation of eventually regaining Florida for Spain.[63] Yet, de la Puente also recognized the importance of avoiding war with the English over the peninsula and the influence of indigenous visits to Cuba in British perceptions of Spanish culpability for any anti-British actions on the part of the Indians. Here, in a report dated March 1773, de la Puente suggests that European and indigenous geopolitics appeared to collide. The agent related "the terrible venom" he observed among the Indians toward the British and was convinced that they would wage a protracted war until even San Agustín de la Florida and Santa María de Gálvez de Panzacola were razed, and the British would lay blame at the feet of the Spanish, "supporting their presumption with the fact that our Fishermen ... travel to the coasts of West Florida and that they travel to this City (Havana)."[64]

The secretary, nervously seeking to allay British suspicions and ensure "that there is no motive which would disrupt the good harmony between the two Crowns," recommended that "the proper method to remedy this problem without angering the Indians (because we are not going to, in any way, shape or form, dissuade them) is to completely prevent our fishermen from passing by the aforementioned coasts of West Florida."[65] The colonial government sought to maintain its alliances at a distance or at least to retain the flexibility of meeting and trading with its indigenous counterparts on tierra firme and keep British eyes away from the island colony. It also sought to cut the rising costs of the many Amerindian parties arriving and staying in Havana by terminating "their frequent visits, which do not cease to be costly to the Royal Estate."[66] The crown, in turn, agreed and urged the government in Havana to "find a way to moderate the repetition of their visits," but gently, "without exasperating them ... so that they do not impede our fishing on their coasts."[67]

From an indigenous perspective, the objectives of the frequent visits of the Creeks to Havana were manifold, politically strategic as well as economic and social, and interrelated. The frequent Creek reassurances to their British allies of gathering intelligence concerning the Havana expeditions and missions notwithstanding, the Amerindians appear just as often to declare their allegiance to their Spanish allies and provide intelligence to the latter when in Havana. Distinctions should be made here, although they were not always clear.

Ultimately, throughout the 1770s and 1780s, the British, the colonial regime in Havana, and the imperial government in Madrid were unable to prevent the Creeks or any indigenous allies from going to Cuba. Divided in their allegiances to the contending European powers, the indigenous peoples of Florida nonetheless remained determined to act in their own best interests. The old Creek leader Emistiseguo repeatedly reassured the British of his and his peoples' allegiance, manifested through the collection of intelligence on the constant intercourse between the Lower Creeks and the Spanish in Havana. Other Creek leaders, like the Young Lieutenant, or Escuchape, of Coweta, also stated that they would provide intelligence.[68] Circumstances intervened, however, and often qualified Creek support for the British. While Escuchape may have "promised to communicate whatever should pass" in his meetings in Havana with the Spanish, he and other Creek leaders appear to have more often than not kept their counsels with the Spanish tightly under wraps.[69] Even Emistiseguo, who reported on the many visits of other Creek leaders to Havana, could or would say little of the substance of the meetings.[70] Stuart's agents Sinnott and Taitt were no more successful, conveying little more than the vague information that the Creeks were treating and trading with the Spanish in Havana.

As de la Puente had reported, the Creeks in Havana were indeed in negotiations, at several levels, trading intelligence and goods with their Spanish counterparts. As geopolitically astute as the Europeans, Creek leaders, their families, and delegations traveled to Cuba to treat with the Spanish toward safeguarding their material, political, and sociocultural interests. Toward these ends, Escuchape, Estimslayche, Tunape, and other Amerindian leaders sought and gained conferences with the governor and captain-general of Cuba, whether solicited or not. The Havana meetings served as a forum for the Creeks to claim their allegiance to the Spanish crown and also, therefore, their right to Spanish attention and consideration.

In one of many such instances, de la Puente reported on a meeting with "Captain" Estimslayche of the Uchise in Havana in February 1773. Estimslayche and other Creek leaders had been calling on the governor of Cuba to convey to the Spanish crown their need for material and moral support in order to evict the British and enable the Spanish to reclaim the peninsula.

In his conference with de la Puente, Estimslayche acknowledged the power of the Spanish crown and then asked that some of that power be conveyed to the Creeks in Florida in the form of weapons and other supplies.[71] The grievances and requests of indigenous leaders like Estimslayche are acknowledged and confirmed in British reports of the early 1770s. In a report dated December 1771, John Stuart observes that the Creeks and other nations "complained of abuses of fraud committed by their traders," "accused me of being wanting in fulfilling the Agreements," and were "uneasy" about growing land pressures and "extensive cessions."[72] De la Puente, also mindful of the sensitive geopolitical circumstances of the region, attempted to diffuse the situation by reassuring Estimslayche that rather than arming them and provoking the British, his people put their faith in the supreme king.[73] De la Puente concludes that his answer satisfied Estimslayche and the entourage, who left to embark on their return "with happy and content looks on their faces," laden with the various gifts and supplies provided on their return to the peninsula.[74]

During the winter of 1774–75, as tensions escalated over settler expansion and war with the American colonists approached, British and Spanish reports commented on the increased frequency with which indigenous leaders in Florida were resorting to Cuba for support. John Stuart conveyed a report along these lines from one of his agents stationed in a Creek town. The report notes that land disputes were intensifying and the Creek leader "the Young Lieutenant is gone in a canoe to hunt for the Spaniards to get ammunition from them if he can find them."[75] He did. In correspondence dated May 1775, the interim senior assistant to the governor of Havana reported on the previous months' activities, chief among them the arrival, again, of Escuchape, the Young Lieutenant, accompanied by a delegation of war chiefs and their families. Through an interpreter Escuchape reported at length to the governor on the increasingly violent confrontations between the English and indigenous nations. He pleaded for the Spanish monarch to "help them under the concept of their pledging obedience to him, as earlier captains general had done, and concluded "by saying that their intention was to settle in the said Tampa Bay with absolute obedience to His Majesty" while also ensuring the continuation of mutually beneficial trade relations with the island colony.[76]

Once again, with reassurances from the governor of Cuba that the issues would be resolved, Escuchape and his delegation expressed satisfaction with the expectation of the traditional gifts bestowed on his people by the Spanish crown as signs of the latter's "acceptance of their solicitude," the king's protection, "and to placate their companions who remain waiting impatiently on the Coast, not having been able to come due to a lack of Boats."[77]

The governor and marquis de la Torre tempered his gratitude and reassurances with mild admonition that "it was not necessary to return there [Havana] with similar solicitations, with respect to the two prior visits being sufficient to give notice of such."[78] Though briefly acknowledging the "incessant bands" visiting Havana, de la Puente thought the expenses of at least some of the many delegations worthwhile, if high, "as they are all important men."[79] The marquis de la Torre latched onto de la Puente's comment, complaining further of the costs of the frequent visits of "unwelcome guests" and their prolonged stays. If they persisted, he sternly resolved "not to administer more than precisely what they need for their subsistence. I will dispatch them without giving them even the slightest gift and will warn them expressly that if they repeat these trips once again, they will have to maintain themselves and their transport at their own cost."[80] A year later, following another in a series of delegations, the marquis warned them "seriously to not repeat the trips so that they would not have to maintain themselves at their own cost."[81] Still, the governor deemed it "pertinent to administer the funds necessary for their subsistence in this and in the food which they were provided for their return, as was done for the other two that stayed here beginning on the 17th of March."[82]

Yet the Spanish needed their friends. Whether dissenting or supportive, each side recognized the regional and global strategic importance, politically and economically, of indigenous allies like the Creeks. Despite his own protestations against the many Creek visits to Cuba, the marquis de la Torre was forced to acknowledge the dependence of the Spanish on their indigenous allies "for their repeated demonstrations of obedience to the King . . . and for the protection which they offered to give to the Spanish boats which fish on their coast, as well as to those which are lost there."[83] The governor was further forced to admit the reality that ultimately, no measures of any substance could be enforced against the Amerindians to deter their coming to Havana. As he himself had admitted, mollification of the Creeks was, under the circumstances, the only logical option, if only to prevent any indigenous interference with Spanish coastal fisheries on the peninsula, an intrusion, he concluded, that could result in "great damage" to the economy of Havana.[84]

Nor were the indigenous allies of the Spanish discouraged or put off by the governor's qualified warnings. Indigenous individuals and delegations continued to come to Cuba, and the colonial government in Havana continued to receive and accommodate them while there. The expenditure of thousands of pesos and local resources speaks to the necessity and therefore, even if reluctant, willingness of the Spanish to continue funding and supporting their Creek and other indigenous allies regardless of the costs of such frequent intercourse in Havana. In turn, Havana became a stage not only for the entangling struggles of European and indigenous politics but for scenes of a form of role reversal in economic relations as well. Conversely, if the practice of gifting, providing lodging for, and otherwise accommodating "the continuous troupes" of indigenous people in Havana cost the colonial government thousands of pesos each year, it also provided stimulation for the local economy in Havana and environs, where many of the necessary items were purchased. Directly and indirectly, indigenous people exercised some influence in the economy and life of the capital city.

In December 1777 another in a series of Amerindian delegations came to Havana, "desirous of a conference with the Governor and Captain General." Like other visits, this delegation of twelve led by the Creek cacique Tunape and captain Talope sought to convey their loyalty to Spain and antipathy for the British. Spanish Indian agent de la Puente reported that they also came for some material aid from their ally, for

> they already completely lack powder, ball, guns, axes, hoes, and other indispensable articles required for defense from their enemies, to hunt animals, build their huts, or to dress themselves in the meager clothes they use, and even at the moment [they lack] provisions, since in the present year the harvests were poor. . . . [I]t is well understood that in [Tunape's] village as well as in others of its neighborhood, there are many Christians who wish that all those who are born may so be also, for which they charged he should ask that the Spaniards should send there priests who could baptize, teach, them the catechism, hear confessions and attend them when dying.[85]

Tunape urged the maintenance of "a friendly discourse" between the Indians and Spaniards, "as otherwise this will be lost with the passage of time and the English, who have desired [to replace] them, will succeed."[86]

De la Puente recommended that the provisions requested be provided and that a competent and reliable interpreter be assigned to the party.[87] Such practices, though of significant expense to the crown, nevertheless served the Spanish in their positioning war with the British. The Creeks and Seminoles were also served in receiving needed provisions and supplies, including weapons, being entertained while in Cuba, and subsequently playing one colonial power against another, though trade with British and Spanish forces would also eventually fracture the unity of indigenous allies. Although the Creeks and Seminoles exploited the Spanish in the interests of their own collective needs, they also took their alliances seriously.

The cacique Tunape declared in a lengthy discourse on his long friendship with the Spanish and hatred of the English that he would "sooner lose his life and that of all the force which accompanies him, before permitting any English to settle between the bar of Aix and the Boca de Ratones, and from the Punta de Tanche to St. Joseph's Bay, which is the territory he is prepared to guard and defend."[88] An old resident of Florida, Tunape spoke to a creole Spanish official well acquainted with the area and its indigenous inhabitants: "He claimed to have been raised to love the Spaniards."[89] For the Creeks, Seminoles, and other long-standing Amerindian allies, such a claim rested on a substantial foundation, as these communities had a long history of familiarity and relations with the Spanish in Cuba, building and cultivating a relationship of mutual trust in no small degree in Havana. The many years of conferences and gifting or provisioning in Cuba reinforced these relations for Spain's indigenous allies, as it did Cuba's symbolism as a place where these relations were developed and reaffirmed. If at times grudgingly or reluctantly, Spain's imperial and colonial governments were forced to acknowledge this interdependence. As Tunape Escuchape, and other indigenous leaders constantly reminded the marquis de la Torre and his fellow colonial officials in their Havana conferences, and as the colonial government also recognized, Spain's dependence on its indigenous allies encompassed several entangled dimensions, from politics to trade.

In fact, to a substantial degree, as the governor had observed, this relationship had long been played out in part in the straits and the peninsular coastal fisheries frequented by Cuban fishermen, fisheries whose productivity, as the Spanish were reminded, was facilitated by the region's indigenous inhabitants, many of whom worked and intermarried with the Cubans. Havana was as dependent on these fisheries economically as politically with respect to access to them. The fisheries played a considerable part in provisioning Havana and sustaining the local economy.[90] That this relationship developed on several levels was consistent, certainly, with indigenous systems of trade that have consistently integrated economic and kinship networks.

At yet another level, various indigenous nations of the region maintained relations over time with the Spanish in Havana through direct trade of various goods in the city. In addition to the use of Cuban fishing vessels to convey groups to Havana, indigenous traders had also long navigated their own vessels to the port city to trade. Although goods traded with the Indians were somewhat restricted, such as no firearms until the eighteenth century, the Spanish eventually opened up trade as their need for certain key products like ambergris to make perfume increased and English competition along with it. In exchange, native traders took tobacco and various implements including axes, hatchets, fishhooks, and knives. By the eighteenth century, trips to Havana and other Cuban sites for trade were becoming commonplace. According to James Covington:

> Many of these Indians traveled from the mainland to Havana in their small canoes, making the journey from the Keys in twenty-four hours, and traded with the people in the city. . . . They carried fish, ambergris, tree bark, fruit, and a few hides or furs to the Cuban city. A very profitable item was the sale of cardinal birds to the sailors at a price ranging from six to ten dollars apiece. The Indians received a princely sum of more than eight thousand pesos during the month of March, 1689. Thus, these half-clad natives in their frail canoes carried on a considerable traffic but, according to the Spanish, acquired very little articles or cultural traits from Cuba.[91]

Following the migration after 1763 of numerous Amerindians from Florida to Cuba, Creeks and Seminoles from the regions of Georgia, Alabama, and northern Florida took up trade with Cuba. In fact, the Seminoles of northern Florida had traded with Cuba well before 1763, traveling in seagoing vessels that carried up to thirty men to the Keys, Cuba, and the Bahamas.[92] Covington explains that one group of Seminoles, "which had roamed as far south as Charlotte's Harbour, traded furs and hides for dried fish which the Spaniards caught and salted or cured on the islands lying off the coast."[93]

William Bartram observed this indigenous trade in the summer of 1774:

These Indians have large handsome canoes . . . some of them commodious enough to accommodate twenty or thirty warriors. . . . [A] crew of these adventurers had just arrived, having returned from Cuba . . . with a cargo of spirituous liquors, coffee, sugar and tobacco. One of them politely presented me with a choice piece of tobacco, which he told me he had received from the governor of Cuba. They deal in the way of barter, carrying with them deer skins, furs, dry fish, bees wax, honey, bear's oil, and some other articles.[94]

Bartram notes the equally significant Spanish trade and industry across the straits: "The Spaniards of Cuba likewise trade here or at St. Marks, and other sea ports on the west coast of the isthmus in small sloops; particularly in the bay of Calos, where are excellent fishing banks and grounds; not far from which is a considerable town of the Siminoles, where they take great quantities of fish, which they salt and cure on shore, and barter with the Indians and traders for skins, furs, etc. and return with their cargoes to Cuba."[95]

In their meetings with the colonial government in Cuba, principal caciques like Escuchape often reminded the Spanish of the multifaceted, albeit uneven, reciprocity between the allies and the active and ongoing trade in Havana and environs, and they vowed to maintain it.[96] While some colonial officials doubted the sincerity of every claim made in this vein in the Havana conferences, there was no doubt of Havana's need for the trade goods that their indigenous allies could and did provide. At the same time, Escuchape and Amerindian leaders insisted on their right to conduct trade in the island colony's capital.

In the summer of 1775, in one of many similar conferences held in Havana with colonial officials, an unnamed speaker representing the Lower Creeks declared that he had come "to renew the loyalty and love which they hold for the King of Spain and all of his vassals" and expressed their desire "to maintain communication and commerce" with them, not the British.[97] The Creeks also had a very specific understanding of the manner and location in which this commerce with the Spanish was to be conducted, requesting that the governor "provide a boat that they themselves would [navigate], and which value would be paid for with the goods they would bring from their coasts to sell here."[98] The government in Havana agreed with the need for continued commerce with their indigenous allies but politely refused to relinquish the boat, suggesting instead that the trade be conducted on the peninsula. This they did, but would not and, in the end, could not realistically prevent the Lower Creeks and other indigenous traders from carrying out their trade on the island. The Creeks and other indigenous peoples in the Florida region reckoned that they had at least as much right to trade in Havana as did the Spanish on their coasts, and they continued to do so: "[I]n their own vessels or in those of Cuban fishermen this was not difficult, and Tonaby, Escuchape, Alligator, and other Yuchis [Lower Creeks] . . . arrived in Havana to barter skins for manufactures and receive presents from Spanish authorities."[99] The governor and captain-general de la Torre considered it "advantageous to our commerce the extraction of the goods that the Indians desire to offer and desirable for this city the introduction of horses, bulls, jerky, and pelts that are the benefit which they offer."[100]

The indigenous preference for trading in Havana became particularly and understandably emphatic as the American Revolutionary War intensified. The Spanish colonial government received repeated pleas from Amerindian envoys in Havana for Spanish vessels to carry trade goods to Cuba and to restore the lines of communication and commerce that war had torn asunder.[101] The governor and captain-general responded in a manner almost formulaic, agreeing to the need to trade but insisting on meeting on the peninsula, a demand, however politely put, not always feasible when war engulfed the region. For the duration of the 1770s and 1780s, whether through the exigencies of war such as the British military presence preventing a Spanish landing or the persistence of their indigenous allies, or both, the colonial government found itself admitting its allies into Havana and conferring with and trading with them.

The Amerindian relations with the Spanish in Cuba were not limited to communications and commerce. Spanish government reports suggest that indigenous delegations in Havana did not always return to the peninsula with their full compliment. Reports indicate that some indigenous women stayed behind to reside in Havana, even marrying there. This was not new, as indigenous peoples of the southeastern regions of North America had long been coming to Cuba, and many made the island colony their home.

Probably the most dramatic example of this was the 1763 evacuation from Florida of Spanish colonial families, including indigenous allies and kin. By the late eighteenth century this process had by no means ended, as colonial government and ecclesiastical officials in Havana continued to address issues concerning refugee indigenous families and the indigenous wives and children of Cuban fishermen. While some adapted to their new environs, others still struggled years after their arrival.

During the early 1770s, the colonial government in Havana pleaded with the imperial government in Madrid for support for a number of indigenous women who, several years after their arrival, de la Puente observes, "live in such a forsaken and destitute state that, not only do they not have anyone who values them enough to take care of them, there does not exist any sufficient reason why they should toil and suffer so."[102] In this report dated July 1771, de la Puente describes some of the range in living and working conditions for Amerindians residing on the island. While some lived in poverty, in a "sad and shameful situation," others, particularly the men, were "strong enough to work, as is verified by their various trades, or to fish, or to cut firewood in order to sustain themselves."[103] A number of Amerindians, mostly males from Havana and environs such as Guanabacoa, served as interpreters for the colonial government, acting as liaisons to translate and at times mediate at the many meetings or audiences that the government in Havana held with indigenous delegates. Spanish documentation suggests that overall and perhaps not surprisingly for the period, indigenous men in Cuba had relatively more choices in livelihood than did the women there.

Other indigenous women survived in Cuba by marrying residents of the colony.[104] A recent study by John Worth further suggests that a small but significant number of these indigenous immigrants and refugees intermarried with Cubans of African, African-indigenous, or indigenous ancestry. As described earlier, some bore children, and some collected pensions at least as late as 1800.[105] Some of these indigenous women may have become entrepreneurs, even slave owners; this was not unusual for the Lower Creeks or other Amerindian nations who traded in captives with their European counterparts.[106] Though the magnitude is unclear, some of this human traffic, indigenous and African or creole, found its way to Cuba.

Before this chapter concludes, some further elaboration is due regarding the indigenous traffic that voluntarily and even assertively made its way to Cuba, specifically with respect to the means by which many tended to arrive: the Cuban fishermen. Though perhaps at first glance apparently merely contemporaneous, in fact, indigenous passage to and trade in Cuba were not merely accompanied by but intermingled with and facilitated by a growing coastal fishing industry. Increasing numbers of Cuban fishermen were attracted to the bounty of drum, sea bass, pompano, and sea trout to be found off the southwestern coast of the peninsula. By 1770, reports estimated that more than thirty Cuba fishing vessels took part in the trade.[107]

The season ran from August to March, during which Cuban fishermen made one of the many coastal islands or keys their temporary homes and processing plants. It was at these *ranchos* (bases) that the Cubans processed the fish for sale back in Cuba. Some Cuban fishermen became so enamored of the Florida Keys that they chose to stay, working for various fishing interests during the season and cultivating small garden plots the rest of the year. The ranchos became important places of interaction between Cubans, Creeks, and Seminoles, with indigenous laborers aiding the Cuban fishermen in processing their catch. In turn, as already demonstrated, the Cubans' fishing vessels often provided transportation for Amerindians wishing to go to Cuba to trade their goods and treat with the colonial government.[108] By the early 1800s, expansionist Americans were understandably alarmed by newspaper reports that Seminoles were acquiring munitions from Cuban fishermen "who swarm uninterruptedly along the coasts."[109] Cuban fishing vessels likewise continued to transport indigenous delegations to Havana until the early 1820s, even for a short time after the 1821 transfer of Florida to the United States.[110] An era had come to an end. Yet, for the Seminoles, Creeks, and Cubans, such relations also transcended political, economic, or financial transactions.

Put another way, Cuban fishermen were not merely enamored of the Keys. Cuban or Spanish women did not accompany Cuban fishermen to the ranchos. Consequently, many of the fishermen had sexual relations with their female Creek companions; many also married them or lived in consensual unions, the progeny of which became known as "Spanish Indians," a culture that integrated Cuban traits and culture. Many if not most of the Cubans who lived at the rancho settlements had Amerindian wives, children, and even grandchildren. Covington has found that most of the offspring of the Cuban fishermen and Florida Amerindians "were born at the ranchos, spoke Spanish, and had not gone ten miles into the interior of Florida."[111] A number of the Seminole men eventually worked as crew members aboard the fishing vessels and "were acknowledged by white observers to be capable sailors."[112]

The Catholic Church and colonial government in Cuba took these relationships seriously and viewed the marriages as legitimate and sacred bonds. Furthermore, although some Seminole communities adopted the Cubans as family members, many if not most of the children of these families eventually journeyed to and remained in Cuba.[113] Although fragmentary, the evidence strongly suggests that these more intimate relations lasted well into the nineteenth century and that a number of fishermen returned to Cuba not long after the United States took possession of Florida in 1819.[114] A petition presented in 1838 by Cuban fishermen sheds some important light on the outcome of these unions:

> The memorial of the undersigned respectfully represents that your memorialists were located on the Gulf Coast of the peninsula of Florida as fishermen and seamen at the time of, and long prior to the cession of the territory to the United States, that it has been a long-established custom among the class to which your memorialists belong, and one which was recognized by the Spanish Government at Havanna [sic] as legal to intermarry with the Indian women of the country. Many of the children, offspring of these marriages were baptized and educated there and recognized as legitimate by the authorities of that city and country. Some of them are now residing there in respectable situations and enjoying all the rights and priviledges [sic] of Spanish subjects.[115]

The petition was presented by some twenty-one fishermen to U.S. Secretary of War Joel Poinsett in an attempt to recover family members deemed "Spanish Indians" by the government and slated for removal to the West, part of the larger and tragic Indian removal policy of the United States.

Many Cuban fishermen who married Seminole women appear to have chosen to settle in the United States. The fates of those who returned to live in Cuba remains unclear, another area in which more research is required. This process raises a number of questions about those Indian and mestizo children who, over a period of more than a century, were baptized, educated, and came to live in Cuba, the legacy of more than two centuries of indigenous passages to Cuba from Florida and the surrounding southeastern region of North America. The outcomes of these social relations and the communities that may have potentially formed around them in Cuba remain for the most part outside the purview of the history of Cuba and of the region.

Nevertheless, it is clear that Cuban fishermen played an obvious and considerable role in enabling indigenous peoples like the Creeks to directly address many of their various needs, whether political, economic, or social—including leisure and entertainment—by consistently providing transportation to Cuba, often against the orders of both Spanish colonial and imperial governments that, although mindful of the need for such alliances, chafed at the rising cost of the frequent and extensive visitations of their indigenous allies. The intimate and complex links developed between Cuban fishermen and their indigenous partners—from wives to crew members—adds a crucial element, one that likely played a significant role in facilitating and perhaps even expediting indigenous passages to Cuba. Finally, it is also clear that, for the indigenous peoples of Florida and the surrounding region, even and perhaps especially amid the tectonic shifts in the continent's geopolitics, many of which bode ill for the indigenous inhabitants, the Spanish Empire, for one, also remained useful to nations like the Creek. Likewise, Cuba had remained an essential venue of great utility: a gathering, meeting, trading, and dwelling place.

For more than two centuries, Havana served as a site of resistance, negotiation, and adaptation for Florida Amerindians as they adopted the great city for their various purposes, whether toward the fulfilment of political objectives in relation to conditions back on the continent, to carry on commerce and trade, or to settle as residents. When in Havana, both parties, empire and Amerindian nation, logically promoted their respective interests, whether candidly or through pretense; each possessed its private and public transcript, so to speak, with Havana as their forum. Put another way, the Pearl of the Antilles and its utility were not exclusively the domain of the Spanish Empire. From the sixteenth through the late eighteenth and even the early nineteenth centuries, diverse indigenous cultures, from the Calusa to the Seminole, journeyed to Spain's largest insular colony, engaged successive colonial and imperial governments, conducted trade in Havana and its environs, and established a small but significant and multicultural indigenous presence in Cuba. For the most part, they did so of their own volition. This may not be said of other, involuntary Amerindian migrations to Cuba that were also the product or outcome of the relations of geopolitics and colonial or frontier wars.

3

"BARBAROUS NATIONS"

Apaches, "Mecos," and Other "Indios Bárbaros" in Colonial Cuba

While many if not most indigenous peoples from the southeastern regions of North America, by the seventeenth and eighteenth centuries, came voluntarily to Cuba for all manner of reasons—trade, diplomacy, the exchange of intelligence with the Spanish, refuge, kinship, and even settlement and residence—this was not the case for other indigenous peoples who came to the largest island in the Caribbean.[1] By the late eighteenth and early nineteenth centuries, when Creek leaders like Escuchape, known as the Young Lieutenant, and their delegations had met, treated with, and were generously accommodated by the governor in Havana, many of their distant neighbors to the west faced considerably different treatment. Unlike their southeastern counterparts, the various nomadic groups labeled "Chichimecos" or "Mecos" as well as Apaches and other "indios bárbaros," or "wild" Indians, of the southwestern regions of the continent sustained their resistance to Spanish colonization of the *provincias internas del norte* (interior or northern provinces). Although some chose to compromise, like those among the Apaches who would succumb to the attempts of the Spanish at pacification, or would choose to negotiate and form strategic alliances with the Spanish colonial government, many others would choose not to submit, instead defiantly persisting in raids against Spanish settlements.

With the exception of those indigenous peoples like the Lipán Apaches and others who negotiated fragile alliances with the Spanish and lived as agriculturalists, to some degree the northern provinces of New Spain arguably otherwise resembled the southeastern regions during the sixteenth century. In these lands many indigenous people defied colonization and assimilation and fought aggressively against the Spanish colonizers, who struggled desperately to introduce some semblance of control and stability in order to be able to proceed with the project of colonization, resource exploitation, and evangelization.

As the commander in chief of the interior provinces of New Spain, Brigadier Felipe de Neve (1783–84) observed that economic development necessitated the subjugation of Indians: "Agriculture, cattle raising, mining and commerce required the pacification of Indians."[2] In both areas, if at different times, the Spanish struggled, while the indigenous inhabitants vigorously resisted. David Weber notes that Spanish government officials "regarded Indian resistance as an obstacle to progress rather than acknowledging that alleged progress provoked Indian resistance."[3] In the case of the Southeast, the Spanish struggled for generations before moving to a policy of greater diplomacy in order to initiate workable relations with the indigenous inhabitants of the region. The same was attempted again among the Amerindians of the northern frontier but with relatively less success. In the interior provinces, by the late eighteenth century the Spanish desperately reverted to a carrot-and-stick policy in the *presidios* (fortified military settlements): offering peace and prosperity to those who reconciled and military repression, imprisonment, and forced exile to those who continued to resist.

Compared to the many Calusa, Creek, and Maya who came to Cuba in the eighteenth and nineteenth centuries, those of northern New Spain came invariably against their will. Unlike the approach to these other groups, Spanish policy made little or no allowance for the options available to the various Apache and other resistant "indios mecos";[4] they were captured, made prisoners, marched in *colleras* (guarded contingents or convoys) to embarkation points like Vera Cruz, and then shipped to the island colony to undergo forced labor in public works and servitude in private households, a process that involved entire families of men, women, and children.

The Apaches encountered by the Spanish were somewhat arbitrarily identified by their general geographic location; those bands and tribes that comprised the larger nation inhabiting the region west of the Rio Grande in New Mexico and the Camino Real in Nueva Vizcaya were broadly characterized as western Apaches. Five principal tribes were recognized: the Mimbreños (Iccu-jen-ne), Gileños (Tjuiccujen-ne), Chiricahuas (Segatajen-ne), Tontos or Coyoteros (Vinniettinen-ne), and Navajos (Yutagenne). East of the Rio Grande in New Mexico and ranging from El Paso to

Chihuahua in Nueva Vizcaya were the eastern Apaches. Here, the Spanish recognized four tribes: the Faraones (Yntajen-ne), Mescaleros (Sejen-ne), Llaneros (Cuelcajen-ne), and Lipán (Lipajen-ne).[5] Though Apache economies centered generally around hunting and raiding, a few groups like the Lipán, incorporated some farming into their array.[6] As the eighteenth century progressed, however, the semicultivation of the Lipán and other Apaches gave way to a growing emphasis on horse herds and bison hunts. Spanish settlements, presidios, and military forces, meanwhile, contended with all of these groups, variously allying with some while defending against and pursuing others who refused alliances and kept up their resistance.[7]

Some scholars have argued that Apaches were intruders in New Spain; historical evidence suggests that they likely did not precede the Spanish in the area by many years.[8] As indigenous peoples in general have done, Apaches adapted to living in the plains environment, penetrating the southern regions east of the Rocky Mountains. Their first encounters with the Spanish took place there, as they met Francisco Vázquez de Coronado and his men in the mid-sixteenth century. It was in what became New Mexico that the principal Apache-Spanish contacts occurred, and it was there that the Apaches initiated their long history of "raiding and trading" among the more sedentary peoples, including Spanish colonists.[9] These complexes of the various Apaches (and Comanches, Kiowas, Navajos, and others) were expansive and extensive. Articles of trade that included horses and captives crossed the southern reaches of the northern continent from east to west, all the way to Cuba.[10] The Spanish may have shared with the Apaches and other regional peoples a heritage of capture, enslavement, adoption, and exploitation, but in the northern provinces the overriding need of the Spanish was a well-defended, stable economy and governable colonial system.[11]

The Apaches themselves were not a monolithic entity. Though they often allied with one another in raids against the Spanish and other adversaries, they were not united under any single national or tribal government, and leaders of individual communities retained their authority only in times of war.[12] All experienced varying degrees of prosperity and privation as well as pressure over territory from competing nations, whether from adversaries like the Comanches or the Spanish or both.[13] The degree to which they were pressured, and by whom, not infrequently determined whether one or another Apache tribe would treat for peace or persist in resisting the Spanish.

By the late eighteenth century, Gileño Apaches, for instance, were deemed relatively stalwart allies by the Spanish. Conversely, the Spanish alternately sought out the Lipán as allies one moment and disparaged them as barbarous enemies the next. Even when alliances were recognized by both as mutually beneficial against mutual adversaries like the Comanches, Julianna Barr has found, "replacing enmity with peaceful alliance did not prove easy."[14] Viceroy Bernardo de Gálvez, a former captain in the Indian campaigns of the 1770s, commented somewhat insightfully, "The Spaniards accuse the Indian of cruelty. I do not know what their opinion would be of us: maybe it would not be any better and maybe with more basis in reality. What is certain is that they are as grateful as they are vengeful. . . . The Spaniard should be impartial and recognize that if the Indian is not our friend, it is because he does not owe us anything, and that if he is vengeful, it is for the simple reason of wanting to get even for the ill treatment he has received."[15]

As scholars have recently made clear, Spanish-Apache enmity was also perpetuated in no small part because of the perceptions, conflicts, and contradictions manifest in the practice of Spanish Indian policy in northern New Spain. Conflicts existed between Spanish officials who favored treaties and alliances and those who opposed these as futile and opted for extermination. In turn, such disputes had their origins in the imperial prohibition against the enslavement of Amerindians, in effect since the compilation of the Laws of the Indies of 1680. The Laws of the Indies reaffirmed that Amerindians captured in battle had to be treated by Spaniards as prisoners of war or as criminals, not as slaves.[16] In 1756 the crown reaffirmed that "in no case, place, or time" could Amerindians be taken as slaves, although it also made exceptions of the various Chichimecos, Caribs, and others.[17] At any rate, official policy, as reiterated by Spanish officers, required that Amerindian captives be relinquished to authorities and treated as prisoners of war and officially sentenced to labor in mines or on haciendas for a period of time, not "claimed as chattel for life."[18] As always, however, the consistency with which the laws were enforced in tierra firme is another question. In the northern frontier, many Spanish, including government officials, found it "economically advantageous" to capture, buy, and sell indigenous men, women, and children, rationalizing their purchases with "the noblest of reasons," most commonly "their conversion to Christianity and freedom within Spanish society," all this even in the face of royal threats and papal orders of excommunication.[19]

In practice, then, these philosophical and administrative disputes had severe consequences for Spanish administrators, colonists, and Apaches alike, ultimately most severe for the latter. The struggles of Jacobo Ugarte and Juan de Ugalde, governors of the interior provinces in the 1780s, are a case in point. Both supported Spanish Indian policy, each in his own way. Each endorsed the capture and deportation of "indios feroces," or "belligerent" (read: resistant), Apaches and other Mecos, but where Ugarte favored a carrot-and-stick approach and distinguished between peaceful, treaty-observing allies and rogue renegades, Ugalde made no such distinctions, often attacking peaceful Apache settlements and imprisoning Apache allies.[20] Nor did Ugalde shy away from deception, agreeing to peace talks and then imprisoning and deporting unwitting Apache leaders and their followers.[21] Numbering among Apache deportees later sent to Cuba, therefore, were not only the most hostile but also would-be allies and peacemakers.

The beginnings of the official policy to physically remove and relocate Apaches and other indigenous resisters from their northern homelands to more remote locations like Mexico City are to be found in the Reglamento of 1729.[22] The policy was a result of an urgent, twofold need to, on the one hand, consolidate an effective, uniform defense system encompassing the northern borderlands of the provincias internas, and on the other, regulate the behavior of Apaches and the frontier population, civil and military, who tended to appropriate and abuse indigenous captives. Still, even after the *reglamento*, captive Apache and other indigenous men, women, and children were parceled out for servitude in Spanish homes, sold as slaves to Mexican mines and labor camps in the Caribbean, or, as very fragmentary evidence suggests, the children sent to Cuba for education and indoctrination.[23]

Nevertheless, the 1729 reglamento at least officially prohibited the act of forcing indigenous captives into servitude, although a variation on this would be reinstituted under later reglamentos. These captives of the Spanish, no longer spoils of war, were now to be sent under a secure military escort to the environs of Mexico City, there to be dealt with according to the royal directives as interpreted by the viceroy.[24] This the Spanish imperial government rationalized as a necessary solution for the "tranquility" of both indigenous resisters like the Apaches and the inhabitants of the northern provinces.[25] By 1739, the first of such forced relocations or deportations took place; an Apache leader known to the Spanish as Cabellos Colorados and thirteen members of his community made the forced march from Texas to Mexico City.[26]

The draconian stick component of Spanish indigenous policy was the desperate resort of the royal government to, once and for all, impose control over the northern provinces of New Spain. By the late eighteenth century, colonial government officials called for the capture and forced relocation of Apaches, Mecos, and other so-called indios bárbaros to locations distant enough from their homelands to discourage their return. In 1772, when the new reglamento establishing frontier presidios renewed the recommendation for the forced relocation of indigenous prisoners of war and their families to Mexico City, colonial officials like Hugo O'Conor and Jacobo Ugarte had openly contemplated the more permanent solution of shipping them away to Cuba or some overseas destination distant enough to discourage escape and return and, therefore, put a definitive end to seemingly endless frontier warfare.[27] In fact, at least as early as 1770, Ugarte urgently pressed for the capture and shipping off of rebellious Amerindians to labor in the crown's work sites in Havana. Even those like the Julimeño who, according to Ugarte, were complicit with the Apaches were targeted as deportees to be sent to Havana as a "pious punishment" for their "enormous guilt."[28] Several years later, Ugarte continued to press for such a solution.[29]

If the crown was initially slow to act on Ugarte's repeated recommendations, the need for such an alternative became all the more vivid in Spanish colonial minds after the incidence increased of Apache and other indigenous captives who had been relocated to Mexico City and other points in central and southern New Spain violently rebelling, escaping, and returning to their communities armed with knowledge of Spanish methods and therefore even more dangerous.[30] The rising incidence of such occurrences coupled with continued Apache raids and resistance to colonization in the north hardened the attitudes of Spanish military administrators. In a report dated January 1780, Ugarte again reacted to Amerindian resistance in the northern provinces by concluding that the only way to "bring about the king's pious intentions for the salvation of these ungrateful nations" was to "wage the most energetic war" against those like the Seri and Lipán Apaches of Sonora who resisted Spanish colonization and to forcibly and more effectively relocate them, "men, women, and children," to Havana.[31]

Moorhead has noted that if Ugarte's recommendation appeared extreme, by the late 1770s, many of his colleagues and contemporaries also considered the expatriation of recalcitrant indigenous nations as imperative, although the crown would take more time to persuade, certain of its policy of attracting the Indians to peace by the use of "pacific means."[32] By the end of the 1780s, however, and the evident inability of the crown's policy to come to fruition, the royal government in Madrid conceded to colonial exhortations.

For the Spanish colonial government in the capital, Cuba was the logical resolution for a festering problem, on at least two levels: the island colony appeared as an obvious alternative precisely because it was an island, and its distance and insularity seemed to offer the much greater likelihood of defusing and deprogramming the more threatening indigenous groups by employing them in needed public works on the island such as roads and fortifications. At the same time, such an insular location might ultimately prove more effective in expediting their assimilation.

In fact, colonial officials in Havana appear also to have long contemplated, along similar lines, the possibilities of relocating "indios infieles" to the island colony. By the early 1780s, discussions moved in the direction of the advantages, merits, and details of such a policy, reiterating many of the arguments propounded earlier by Ugarte.[33] Agreement on the utility of Cuba as an optimal site was not unanimous, however. Most colonial officials appear to have supported the enterprise, some saying that residents of the island, particularly in Havana, eagerly requested Amerindians as workers in domestic and other tasks while also expressing their heartfelt intentions to educate and instruct their wards in the Catholic faith and Spanish customs.[34]

Some colonial officials in Havana had misgivings; the short-lived governor Luis de Unzaga y Amezaga harbored doubt about the likelihood of such a policy's success, and he warned against underestimating the "fierce character" of resistant Amerindians like the Apaches, while his successor, the marquis de Someruelos, complained of the Spanish crown's introduction of "such evil elements" into Cuba.[35] These opponents warned further that the notion that wild Indians would be tamed and therefore more effectively assimilated to the labors and general environment of colonial society in a distant island colony left much to be desired. The captives were more likely, opponents argued, to remain wild and perhaps become even more volatile and vengeful, escaping into the countryside of the island. Unlike their urban compatriots, the argument went, farmers had reason to be concerned about

conflicting opinions about relocating Amerindians to Cuba

their safety. Unable to escape from the island, the Amerindians were likely to "disturb the tranquility of the farmers, their women, and families," setting fire to the sugar mills and "committing other atrocities that their vengeful savagery incites."[36]

Opposition notwithstanding and based on the relative continuity of the shipments, the extent of opposition to deportation does not appear to have been all that significant; the proponents of insular relocation prevailed. The policy of forcibly relocating Apaches, Mecos, and others deemed indios bárbaros to Cuba eventually became generally accepted and commonly practiced. In 1783 the crown endorsed an order by Teodoro de Croix, commandant general of the internal provinces, supporting the deportation or forced relocation of some ninety-five Apache prisoners of war to Cuba.[37] In December 1785 another order for the transport of indios Mecos to Cuba was endorsed, destined for El Morro fortress in Havana.[38] By 1789 the deportation of Apache and other indigenous combatants was a generally accepted policy; dissent was, for the most part, eventually silenced by the imperial government, as deportation policy was formalized in April 1799 and subsequently augmented.[39] Cuba was to be the prisoners' central and final destination.

Between the complexities, inconsistencies, contradictions, and confusion of Spanish Indian policy in the northern provinces and indigenous responses to it, the conflicts between colonizer and indigenous inhabitants like the Apaches persisted through the late eighteenth and into the early nineteenth centuries. As a result, in the course of the 1790s, many Apache, Meco, and other indigenous combatants and their families, captives of Spanish military expeditions, made their way in a series of colleras to Altamira (Nueva Santander province, present-day Tamaulipas and Veracruz). Mark Santiago, in a recent and important study of the deportation of Apache prisoners of war to Mexico City, concludes that "it is likely that many, if not most, Apaches who were sent into exile did not remain at Veracruz, but were sent off on a third and final journey to Havana, Cuba."[40] The evidence contained in government accounts, correspondence, and reports bears this out: hundreds of Apache men, women, and children were transported routinely on warships from Veracruz to Havana.[41]

A number of colleras of Apaches were conducted by Spanish military officials throughout the 1790s, several, for example, in 1796.[42] In another of many such instances, in late 1797 some seventy-one Apaches from the region of Chihuahua in Nueva Vizcaya, fifty-seven women, thirteen men, and one child, were conveyed under a guard of twenty-four Spanish troops to Veracruz, to be subsequently transported to Havana.[43] In August 1798, another collera of some forty-two Apache men, women, and children ranging in age from nine to more than seventy years old, all characterized as prisoners of war, were conducted to Mexico City to be processed for shipment to Cuba.[44] In September of the same year, a contingent of twenty-seven Apache males were conveyed for transport to the island colony.[45] In April 1799 still more "indios bárbaros prisioneros de guerra" found themselves forcibly relocated to the island colony of Cuba.[46]

The conditions of these forced journeys were, of course, extremely harsh. Bound, shackled, and guarded, Apache men, women, and children were force-marched considerable distances over often unforgiving terrain to their port-city destinations and from there placed on ships bound for Cuba. If conditions on the ships were relatively better than they were for African slaves, a number of Apache deportees still succumbed and perished on the passage. Whether over land or on board ships, death came as a result of mortal wounds received in struggle and resistance, disease, despair, or a combination of these. In one such shipment in 1798, eleven Apache prisoners died, part of a larger party of some sixty souls in transit from the Hospice of the Poor in Mexico.[47]

Regardless of the death toll, Apache and other Amerindian deportations proceeded apace. Based on admittedly incomplete Spanish accounting records, Santiago estimates that out of a conservative total of some 2,266 Apache deportees, more than 50 percent, at least 1,133 Apaches made the journey to Cuba.[48] He also comments, "Although Havana was not as susceptible to disease as Veracruz, the tropical climate, poor nourishment, and backbreaking labor led to a relatively high mortality rate there as well."[49] The basis for this assertion is unclear, especially, as Santiago also notes, as many of the Apache deportees to Havana and environs were women, the large majority of whom were assigned to domestic service. In at least a few cases, Apache men also worked in plantation and urban households. Further evidence suggests a longevity as the result of an ancient culture of adaptation and resilience.

From 1800 to 1802, various Apache colleras made the forced trek, some from as far west as the province of Sonora in Nueva Navarra, others from Nueva Vizcaya, and some from Nueva Santander.[50] More than a decade later, Apaches and other so-called wild Indians continued to be forcibly transported by their Spanish captors to insular exile in the Caribbean. In one typical shipment in 1816, "varios piezas" of Apache prisoners of war, amounting to thirty-five Apache men, women, and children, were sent to Havana.[51] Throughout the year 1816 and beyond, government reports account for the colleras of indios bárbaros conducted by the Spanish military to eastern ports on the Gulf of Mexico and from there to Havana.[52] This human traffic, fueled by Apache defiance, Spanish policy, and insular demand, would continue at least until Mexican independence in 1821. Even after independence, though, republican governments continued to entertain the idea of Apache relocation and deportation.

The specific objectives of deportation to Cuba included relocation and placement of the indigenous captives for employment and instruction under the oversight of the institutions and eminent residents of the island colony, primarily if not exclusively in Havana.[53] The interested citizens and institutions included the small and incipient middle classes of colonial Cuba, ostensibly extending their hands to provide education and instruction in the tenets of Christianity, while the colonial Catholic Church held precedent in the latter area of instruction. It too petitioned the colonial government, offering its services in the provision of religious instruction of the Apache "bárbaros." In one such instance in 1800, the Bethlehemite religious order in Havana arranged with the imperial government in Madrid a program of instruction for the children of the Apache and other Meco families transported to the island colony.[54] Whether among elite families or the church, indigenous labor mixed with Christian instruction, although, arguably, the Catholic Church orders tended toward a more genuine attempt at Christianization and assimilation than the various families claiming Christian benevolence and, in practice, desiring nothing more than domestic laborers for their respective households, in which indigenous women and children were favored.

While also presumably the recipients of benevolent Christian instruction, adult Apache and other Meco males were to take their places alongside African slaves and the fewer but significant numbers of Maya and other indigenous laborers, contributing to the harvest in the cane fields and tobacco vegas, and to the maintenance and repairs of public works in fortifications, roads, and various other tasks. Fortification work sites offered no shortage of digging of trenches and foundations, hauling of stone, earth, sand, and other construction materials, building of batteries, and quarrying and stone cutting. Labor also included the working of ovens and carting of lime and charcoal. Some of the laborers were assigned to work in warehouses, while a few might be assigned to work with skilled tradesmen as apprentices in carpentry or metalwork.[55] Outside of fortifications, enslaved workers could be found in various sites around Havana such the royal shipyard, arsenal, and tobacco factory.[56] Some were even assigned to work in hospitals.[57] One of the central priorities, however, especially after the British occupation and Spanish retrieval of Havana in 1763, was defense works.

In fact, Evelyn Jennings has found, "the scale and urgency of defense projects after 1763 forced the state to recruit and deploy many of its enslaved workers in ways that were to anticipate the work regimes on sugar plantations in the nineteenth century" as well as to affect subsequent deportation policies.[58] Though the defense work was scaled back somewhat by the 1780s and 1790s, thousands of enslaved workers were sent to Cuba during the mid to late eighteenth century to shore up an economy "perpetually short of labor."[59] Africans may have represented the largest single group of enslaved workers, but indigenous laborers from throughout Mexico, categorized variously as "reos" (offenders), "presos" (prisoners), "presidiarios" (convicts), and "prisoners of war" provided significant reinforcements, filling the ranks of forced labor in Cuba; throughout the 1760s alone, hundreds were transported to the island colony.[60] Though less is known about this indigenous traffic, in part due to the inconsistent identification of the trafficked, the available evidence indicates that many were Mesoamerican in origin.[61] Nonetheless, they had helped set the precedent, set the stage for the treatment of "indios bárbaros" of the north. By the 1780s, Apaches and other indigenous prisoners from northern Mexico reinforced these groups, joining them at various public works sites like El Morro fortress. Apache or Meco adults were not the only ones deemed useful for colonial administrators' plans for the development and security of the island. Apache children were, as well.

Amerindian children were deemed by the colonial Church to be the most promising subjects for colonial labor needs but also and especially for conversion and assimilation. They were therefore systematically singled out for their malleability as well as for their utility as conduits through which adult Apache and other Mecos who were relocated to Cuba might be acculturated. In a letter dated January 28, 1800, the Bethlehemite religious order in Havana proposed just such an arrangement to the captain-general. The religious order recommended that of the numerous Indians arriving in Havana harbor from Vera Cruz, Apache and other Meco youth be placed under the guidance and protection of the Church to be given religious and secular training as servants of both God and society. Practically, this translated into the training and placement of a number of young Apache workers in various local establishments in places such as the new settlement of Casablanca, adjacent to Havana.[62] Spain approved of the order's proposal, endorsing it by royal sanction a couple of years later, notably at about the same time that the commandant general for the interior provinces decreed that all presidios were to have primary schools for children under twelve years of age, a practice that also encompassed Apache children.[63]

Such sentiments appeared to be consistent with the intentions and wishes of the Spanish imperial government and other colonial institutions and citizens, if not always the colonial government itself. Colonial government officials had not consistently supported the enterprise of importing Amerindians into the island colony; the example of the various indigenous refugees accompanying Spanish soldiers and colonists from Florida during the early to mid-eighteenth century, including the evacuation of 1763, serves as an extended instance of some resistance to imperial orders. Although the Spanish crown insisted on the colonial government's facilitation of indigenous immigration from the coastal colony, colonial officials in Havana responded with a variation of the *obedezco pero no cumplo* response, in this case, delaying a response for many years. Still, if not consistently, the imperatives of the imperial government would nevertheless hold sway. Colonial government resistance, meanwhile, would slacken somewhat as the need for labor and related concern for racial balance became juxtaposed with stunted Spanish immigration amid a growing and potentially threatening slave and freed person population.[64] Production and defense, and the concomitant profits and security, eventually imposed their own demands.

Notably, even at the height of the slave trade in Cuba and amid the rise of Chinese indentured labor, a considerable demand for indigenous labor prevailed and endured in colonial Cuban households, royal government public works, and private establishments and enterprises, including, if to a lesser extent, staple crops like sugar and tobacco. While many of the petitions or requests for indigenous laborers, especially domestic servants, were made as overtures for Christian Samaritanism, arguments for leading Apaches and fellow indios infieles to the Catholic Church, these appear for the most part to have been little more than pretenses for gaining free labor, as the numerous written requests make clear. A number of these were solicited by widows or relatives of widows, the case made for help needed in the household or on the estate, help that probably came considerably cheaper than the market prices for African slaves, especially after the British abolition of the transatlantic slave trade in 1807.

Apache and other indigenous workers were demonstrative of the small yet significant groups that contributed to the diversity of forced labor in colonial society in Cuba. In turn, whether in the face of colonial government or indigenous opposition, the Spanish imperial government persevered in its mission to relocate and rehabilitate the Apaches. Demand in Cuba reinforced this mission early on, as a wide assortment of individual and corporate interests, largely in Havana, submitted their requests, not a few of them in somewhat desperate tones, for indigenous workers. Accordingly, Amerindian men and women were either assigned by royal sanction or granted through such *peticiones* (requests). The petitioners encompassed a broad array of social classes that ranged from royal officials and colonial and other institutional administrators to professionals, entrepreneurs, and similar members of colonial Cuba's fledgling middle classes.[65] Next to field and fortification laborers, some of the greatest demand was for domestic servants.

The placement of indigenous prisoners of war or otherwise captured Amerindian men, women, and children in Spanish households had become a common practice in New Spain and had its origins with captive Muslims in Iberia. David Weber summarizes this precedent: "Like Muslims, Indian captives taken into Spanish homes became *criados*, a word that meant both 'reared' and 'domestic servant.' Both meanings of the word applied. First, criados were reared by Spaniards, who fed and clothed them, baptized them, gave them religious instruction, and tried to acculturate them. Second, criados served Spanish masters."[66] A large number of Indians sent to Cuba were designated specifically for domestic service. In a letter to the governor and captain-general dated February 9, 1802, a colonial government official acknowledges instructions to receive from Veracruz "various Indians" who were "destined for domestic service in private homes" in Havana and were to be "instructed in Christian doctrine and some occupation that would make them useful in society."[67]

The demand for Apaches and other Mecos in domestic service could be particularly heated, and numerous *habanero* families as well as those elsewhere in Cuba submitted their requests for such servants either before or after the ships' arrival in the city harbor. In one such instance, upon news of the arrival of a ship in early 1802, several families submitted their requests for indigenous servants. Among the first was an order dated February 9 from a ministry official who, while noting the challenge and opportunity of assimilating the relocated Indians to God and country, indicated an interest in male and female indigenous servants whom he would attempt to have "conform to the sentiment that our holy religion inspires."[68]

That same month, within the first week, residents notified the colonial government to make their particular claims on individual indigenous arrivals. One resident, represented by a local military official, firmly reminded the government of her entitlement to one arrival among some twenty-one "Indias Mecas"; she specifically identified "la India" María del Carmen to replace the petitioner's black servant, "who had gone crazy."[69] In another such request, José Antonio de Abreu y Marques noted the arrival of "una Yemesa de Indias Mecas" and conveyed the wish of another resident to receive one "Meca," consistent with the orders and acknowledged obligations for employing the indigenous arrivals.[70] Ana Gamonales, "widow, native of Cadiz and resident of this city," with three sons in the military, "lacking the indispensable service of a slave because of her limited wages" and "knowing that some Indians have arrived in the ship San Ramón," submitted her urgent request for such a servant.[71]

Later that month, additional and similarly worded requests were submitted for distribution of one or more of the "varias Mecas" delivered to the city. The letters are almost formulaic in their requests for indigenous servants and their ostensible wish to fulfill their Christian obligations. On February 10, Juan Díaz, judge and reeve of Casablanca, conveyed a request for a "Meca," citing the orders and obligations decreed by the imperial government "to teach and indoctrinate" the arrivals.[72] In a letter dated the same day, Manuel Mario Lazo de la Vega, a presbytery teacher at San Cristóbal Cathedral, related having been informed of the arrival of "diferentes indias" and being in dire need of one for his "aged mother." Lazo further promised to fulfill the crown's decree toward the Christianization and assimilation of the prospective servant.[73] Anselmo de Gamón, an official of the Ministry of Royal Works, requested an Indian servant, ensuring that he would honor the crown's wishes.[74] Numerous letters put considerable emphasis on the need for servants, some with no little sense of entitlement.

In addition to Samaritan Christian overtures, colonial residents also ensured in their correspondences that their credentials clearly met the crown's wish to distribute indigenous servants to upstanding citizens. In February 1802, Rosalia Peñalver wrote to the captain-general acknowledging the arrival of "algunos Indios Mecos de ambos sexos" and, in noting the planned distribution of them among "honorable citizens" of the city, endeavored to ensure in writing that she was one of these; she requested her compliment of "one male and one female" and concluded with the obligatory promise to "educate them in the principles of our holy religion."[75] Gregoria Puebla, native and resident of Havana, in her request for one of the Mecas being distributed, put particular emphasis on her own honesty and good conduct— including devotion to the care of her indigenous servant—and therefore her merits as an "honorable citizen" worthy of this particular repartimiento.[76]

Other Cuban residents, in addition to insisting on their merits and commitment to educate and indoctrinate their indigenous wards, accentuated their great need under circumstances of want and relative privation. Widows commonly applied in this manner, as did others on account of illness, old age, fixed incomes, and the various encumbrances of large families. Having a household of sons was apparently the grave circumstance of Francisco de Rus, a local accountant who pleaded for an indigenous servant to provide some relief from the burdens of his family, "a woman, three sons, and an orphan."[77] In another request, a regiment officer respectfully insists that he needed an indigenous servant as a nanny to aid him in raising his child.[78] Havana resident Josefa de Castro, "being ill, with daughters, an absent or missing husband, and without means of support for a black [servant] indispensable for her service," conveyed a dire need for one of the "varias mecas" who landed in Havana while also noting her own obligation for ensuring the Christian education and well-being of such a servant.[79] Similarly, María del Rosario de Acosta, "being ill, with sons, her husband absent in performance of royal [military] service, and without a servant," also urgently requested one of the indigenous captives who arrived in the city.[80]

Among those claiming special need for indigenous servants, widows tended to be particularly well represented in the documentation, many exuding a considerable air of entitlement, merely identifying themselves as widows as adequate grounds for justifying the grant of a servant. In a letter dated February 12, 1802, Clara Cortes, "widow and resident" of Havana and burdened with two children, requested a "Meca" servant "for the service of her house."[81] Likewise, María Josefa de Velasco, widow of a militia member, requested delivery of one of the "Indias Mecas" distributed by the crown.[82] In the written request of María Magdalena Lazo, also widowed, she stated that she had been stranded with children and family and was therefore in especially urgent need of a servant, meriting because of her own reputable demeanor "una India . . . del Reyno de Mexico."[83] Similarly difficult circumstances apparently accounted for the plight of María Loreto de Castro, widowed, "ill and without a servant that is indispensable for her service."[84]

In February 1802 alone, the colonial government received more than twenty claims or requests for indigenous domestic servants. In the months and years that followed, this pattern of requests and veiled entitlements directed to the captain-general and then the distribution of Indians in Cuba is repeatedly reproduced, effectively creating a market and reinforcing the process of indigenous captives being forcibly relocated to Cuban households. For the duration of 1802 and afterward, the Spanish imperial government transported indigenous captives to meet a continuous demand from colonial residents in Cuba. Requests arrived throughout the early 1800s, many based solely on the purported wish to Christianize and assimilate the captives; some were based on reportedly urgent circumstances, while still others appear to have been either tenacious in their requests or perhaps proverbial repeat customers.

Such circumstances may explain the cases of Ana Gamonales and María de Africa Albuquerque. The widow Gamonales, in a letter sent in August 1802, stated that she had not been included in the repartimiento of indigenous servants back in February and therefore assertively reiterated her case and her request.[85] María de Africa Albuquerque was merely one more in a line of applicants who submitted their claims for indigenous labor based on a lack of the necessary resources to purchase a servant she considered "indispensable" for the care of her family. She assured the imperial government of the family's commitment to educate and indoctrinate "la India Meca," with a more explicit promise "within a short time" to baptize their ward.[86] Nor was it uncommon for suitors, perhaps as a contingency of marriage, or newlyweds to make less urgent requests for "useful" Apache house servants to maintain their households.[87] Throughout the spring, summer, and autumn of 1802 and into the following year, habaneros pressed their various claims to one or more of the Apache and other indigenous prisoners disembarking at Havana harbor.

Transports of relocated indigenous captives persisted throughout the late eighteenth and early nineteenth centuries in Cuba, and so too did public interest in acquisition and exploitation of the labor of these exiles, some *vecinos* (residents) applying more than once or for more than one or two individuals.[88] Wenceslao del Cristo, administrator of the San Francisco de Paula Hospital, requested at least four indigenous workers to be employed in the hospital.[89] During this period, many indigenous people landing in Cuba were identified as Apaches, Mecos, or of other northern nations of New Spain; a few are characterized as "guachinangos," a term that in Cuba more commonly referred to indigenous deportees from central Mexico like the Nahuatl-speaking peoples and could include peninsular Yucatec Mayas.[90]

It is perhaps a truism to observe that the distribution of indigenous laborers corresponded to the needs of the various social classes and economic sectors of colonial society and economy in Cuba during this period. That is, the captive men, women, and children were directed to work at various levels and in various economic sectors of the island colony of Cuba. Perhaps similarly to the earlier colonial labor system of *encomiendas*, the extent of Cubans' concerns for Christian charity relative to residents' practical considerations of labor, servitude, and profit is not easily determined. Based on the cases examined here, however, the overwhelming majority gave consistent priority to and emphasis on the needs of the households and enterprises, as Weber also observes: "Beneath these altruistic and strategic reasons . . . lay a fundamental economic truth: Indian laborers brought profits."[91] Furthermore, as noted, they were also favored as a necessity by those unable to afford the rising prices of African slaves with whom Apache and other indigenous servants shared much the same conditions and status. Some residents were quite explicit about cutting their labor costs by acquiring a Meca in place of a more expensive slave.[92] Spanish officials even used the term "piezas Apaches" to quantify Apache labor shipments just as they did "piezas de esclavos" for African slave transports.[93]

Most Apache men often found themselves directed to royal infrastructural works in Havana and Matanzas. Others were sent to the fields and mills of the rural areas. Almost all Apache women worked as house servants and possibly even as wet nurses. Of the conditions of "employment," a dubious term, as this was enslaved labor, of these indigenous forzados we know too little. However, some significant if fragmentary evidence can be gathered from the correspondence and reports of colonial officials and others in Cuba and Mexico. Filtering such documentation can also result, to some extent, in acquiring at least some understanding of conditions for indigenous laborers in Havana and environs and the perspectives and responses of the Amerindians themselves.

At least as early as 1783, colonial officials in Cuba were almost boastfully confident that they were more capable of handling the colleras of indios infieles that authorities in Mexico were having trouble keeping incarcerated or in work gangs at fortifications there. Officials in Havana, receiving news of the various desertions of Apache and other indigenous prisoners from within and around the prison San Juan de Ulúa in Veracruz asserted to imperial and colonial governments in Veracruz that their island system and facilities were more likely to be successful in keeping Apache and Meco laborers tied and occupied, while the insular nature of the colony would force them to become resigned to their fates and therefore more likely to be assimilated.[94] In a report to officials in Mexico, the colonial government in Havana expounded on the merits of sending Apache and other indigenous forzados to the island colony. The likelihood of their eventual docility and assimilation to Spanish colonial society, colonial officials in Havana argued, was considerably greater under the conditions in Cuba.[95]

Documentary evidence indicating circumstances of the dynamic and specific conditions of "indios bárbaros" in Havana and elsewhere in colonial Cuba is fragmentary. Still, it is possible to excavate some sense of the circumstances surrounding labor conditions for indigenous forzados in late colonial Cuba. It is clear that those indigenous captives who arrived in the island colony during this period were assigned to various sectors of labor in and around Havana. Although, in practice, men were usually assigned the heavier labor of royal public works such as fortification and road construction and repair while women and children were directed to work as domestic servants in the homes of "vecinos distinguidos" (distinguished residents), all could be designated for various labor duties "suitable to their disposition."[96] Based on the experiences of various indigenous forzados from other regions who labored in Cuba, rebellious Yucatec Mayas and others, for instance, it is probable that indigenous work assignments in Cuba during this time also encompassed other economic sectors. One of these likely included the shipyards of Havana, a center for the construction of some of Spain's best warships.[97]

Evidence for the daily working and living conditions of Apache and other Meco laborers in Cuba, although less clear, does suggest that some Amerindian exiles appear to have conformed or resigned themselves, at least to some extent, to their imposed conditions. A substantial part of the basis for this argument lies, to begin with, in the continued deportation of Apaches to Cuba along with the ongoing abundance of requests from residents in Cuba for Apache or Meco laborers for domestic and other work through the late eighteenth and early nineteenth centuries. Arguably, if problems with Apache resistance in habanero households were serious and widespread enough, such repeated requests likely would not have continued. During those years, however, the requests did continue. Groups of "indios Apaches" continued to come to Cuba through 1816 and at least until the end of Spanish rule, although, again, even governments of post-independence Mexico at least considered maintaining the enterprise and in fact did take it up again, this time victimizing Yucatec Mayas and others.[98] At a minimum, therefore, it may be inferred that overall, Apaches and other Amerindians in Cuba were employed according to their respective assigned labors and, for the most part, conducted themselves accordingly, if grudgingly.

Many if not most Apache women and children as well as some men worked as domestic servants in urban households. Weber suggests that in similar arrangements in New Spain, indigenous servants, especially women and children, not only worked cooperatively and efficiently but also eventually became attached to their new Spanish families, viewing them as a kind of foster family and their guardians, in turn, regarding them more as foster children than as servants.[99] As Weber points out, however, it is difficult to determine "where bonds of affection ended and self-interest began."[100] It is entirely plausible that such bonds also developed in Cuban households.

At the same time, based on the voluminous correspondence of habanero and other residents anticipating delivery of their respective Mecas, such requests or claims consistently put at least equal emphasis on their need for servants or slaves as Christian charity. Indeed, many requests put the initial emphasis on domestic service. Reconciling the two in practice is another question: "Whether or not criados became 'content,' the law made clear that criados were not the slaves of their guardians and could not be bought and sold 'as if they were Negroes or trade goods.'"[101] Indigenous criados had rights under Spanish law, as did slaves under the slave code. Some indigenous servants did in effect become slaves, although their Spanish masters, aware of the prohibition against slavery, referred to them as criados or *indios de depósito* (indentured Indian servants).[102] Others, especially Apache children and youths, worked as wards of the Catholic Church or under one of the religious orders.[103] Apache men, meanwhile, toiled primarily under the rigorous conditions of work sites like El Morro fortress and the king's highway. It is here that we have some of the more substantial evidence of conditions and indigenous responses.

The paradox of Apache existence in Cuba, arguably no less so than in the northern provinces of New Spain, lay in the dual responses of conformity or submission and active resistance—and everything in between. In contradiction to the boasts of overconfident colonial officials in Havana, Apaches may have adapted to their new surroundings as laborers and domestic servants, but some also resisted, likely covertly, subtly, but also aggressively and violently. Obviously not all Apaches submitted to a fate of servitude, at least outwardly. Numerous Apache and other indigenous captives not only attempted to escape en route to the island colony but were no less determined to assert their will to resist when in Cuba. Though in more qualified ways, Apaches were, Christon Archer argues, "no less dangerous in Cuba than they had been in their homelands in the internal Provinces."[104]

While some indigenous house servants probably found ways to exercise their rights under Spanish law against the abuses of their guardians, other Apache and Amerindian prisoners and slave laborers attempted to achieve freedom as determinedly as did African or creole slaves and Chinese indentured laborers.[105] The work sites that serve as demonstrations of some of the most substantial evidence of open resistance include public works locations like roadways, fortifications, and other defense works. A number of incidents were reported throughout the early 1800s, one in 1802 about the flight of several Amerindians from munitions works in Havana. The reported *cimarrones* (runaways) raided various local farms in the territory surrounding Havana, stealing and slaughtering livestock for food, while aggressively resisting arrest.[106] Further, the indigenous escapees had reportedly established a fugitive settlement in the forest near the village of San José de las Lajas. In the course of what became a violent manhunt, an African slave named Pascual of the sugar plantation San Rafael was killed, as were a militia captain and two of the Apaches.[107] The surviving fugitives were eventually tracked down and captured by the pursuing slave hunters and later convicted. The captain-general fully intended shipment of at least one of the prisoners to Veracruz but was firmly rebuked by the viceroy of New Spain José de Iturrigaray; without exception, "Indio" prisoners were "never" to be sent back to tierra firme.[108]

That same year, according to colonial government reports generated in October through December 1802, Apaches, indios Mecos, and other unidentified "indios feroces" (ferocious Indians) were causing "grave damage" within a radius of ten to eighty leagues beyond Havana.[109] These indigenous exiles had managed to escape from forced labor in fortification and other public works in the capital and fled to el monte (the woods), along the way arming themselves with "arrows and other arms" and otherwise supplying themselves with necessary provisions through pillaging area farms and plantations.[110]

Whether in New Spain or Cuba, exposed to enough oppression and privation, Apache people acted in defense of their interests.[111] Given the inability noted by Laird Bergad and others of sugar planters and other employers to distinguish between the treatment of African slaves and indentured laborers and the concomitant propensity of employers in Cuba to use excessive force consistent with their treatment of African and creole slaves, it is likely that Apaches in Cuba received similar treatment and responded as they would have under oppressive conditions in their homeland regions.[112] Whether they lived in freedom or as prisoners, Apaches' violent resistance to Spanish Indian policy could be relentless. In their homelands in the interior provinces, during the sea voyage to Cuba, and once in the island colony itself, numerous Apache men and women were determined in their bid for freedom. Escape attempts en route to Havana sometimes took heavy tolls on Apache and Spaniard alike. In one such attempt reported in 1799, some fifty-one Apache women in a collera destined for Havana rioted and escaped from custody in Veracruz.[113] In some areas of western Cuba, the intensity of Apache attacks and raids can be measured by the abandonment of certain agricultural operations such as tobacco vegas.[114]

Based on the available reports, the "rebellious Indians" of Cuba appear to have been predominantly males. The escaped indios feroces who were pursued and sometimes captured were men. This has significant implications for issues of gender and considerations of indigenous resistance. On one hand, it suggests that Apache women appear largely to have conformed

everyday vs. outward forms of resistance

to their work routines, while Apache men did not do so as consistently and continued to resist, with violence. This by no means negates the potential for the resistance of Apache women but instead suggests that if Apache women resisted their confinement in Cuba, which they likely did, they did so more covertly, along the lines of James Scott's "everyday forms of resistance." Though the paucity of direct evidence for this forces an inference, a reasonable one may be made.

Even in the context of indigenous cultures like those of the Apache, Comanche, and other indigenous peoples of southwestern North America whose communities possessed clear divisions along lines of male authority and dominance, women played significant roles as mothers, medicine woman, and guardians not only of future generations but of indigenous custom. In the diplomatic and martial struggles between Spaniard and Amerindian in the interior provinces, Apache and other indigenous women were "sometimes pawns, sometimes agents."[115] Used and often sold as captives by both Apache and Spanish males, indigenous women adapted and even as captives, acted as mediators between the two groups.[116] Such acts not infrequently worked to the women's benefit. It is plausible that with the rough transplanting of these interior struggles to an insular environment, indigenous strategies employed in the provinces could have been adapted to the new environment in the island colony. That this may indeed have been the case is suggested by scant, fragmentary evidence in the form of correspondence in the 1760s from the governor of Louisiana describing "captive plains women" to be sent to Cuba, presaging the official deportation policy.[117] James Brooks rightly surmises that "these anonymous Plains Indian women presumably spent their lives in Cuba."[118]

A half century later, indigenous women of the Plains continued to arrive Cuba as captive "prisoners of war." These "Indias Mecas" were destined for servitude in Havana and its environs. If they did not already have Christian names, they received them along with occupational designations, predominantly that of domestic servant.[119] If the extent to which Juana María, María de los Angeles, Paula Gertrudes, Dorotea Nicolasa, and numerous other indigenous women resigned themselves, at least outwardly, to their fates is unclear, it is probable that they employed some agency in that fate through varying degrees of negotiation and perhaps covert resistance.[120]

It is also probable, furthermore, that Apache and other indigenous men referred to in Spanish deportation reports likewise adapted, negotiated, and resisted in the context of their new conditions in Cuba and that they did so as individuals and in unison with other forzados. Not surprisingly, the more readily available record is not that of the relatively peaceful instances but of the more violent cases of resistance, as these not only made official reports but the local news as well. In an important study of runaway slave settlements in Cuba, the Cuban anthropologist Gabino La Rosa Corzo notes these incidents of violence (some cited here earlier), albeit briefly, in the broader historical context of fugitive slave experiences in Cuba. The cases cited, while fragmentary, are instructive and speak to certain key aspects of this indigenous presence in colonial Cuba. In at least one instance in the autumn of 1802, more escaped and "violent Indians" were reported plundering plantations in the Filipinas region west of the capital. Two years later, as they continued to elude capture, the ranks of these indigenous fugitives were reinforced by other "Mexican" Indians as well as by fugitive slaves.[121] While the result of this episode is uncertain, it was by no means an isolated incident, as similar reports were repeated throughout western and eastern Cuba.[122] The fugitives were probably Apaches, at least with respect to "indios bárbaros" in the western region, an inference consistent with the reports of colonial officials and other witnesses at the time.[123]

Nor were they alone. In reference to the Apaches, indios Mecos, and other unidentified indios feroces who had caused "grave damage" in the area surrounding Havana in late 1802, the *fiscal protector de indios*, Governor Someruelos, also reported that the "malefactors" became even more dangerous as they united with others "of their nation" as well as various other renegades they encountered along the way.[124] Someruelos contrasted this "reality" with the intended policy of the Spanish crown to instruct, indoctrinate, and assimilate the Amerindians. The imperial government was neither amused nor flexible and firmly reminded the governor of his responsibilities under the decree of 1799.[125]

Throughout the early nineteenth century, reports abound of "fierce" and "wild" Indians terrorizing the Cuban countryside. "The case of the rebellious Indians," La Rosa Corzo notes, "was notorious at the beginning of the nineteenth century," as the incidence of escapes and attacks appears to have escalated from 1802 to 1805 and later, while also suggesting a regional pattern.[126] Furthermore, contrary to earlier understandings, Amerindians like the Apache exiles in Cuba did sometimes favor alliances with escaped African slaves as well as with other indigenous fugitives. In the early nineteenth century, according to reports of slave hunters, "rebellious" or "wild" Indians sometimes allied with or even led mixed groupings of African slaves and fellow fugitives.[127] This should come as no surprise; such alliances could prove vital for short- and long-term survival. Francisco Pérez de la Riva has demonstrated in his classic essay that settlements of "rebellious Indians" dotted the Cuban landscape and therefore Cuban history from the sixteenth through early nineteenth centuries, if less so the historiography.[128] In some cases, Amerindians reportedly led *cimarron* (runaway slave) communities.[129]

Of the outcome of these events and the communities that became products of some, we know little. Certainly, some runaways were captured or killed, while others appear to have successfully eluded their pursuers, perhaps living as solitary fugitives or becoming incorporated into *palenques* (underground communities). These fugitive communities were later either abandoned or incorporated as rural towns or neighborhoods like Consolación del Sur in Pinar del Rios province or Jovellanos in Matanzas.[130] The identities of survivors raises yet another question. Here, a combination of earlier evidence and more recent studies may shed some light on enduring, although relatively rare, identification as "indio" or "indígena," both confounding and engaging the issue of *mestizaje* in Cuba.[131]

Of the survivors among Apache and other Meco exiles, therefore, a number of possibilities remain, with important implications not merely for understanding Cuba's understudied indigenous history but also for the history of race and mestizaje on the largest island in the Caribbean. Considerably clearer is the degree of endurance of Spanish policy and practice and also of the resilience and determination of Apache and other indigenous people in their negotiation, resistance, and adaptation to conditions imposed on them as captives and forcibly relocated immigrants.[132] Also clear is the continuation of all of the above and more after Mexican independence in 1821. Until U.S. annexation of northern Mexico and then liberal reforms in Mexico in the 1850s, deportations of Apaches continued under the new republic, as Mexico followed its colonial predecessors' policy of capturing indigenous men, women, and children and deporting them, possibly to Cuba.[133]

By this time in the island colony, sugar production and a plantation economy driven by slave labor had become the norm. Though the mass importation of enslaved Africans predominated as a source of labor in Cuba, a perennial shortage perpetuated by rising slave prices, active British abolitionism, and a growing freed-person population kept planters' minds open to a range of labor forms and prospective laborers. By this time too, amid the exigencies of war, Mexico had approved the deportation and forced reloca-tion of other indigenous peoples, also as prisoners of war, to Cuba. Like the Apaches, the Mayas of Yucatan, rebelling against a new order aggressively imposed upon them, became captives and unwilling immigrants in a sys-tem of human traffic bound, literally and figuratively, for Cuba. At the same time and also like the experiences of the Apaches, the Mayas' encounters, concomitant struggles, and resistance to a policy of captive commerce was a generational one begun several centuries earlier.

4

MAYAS AND THE MESOAMERICAN
PRESENCE IN CUBA

In a street scene in late sixteenth-century Havana depicted by Alejo Carpentier in a collection of his essays, the Cuban novelist describes a fascinating scenario: "The Indians play *pelota* [a ball game] in a plaza of the barrio of Campeche."[1] The reference is to a significant but little-known area of Cuban history: the barrio of Campeche and indigenous game of pelota are both real and symbolic manifestations of the multifaceted, complex, and enduring instance of the Maya presence in the history of Cuba, a story of migrations, diaspora, adaptation, and survival.

The Maya diaspora, Christopher Lutz and W. George Lovell have pointed out, "has a transmigrant dimension dizzying in its scale, complexity, and local and national impact."[2] Migration, "in one form or another," constitutes "a recurrent theme in the shaping of Maya history."[3] From an archaeological perspective, "Maya origins begin with migration," from the earliest peopling of the Americas; from an ethnohistorical and cultural perspective, migration is of intrinsic and spiritual essence, as is suggested in the Popol Vuh's reference to "semi-mythic migrations."[4] Historically and demographically, the scope of the Maya diaspora transcends its more commonly studied continental dimensions, extending into and encompassing the Caribbean basin, especially on the region's largest island, Cuba.

Migration plays a vital role in the story of Maya adaptation and survival. Whether forced or voluntary, Lutz and Lovell observe, Maya migration may be seen as

a rational, multidimensional reaction to the daily challenge of survival, whether the challenge arose last year, a decade or a century ago, or in the wake of the Spanish conquest almost five hundred years ago. Continuity in certain key patterns of survival comes as a surprise only if we fail to identify, analyze, and at least try to unravel the complex web of past and present migration experiences. Migration, in fact, is such a ubiquitous feature of Maya life that it would be possible to envision a cultural history that harnesses the theme as its principal organizing concept.[5]

The Yucatec Maya diaspora in colonial Cuba constitutes one case study in the dynamic of the diverse Mesoamerican presence in the Caribbean; it is also a study of the relationship linking Maya migration, survival, adaptation, and negotiation within domination. Further, the Maya presence in Cuba was reinforced by the presence of other Mesoamerican peoples such as Nahua from central and southern Mexico. The evidence suggests that over half a millennium, Yucatec Mayas predominated as the largest and most consistent Mesoamerican presence in colonial Cuba. Geographical proximity is one explanation; imperialism is another. The barrio of Campeche is one of the earliest manifestations of the Maya presence in Cuba during the colonial era. The earliest beginnings of Cuba's colonial existence, the barrio of Campeche in the city of Havana, represents yet another component in the "dizzying" dimension of the Maya diaspora's range and impact. Through the next five centuries, the Mayas of Yucatan, whether as individuals, families, or communities, journeyed to Cuba, voluntarily and involuntarily, under various circumstances and conditions, well into and in fact, beyond the late nineteenth century.[6]

In this chapter I trace the dynamic and significance of Maya passages to Cuba in the context of considerations of continuity and change. Perhaps more obviously in the case of colonial Cuba, the migrations of Yucatec Mayas to the island colony exemplify continuity with the past and are consistent with precolonial indigenous passages between the island and the peninsula.[7] Less obvious is that even under the domination of Spanish colonists, Mayas continued to find ways not merely to survive but more importantly to assert, through various forms of negotiation and resistance, their needs and interests as much as possible under circumstances of colonial social control. These were indeed times of great change and transformation in the Spanish Caribbean and tierra firme, change that too often boded ill for the region's indigenous inhabitants.

The earliest colonial era indigenous migrations to the Caribbean followed the Spanish conquest and colonization of Cuba in the early 1510s. As the ranks of indigenous Arawak Taíno laborers diminished on Spain's first two Caribbean colonies, Cuba and Hispaniola, expeditions were launched throughout the circum-Caribbean in search of slaves to resolve the deficit. By the early 1540s, more than two hundred thousand Amerindians from the American mainland had been captured, enslaved, and delivered to labor in the fields and mines of Spain's Antillean colonies; many were taken from the coastal regions of present-day Central America and Mexico.[8] Among the thousands of Mesoamerican captives, many were Mayas, transported to Havana through Campeche, the site of what would become a major port city on the western coast of the Yucatan peninsula.

Long before the official designation of Spain's largest Caribbean colony as a depot for the delivery of recalcitrant Amerindians in the late eighteenth century and before the more substantial flow of African slaves, Cuba received hundreds of indigenous slaves as laborers into its towns, settlements, fields, and mines. Increasingly, these filled the growing *poblados indios* (Indian settlements and towns) initially populated by indigenous Arawak Taíno, effectively rounded up by Spanish colonial authorities under the reducción policy of the crown. After several decades of aggressive resistance against *conquistadores* and colonizers like Fernando Hernández de Córdoba, Juan de Grijalva, Hernán Cortés, and then Francisco de Montejo, a captain of Cortés, the Maya of the unconquered Yucatan peninsula finally capitulated.[9] Even then, however, the conquest of the Maya remained relative; those in the northern part of the peninsula in regions surrounding the Spanish settlements of Merida, Campeche, Valladolid, and Salamanca de Bacalar as well as Mayas to the south and those who escaped to the south remained staunch in their resistance.[10] Many of the Mayas taken captive were transported to Cuba as a dual solution for Spanish administrators who wanted resistant indigenous people out of the way of mainland colonization and who also needed laborers in the island colony. By the mid-sixteenth century, Yucatec Mayas gradually but prominently came to reside in sites in western Cuba such as Guanabacoa, Regla, and what became known as the barrio of Campeche.

The Havana that became the capital of Cuba by the beginning of the seventeenth century was still only an embryonic city when in 1553 the Council of the Indies ordered the governor of the island colony to move his residence there from the old capital in Santiago de Cuba.[11] The barrio of Campeche was one of the two founding barrios of the colonial settlement of San Cristóbal de la Habana (the second being La Punta, known as the Spanish barrio). The Maya pueblo that became the "indio" barrio, although founded earlier, was first recorded in the Actas Capitulares del Ayuntamiento de La Habana of 1564.[12] Mayas in fact arrived as laborers in Havana considerably earlier under crown sanction, which, though declaring for the good treatment of the indigenous, did allow for the enslavement of those who resisted. Some of the earliest arrivals of captive Mayas landed in Cuba in 1517 under the conquistador Hernández de Córdoba after his first expedition to Yucatan. The Maya presence was not limited to the "Campeche ward"; colonial records indicate that many lived and worked in various parts of the island, including as far east as Puerto Príncipe.[13]

In an island colony where indigenous populations were becoming decimated as greater numbers of *encomendados* ("commended" laborers) found their ultimate relief from harsh labor through flight or death, *encomenderos* welcomed reinforcements of "red captives."[14] Like the indigenous Arawak Taíno, Yucatec Mayas labored under several worker classifications, from slavery to indenture. After the New Laws of 1542, it appears that many if not most Mayas in Cuba labored as "indios libres" and lived in their own humble residences in perpetual servitude to the Spanish crown.[15] As indentured laborers, Mayas were "owned" by various employers and through the cabildo, by the protector of Indians, or on their own by an *escribano* (clerk or notary public) were contracted out for periods that spanned months or years.[16]

Though many Maya forzados slaved away as laborers, indigenous deployment in Cuba exhibited a degree of social heterogeneity; not all Mayas or other indígenas worked in the colony's defenses, public works, fields, and mines. Some of the newly arrived Mayas were destined for other forms of servitude and trained to become interpreters for the Spanish in tierra firme or, in the case of Maya women, worked like other indigenous women commended to colonial estates as domestic servants.[17] Some Mayas trained in Cuba played a considerable role as interpreters and mediators in what became known as the Spanish Main.[18] Others, like their Arawak counterparts in Guanabacoa and similar pueblos, may have been appointed as *alguaciles*, officers responsible for the administration of their local communities, a duty roughly similar to that of the Maya *batab* (cacique).[19]

The greatest need, however, was for workers. Under the conditions of a growing demand for labor, a recurring theme in the colonial history of Cuba, the traffic of Mayas to the Antilles escalated, and Cuba became the principal destination. As a result of the campaign of Merida, formerly the Maya city Tiho, for example, some one thousand Mayas captured by Montejo were transported to Cuba and traded for clothing and other goods from Spain's Antillean colonies.[20] This settlement of Mayas in Havana's barrio of Campeche may even have predated the establishment of other indigenous settlements in the region such as the pueblo of Guanabacoa.[21] Transported by way of the port of Campeche on the Yucatan peninsula, many of the Mayas who arrived in Havana became known as the "indios de Campeche"; they were settled in the town and its environs and forced to work in public works and construction, among various occupations.

The Campeche barrio was predominantly "indio" and overwhelmingly Maya. A later government report lamented that the barrio was "composed of huts with miserable conucos [cultivated plots] . . . and inhabited by Indians who came from Campeche."[22] The huts were constructed of guano and wood, structures identical to those found in Yucatec Maya communities on the peninsula; such dwellings would later be banned by the cabildo of Havana because of their flammable nature.[23] According to Cuban scholar Fernando Ortiz, in the early stages of Havana's development, the Mayas were the principle inhabitants of the fledgling colonial city.[24] This is entirely consistent with conditions in Havana and most other towns and settlements in Cuba at the time. After the initial and tragic decimation of the indigenous population, the successive conquests of Mexico and then Peru in the early to mid-sixteenth centuries launched one exodus after another as Spanish colonists left the island for the material and financial promise of tierra firme, and these ventures, in turn, resulted in a significant diminution of the island colony's Spanish resident population.[25]

Imperial sanctions against emigration failed to deter exiting colonists, and eventually only several hundred Spanish settlers remained among thousands of surviving Amerindian people, both indigenous and later arrivals.[26] Demographically, qualitative evidence for the predominance of Mayas in the barrio of Campeche is more accessible than quantitative estimates. Early colonial records documenting the hundreds of Mayas forcibly transported to western Cuba and concentrated in and near Havana have been reinforced by more recent archaeological evidence demonstrating their insular presence. Excavation and analysis undertaken by Karen Mahé Lugo Romera, Sonia Menéndez Castro, and Roberto Valcarcel Rojas, for example, demonstrate a substantial material culture of early Mesoamerican Amerindian origin in Cuba's western regions, while artefacts and human remains dated as late as the seventeenth century provide further evidence of this presence in the east.[27]

As Spain's continental American empire grew and as imperial competition intensified in the hemisphere, above all in the Caribbean, Cuba's status gradually rose in the eyes of the Spanish crown from imperial backwater to strategic defense and shipping point. The augmentation of the indigenous and Mesoamerican populations in colonial Cuba by injections of additional, primarily forced, inmigrations of Amerindian groups and individuals coincided with the gradual rise of Havana and western Cuba in the expansionist and geopolitical strategies of the imperial government in Spain. Over the next two centuries, the Spanish crown dedicated more resources toward reinforcing the island colony's defenses. At a time when African slavery was still less utilized and labor remained at a premium—most of it deflected to the continental colonies—Amerindian people, increasingly from abroad, remained a principal source. In the ensuing centuries, the Mesoamerican contingent would remain a significant contributor even amid the rise in slave shipments from Africa.

As early as the sixteenth century, the Mayas of Havana, alongside a diminishing but still extant Arawak Taíno and a tiny but growing African creole population, provided some of the incipient city's principal labor needs. The Mayas of Campeche barrio were routinely conscripted into building and repairing infrastructure including roads and fortifications. In February 1575 the cabildo ordered Indians from the pueblos of Campeche and Guanabacoa to provide labor for the Spanish crown's public works needs in defense and transportation infrastructure.[28]

The work done by the Mayas and other indigenous laborers aided in shoring up the colony's defenses while also maintaining and augmenting infrastructure and facilitating economic growth, at least of the western region. An example is the indigenous labor summoned to work on the Chorrera ditch, a channel that habaneros needed "badly" as a conduit for fresh water.[29] Another typical instance is indigenous labor in the construction of a roadway intended to facilitate the opening of Havana to greater regional trade and commerce.[30] Mayas also worked in the increasingly important

Havana shipyards, on repair crews for El Morro fortress, and as masons for the garrison of Havana.[31] Mayas in the barrio probably also supplied some of the labor needs and services for Spanish colonists who increasingly took up *solares* (lots), in Campeche barrio in the late sixteenth century and early seventeenth centuries, when Cuba was undergoing a housing boom of sorts. This is suggested in various *actas de cabildo* (town ordinances), indicating the growing number of residents who gained entry into the barrio with the sanction of the Havana cabildo and who no doubt came into contact with their Maya neighbors.

That Mayas worked alongside other indigenous laborers in and around Havana suggests further that the *indios yucatecos* came into contact and likely interacted with these other Amerindians in Cuba, including the Arawak Taíno as well as *indios foraneos,* those from elsewhere such as Florida, some Apaches, and Nahuatl-speaking people from central Mexico, in addition to residents of Spanish, African, and other descent.[32] This, in turn, is suggestive of an array of encounters and relationships that developed during the early to mid-sixteenth century among Cuba's multicultural Amerindian population that ranged from co-workers at defense work sites and allies in flight from some of the same work sites to adversaries in violent conflict and spouses in mixed marriages. When then Governor Gonzalo Pérez de Angulo reported on the conditions of the indigenous population in colonial Cuba, he found at least two hundred "foreign" Amerindians living among the Arawak. How many exactly, the governor was uncertain. He sometimes found it difficult to distinguish between them, I. A. Wright notes, as immigrant Amerindians "had become so identified with the [Arawak Taíno] through intermarriage."[33] Some of the more intimate and enduring interactions, those of marriage and child rearing, are indicated in the marriage and baptism records of the parishes of Havana and western Cuba.

The "indios de Campeche" were no exception and likely counted among these groups. In his brief but important quantitative study of the barrio of Campeche, the late Cuban scholar Enrique Sosa Rodríguez found further evidence of Maya intermarriage among the cultures of Cuban colonial society. Parish records for the Espíritu Santo church, constructed in the heart of the Campeche barrio in the 1630s, document the registered marriage of Juan Alonso de Los Reyes, "indio natural de la Ciudad de Merida," to Eufrasia de Coca, slave of Luisa de Oporto in 1679.[34] Parochial records suggest continuity of the Maya and/or Mesoamerican presence in Cuba through intermarriage, reproduction, and sometimes livelihood. Children were born to couples of at least one Maya spouse, originating from in or around the Yucatecan capital, Merida.[35] As noted, the available evidence further suggests that some Mayas joined other Amerindians in Cuba in consensual unions.[36] Later, during the seventeenth and eighteenth centuries, when African slavery was on the rise in Cuba, many entries in the baptismal registers record the births and baptisms of infants born to slaves as well the baptisms of adult slaves and the names of the slave owners.

Relations among Amerindians, Spanish colonials, and African and creole slaves also existed in the context of the violence of colonialism as manifested in a number of ways and at various times throughout the early colonial period in Cuba. Some of the earliest indigenous uprisings against the brutalities of colonial working conditions under the forced labor system of encomienda—an institution that was banned in Cuba by the mid-sixteenth century—were conducted by multicultural Amerindian alliances that included Mayas as fellow combatants.[37] As early as the sixteenth century, Mayas in Cuba joined in the colonywide indigenous uprisings that "threatened Spanish settlements with extinction."[38] Some two centuries later, under an incipient plantation economy buttressed by African slavery, Mayas continued to play a role in resistance, figuring among the members and even the leaders of fugitive African slave groups that formed underground communities known as palenques in the forests and mountain ranges of western and central Cuba. In at least in one such instance in the 1790s, colonial officials reported the capture of a "Yucatecan Indian" by the name of "Guachinango Pablo," one of the leaders of a palenque near the western town of Jaruco.[39]

During the eighteenth century, Mayas arrived in Havana as prisoners of war captured while resisting Spanish colonizers on the Yucatan peninsula. Significantly and convergently, Mayas were also accompanied by Amerindians from the interior of Mexico. Overseas presidio confinement at this time encompassed a range of offenders of Spanish law, from common criminals to those who engaged in uprisings. Many Amerindians served their sentences in presidios in Mexico, most commonly in Veracruz. Increasingly, however, "hostile Indians" were sentenced and dispatched to do forced labor in overseas presidios; "Guachinangos" or "Mexican" Amerindians and, by the end of the eighteenth century, Apaches and other indios mecos from the northern frontier were deported as criminals and prisoners of war.[40] While prisoners were sent to various locations—Acapulco, Pensacola, and even the Philippines—the majority were sent to Cuba.[41] At about the same time, under the monarchies of Charles III (1759–88) and Charles IV (1788–1808) and in the aftermath of the 1762–63 British attack on and occupation and relinquishment of Havana, the Spanish crown frantically invested ever more enormously in the defense works of its Antillean pearl.[42] Labor needs on the strategically essential island colony rose significantly, coinciding with the rising number of revolts by Mayas and other Amerindians in the peninsula and interior of Mexico.

The Maya revolt of 1761 was one more instance in which Maya individuals and families found themselves gathered up and relocated, deported from the Yucatan, and sent to Cuba. The details of the revolt directed by Jacinto Canek Uc, a Maya shaman and self-proclaimed divine monarch from Campeche, Mexico, are beyond the scope of the present study. Of importance is that this was an uprising supported by Mayas from numerous villages in the northeastern region of the Yucatan peninsula, a conflict generated as much by socioeconomic grievances as by cultural factors, as much by colonial oppression as by the great need for "independence and separation from the Spaniards."[43] This was a fledgling revolutionary revitalization movement whose revolutionaries "asserted their right to rule themselves and have their own Maya king as their ruler."[44] As it increasingly controlled local Maya government and threatened the colonial order in peninsular New Spain, Spanish forces eventually resorted to violence to crush the movement. In the trial the following January, of the 134 prisoners who received sentences, many were executed, while others were sentenced to corporal punishment and hard labor in Yucatan and Cuba; nine prisoners were dealt two hundred lashes each and sentenced to eight years of penal servitude in the shipyards of Havana; six more Mayas had their death sentences stayed and instead were likewise sentenced to two hundred lashes and eight years of forced labor in Havana.[45]

Indigenous uprisings against colonial authorities in New Spain were widespread during the eighteenth century, and Cuba remained a central consideration in the minds of colonial Spanish administrators who found themselves faced with the stark dual realities of potential colonial conflagration in tierra firme and the abiding need to ensure Spanish American security by rebuilding and reinforcing Spain's defenses on the strategic isle and key to the Caribbean. Unstable conditions in the frontier lands of the northwestern provinces of New Spain, where colonial authorities also struggled with aggressively resistant Apaches and other "bárbaros," encouraged Spanish administrators to broaden policies that in practice had long been applied to Amerindians who were judged in violation of the empire's authority. By the 1780s, the deportation of Amerindian prisoners of war to Havana for forced labor was a generally accepted policy.[46] By 1799, the Spanish crown issued a royal *cédula* (royal order or decree) endorsing existing deportation procedures.

Though the extent to which Mayas were represented among the hundreds of Amerindians transported to Cuba during this period appears unclear, the consequences of the Maya revolt of 1761, along with the fact that rebellion still simmered in the eastern regions of the Yucatan peninsula,[47] suggest that the Yucatec Mayas probably continued to form a contingent among the colleras sent to Havana, convicted and sentenced for revolts, banditry, and other criminal behavior for which forced labor overseas to Cuba was the punishment. If the flow of Maya deportees and immigrants to Cuba appeared to thin by the late eighteenth and early nineteenth centuries, this was to some degree mitigated by the arrivals of various groups of other Mesoamerican peoples. During the same period, according to the records of legal authorities like the Royal Tribunal of the Acordada and the Real Sala de Crimen, the criminal section of the *audiencia* (royal court), hundreds of "indios" were transported from various regions of central and southern Mexico to Cuba.

While distinguished from "esclavos," the diversity of the broader collective of "forzados" is often masked in colonial government records, variously categorized as "Guachinangos" or "Mexican" Indians, "Guachinangos forzados," "presidiarios," "Guachinangos Presidiarios," "presos," and "reos."[48] Labor and other official reports refer distinctly to "Whites," "Guachinangos," "Mulatos," "Blacks," and "Cimarrones" and others, often, if not consistently, distinguishing among various forzados.[49] On closer examination, one finds that many of these people were convict laborers, among them "indios" who hailed from the Yucatan but also Puebla, Cholula, Oaxaca, Querétaro, Guanajuato, Texcoco, Actopan, and various other areas in and around the Valley of Mexico. As noted, in the lists drawn up by the courts, forzados are not always clearly nor consistently identified; their numbers and names are more often indicated than additional forms of identification. The more complete records that do exist and include place of birth or origin and residence, however, indicate a broader, multicultural Mesoamerican presence in eighteenth-century Cuba.

As such, the available evidence strongly suggests that Yucatec Mayas in Cuba were accompanied by Nahuas from Puebla and Cholula, Otomis from Querétaro and Guanajuato, and Mixtecs and Zapotecs from Oaxaca, among many others.[50] Nahuas and other Mesoamerican people crossed the channel to Cuba as convict laborers, skilled and unskilled, throughout the late eighteenth century. Predominantly male and ranging in age from twenty-five to fifty-five years, these indigenous Mesoamericans served sentences of hard labor in Havana and surrounding areas that stretched from two to ten years or more, coinciding with a corresponding range of offenses, from illegal sale of alcohol to adultery to murder. During October and December 1780 alone, more than twenty known cases exist of Mesoamerican "indios" sentenced to labor in the fortifications of Havana.[51] Depending on factors like the severity of the crime and rate of recidivism or attempted escape, some offenders were banished permanently.

In one of numerous such cases, on December 23, 1780, the Royal Court of Criminal Offenses in Puebla sentenced Severino Antonio, "indio" of Texcoco, in the present state of Mexico, to two years of service in the military installations of Havana, Cuba. The twenty-five-year-old indígena bricklayer had been serving time in the royal jail in Puebla after being arrested for drunkenness and illegally dealing in pulque.[52] As commonly occurred then, the court saw fit to transfer Antonio to Havana, where labor was in perennially short supply. Further, when in Havana, Antonio may possibly have encountered Pascual Felipe, "un Indio" from Santiago Teanquistengo (or Tianguistenco), Mexico, convicted and sentenced about three months earlier. The same age as Antonio, the young and married Felipe had been sentenced to ten years hard labor in El Morro fortress in Havana for the death of Antonio Ramón.[53] Felipe may have been one of those offenders whose crime was severe enough and his offenses possibly numerous enough to warrant a warning from the judge that his sentence would be extended to life if he escaped or otherwise failed to fulfill his term at El Morro. That the court's warning was an effective deterrent is less clear.

According to Spanish forzado labor reports, desertions or escapes were at times a problem of epidemic proportions. During the spring and summer of 1768, nearly one hundred "Guachinangos" reportedly abandoned

(*desertaron*) their work sites at fortifications in Havana.[54] The rising incidence of forzado escapes forced an additional and unwanted expenditure of
funds and resources for the Spanish crown, as guard duties were reinforced
at work sites and deserters were pursued and sometimes apprehended and
returned to the labors they had sought to escape.[55] For the duration of the
eighteenth century, desertions by forzados in Cuba persisted, along with
the concomitant, if not always successful, manhunts by colonial authorities.

As for Severino and Pascual, both offenders joined the ranks of thousands of other forzados, many of them also indigenous Mesoamericans sent
to Cuba to serve out their sentences through hard labor in the fortifications,
roads and other public works, and even military service. Many Mesoamerican people filled the ranks of forzados at least as early as 1763; through the
1760s alone, hundreds were transported to the island colony.[56] In just one
of those years, 1768, more than 350 "guachinango Indians" were transported
from Mexico to Cuba.[57] On June 20, 1772, the marquis de la Torre received
news that twenty-five "Guachinangos Forzados" were on their way to Havana, more hands for the unrelenting needs of the island colony's fortifications.[58] In the summer of 1780, some 800 forzados, "Desterrados del Reino
de Nueva España" (exiles from the kingdom/New Spain) were assigned to
labor in and around Havana.[59] Though the number of indígenas in such
groups is often unclear, the various *acordada* and other court documents
that do provide more complete information suggest that the proportion of
indigenous forzados could have ranged as greatly as 10 to 50 percent of the
total.[60] At bottom, for the duration of the late eighteenth century, Mesoamericans continued to number among the ranks of the various Havana-
area work brigades.

By the end of the century, as the Spanish crown's insular defense priorities became less urgent, this broader Mesoamerican human traffic appears
to have diminished appreciably. The role and contribution of the convicted
indígenas, perhaps most of them from the Valley of Mexico, if more historically episodic, paralleled that of the Yucatec Mayas whose journeys,
although periodically ebbing and flowing, nevertheless persisted over the
centuries. The number of Mesoamerican Amerindians transported to Cuba
in the late eighteenth century was, therefore, considerable. Yucatec Mayas
were also still evident in the island colony, part of the multicultural indigenous presence in late colonial Cuba that included Creeks and Apaches as
well as Mesoamericans such as Nahuas. Albeit waxing and waning, the Maya

presence in Cuba nevertheless remained the most palpable Mesoamerican presence, enduring through the centuries and continuing to manifest in both free and unfree labor.

It is important to note that not all Mayas or other Mesoamericans were in Havana against their will. Records like those of municipal actas de cabildo provide testimony to the continued Maya presence or survival and reproduction, predominantly in western Cuba.[61] Mayas did come to Cuba predominantly as laborers, but they also cultivated the land and farmed, whether on smaller plots in and near Havana or out in *el campo* (the countryside), an occupation in which they predominated in Yucatan and colonial Cuba over several centuries. During the early colonial period, transplanted Mayas appear to have persisted in their agricultural practices, cultivating *milpas* (intercropped farm plots) and growing *maíz*, beans, and yucca. In a petition presented to the cabildo of Havana in 1569, "el Indio" Juan Campeche, Alonso Baas, "also Indian," and others requested a piece of land in the woods "to farm [a]conuco and [grow] maize for their sustenance."[62] This scenario was reproduced even as late as the nineteenth century.

The records of proceedings of the city of Matanzas in western Cuba provide us with still other instances of Maya presence and occupational diversity in Cuba's labor system. One of the more dramatic examples is the case of the Yucatec Maya Felipe López, who was summoned to appear before the Matanzas cabildo in 1773. López, "Indio natural de la ciudad de Merida," worked as a *sangrador* (bloodletter).[63] A formal complaint filed by the master barber Rafael de Sotolongo effectively accusing López of malpractice landed him before the cabildo. Being neither formally trained nor therefore licensed to practice phlebotomy, the Maya healer was accused of breaking the law and endangering the public.[64] López reportedly responded at length, vehemently accusing the master barber of calumny, insisting that he obeyed the municipal laws, citing the Recopilación de las Indias in his defense, and invoking his right, "como Indio natural," to the protection of the municipal authorities of the kingdom.[65] While the outcome of this case is unclear, the Maya sangrador serves as a case study in the ability of the indigenous immigrant to adapt, negotiate, and exercise resistance in various forms in the context of the dominant colonial society. He is also an exemplar in the context of Maya and Mesoamerican social heterogeneity in Cuba.

Matthew Restall has noted of the Mayas of Yucatan, "The fallacious notion that colonial Mexico's indigenous communities were so culturally and economically impoverished by Spanish rule that all inhabitants were reduced to the level of commoners tends to be rooted in the misapplication of a sense of outrage over the injustice of colonialism, in the adoption of a Spanish point of view as a result of approaching indigenous society via Spanish sources, and in a literal reading of indigenous claims that they were indeed reduced to the equalizing poverty of the lowest common denominator."[66] Far from it, Restall concludes, "in Yucatan—indeed, wherever Spaniards ruled indigenous peoples—colonial rule facilitated rather than depressed class differences in indigenous society."[67] This was no less true of Mayas in Cuba.

By the eighteenth and nineteenth centuries, class lines were effectively transplanted and reproduced, albeit on a smaller scale, among the Mayas of Cuba, creating and reinforcing Maya social heterogeneity in Cuba. Recent anthropological and historical research, including from documentation in the notary records of the Archivo Nacional de Cuba, testifies to the importance of Maya surnames as the most reliable, though not exclusive, indicator of group membership.[68] In Cuba, this approach can facilitate not only the identification of Yucatec Maya immigrants, involuntary and voluntary, but in tandem with additional documentation, elucidate questions of identity, social class, and other indicators. Mayas lived and worked in Cuba as indentured, enslaved, or forced laborers, but some also occupied such rungs on the social ladder as healers or sangradores, as shopkeepers, or even possibly as slaveholders, in any one of the various sectors of the plantation economy. Mayas in Cuba could be laborers as well as proprietors, a few penetrating and occupying the higher realms of colonial Cuba's elites. For instance, the Maya Agustín Vicente Chan, one of a number of transplanted Mayas, became a member of the small renter or propertied class.[69]

Maya occupational and social diversity in Cuba is further illustrated in the situation of Polonia May y Cab.[70] The example of Polonia May y Cab is particularly instructive for its implications for social class, questions of class and ideological divisions among Mayas, and finally, the influence of factors such as these in the Maya diaspora in Cuba and in relation to the experiences of Mayas living in Cuba. According to testimonies in the *escribanías* (notaries) concerning the sanctioning of a marriage authorized as socially acceptable by the state, Polonia May y Cab immigrated to Cuba with her mother, Juana Cab, and settled in Havana sometime between 1851 and 1852.[71] The surnames May and Cab are unquestionably Maya in origin, while the references to Doña Polonia May y Cab and her father, Don Pablo, and her wish to contract, by official church sanction, marriage with a Don Luis Morales y Lopez, a reputable Spanish barber from Cadiz, hold various clear indications of social class.[72] The conclusion of colonial government officials that "no obstacle exists to legally impede said marriage" indicates further the acknowledgement of the state of the social acceptability of marriage between families of Cuba's small, incipient middle class.[73]

Just as complex was the relationship of Maya social class to identity, as implied in May y Cab's explanation for immigrating to Cuba in the 1850s. A Maya woman from a Yucatecan pueblo, May y Cab had apparently narrowly escaped with her family from the area when it was overrun by rebel "indios."[74] Polonia and her mother gave testimony to the complex, nuanced realities of the Maya rebellion, or Caste War, that began in the mid-nineteenth century in Yucatan. While historic exploitation united many Mayas, *colonos* (farmworkers), and elites against the Yucatecan state, as scholars have demonstrated in recent and important research, Maya responses to state exploitation were far from monolithic. In turn, this reality found expression in the Maya diaspora far from the peninsula—voluntary passage in the case of Maya elites, largely involuntarily for Maya *macehualob*—to destinations like Cuba. This is further suggestive of ways in which social class divisions among Mayas in Cuba were effectively maintained and reproduced. While it is less clear that immigrating Maya elites held onto traditional authority over Maya *macehualob* in Cuba, although arguably that is likely, it is at least apparent that Maya elites in the island colony differentiated between themselves and the masewalob Mayas whom they identified as "los Indios."[75] Finally, there is also evidence that Mayas in Cuba were represented in the full range of social classes from elites to working classes to what Karl Marx called the lumpenproletariat. At the lowest rung of the social ladder, or perhaps just below it, were the likes of Antonio Can, found in the streets of Havana "without work and vagrant," apprehended, and detained by colonial authorities.[76]

While Maya social class in Cuba demonstrated some variability, so too did immigration patterns. The Maya presence in Cuba from the sixteenth century through the eighteenth and nineteenth centuries tended to ebb and flow in tandem with developments both in the Yucatan and in the island colony, labor being a fairly consistent consideration in the equation. This remained true for the nineteenth century, as the Mesoamerican migration flow to Cuba during the eighteenth century erupted into a considerable torrent by the mid-nineteenth century. Once again, rebellion in the peninsula and the chronic labor needs of the island colony were motivating factors, as the Yucatec Maya rebellion known as the Caste War and a booming sugar economy in Cuba proved mutually reinforcing.[77]

As independence wars ended the reign of Spain in most of the hemisphere, the transition from the Spanish complex of patronage, paternalism, and repression to post-independence breakdown and then fractious republican governments renouncing corporatism and indigenous communalism, along with indigenous cultures more generally, the ancient moral economy of indigenous peoples like the Maya came under attack, rural stability was undermined, and the conditions for war ripened. Ongoing burdens on the Mayas were exacerbated after independence, contributing to a deepening alienation as the Yucatecan agrarian society evolved unevenly and violently from a colonial tributary society to one based on an aggressive agrarian capitalism.

In the last half century of the colonial period, the principal export industry in the Yucatan peninsula was cattle raising, and Cuba was the most important market for Yucatecan beef and cattle products. Concentrated in the northwestern region of the peninsula, cattle raising was a labor-intensive industry but one that allowed the Maya laborers who worked on the cattle haciendas enough time off during the year to work their own fields and raise their crops.[78] With Mexican independence from Spain in 1821, Yucatecan cattle raisers lost the right to sell their goods to Cuba, as it was still a Spanish colony. Sugar and rum imports from Cuba ceased altogether. Investment capital was therefore diverted from cattle into sugar, for which the best lands lay in the east and south, lands that had until then been devoid of haciendas and Maya peonage to *hacendados* (landowners).[79]

After 1825, conditions changed profoundly for Mayas in these regions; new laws smoothed the progress of land acquisition for sugar production, and land tenure was transformed from semisedentary slash-and-burn agriculture and the small milpa holdings predominated by the Maya peasantry to large concentrations of land and *latifundismo* in plantation economy.[80] By the 1840s, millions of acres of land had passed into the hands of a small elite of entrepreneurs, and, Terry Rugeley notes, "settled villages found themselves boxed into increasingly circumscribed and inadequate pre-serves. Peasants could no longer meet subsistence needs, let alone the con-tinued tax demands of church and state."[81]

Politically, taxation remained a volatile issue for decades, pre- and post-independence as the subtext of Maya relations with church and state.[82] For more than thirty years, tax resistance and revolt provided the Maya peas-antry "with ample occasions to rehearse its eventual role as a revolutionary force."[83] Compared to the few Maya elites, who also later joined the war, the great majority of Yucatec Mayas enjoyed little or no patronage from either the church or state, whether under colonialism or the new republic. The Mayas "groaned under well-documented tax and labor burdens" and paid staggering amounts in taxes, rents, and fees for myriad services while also being obligated to provide labor for state projects and under the "unappeas-able moral scrutiny" of the church and state, which monitored everything from marriage to personal travel.[84]

Peasant grievances remained relatively manageable so long as peasant leaders and marginal creole elites stayed content with the broader political arrangement.[85] The transition from the Spanish complex of patronage, pa-ternalism, and some measure of protection to a post-independence break-down wherein Yucatecan creoles acquired wealth and power and fought among themselves and with the center in Mexico disrupted the ancient moral economy of the Mayas, undermined rural stability, and fostered con-ditions for war in 1847. Maya expectations of tax relief, land security, and autonomy—and creole promises to this effect—came to naught.[86] What began in 1839 as a separatist revolt by Santiago Imán and his following of Yucatecan elites to overthrow the centralist regime and declare an indepen-dent Yucatan ended in 1847 with political violence and a massive uprising of disaffected Maya peasants.[87] Begun in the east, the initial Maya rebellion resulted in local government repression followed by social protest, banditry, and killings, which then culminated in more massive government repres-sion throughout the Yucatan "of all those recognized legally as Indians."[88] Active fighting began in earnest in mid-1847; a few months later, Dumond notes, "the conflagration swept over most of the eastern three-quarters of the peninsula of Yucatan."[89]

If Mayas in the eastern Yucatan were the predominant participants in a rebellion against injustice, that was not how state and regional elites saw the crisis. Mayas throughout the peninsula were painted in broad brushstroke as "bárbaros," and the rebellion was almost immediately portrayed as a race war, described by Karen Caplan as "one in which not only the rebels but all indígenas were complicit."[90] While rural revolts in the rest of Mexico prompted national elites to debate the "Indian problem," nonindigenous Yucatecan political and economic elites moved swiftly against enemies real and perceived. A few short weeks after the initial attack in the eastern town of Tepich, the state enacted the decree of August 27, introducing legislation that would fundamentally change, or perhaps more accurately reverse, the status of Mayas and their relation to the nonindigenous population and the state. The decree asserted that Mayas did not "have the aptitude necessary to continue in the enjoyment of the rights consigned to citizens in the constitution of 1841."[91] The state declared that the peninsula's indigenous people had "misused" their rights and were now to be subject to the law as wards to protect them and the rest of society, laws against "vagrancy and idleness," laws that forcibly broke up Maya communities and relocated their populations to other towns and haciendas.[92] The decree's application extended indiscriminately to include noncombatants, opening the door to persecution, incarceration, and summary execution.

unjustified persecution

Historian Eligio Ancona has observed that "under cover of these laws, and above all with the pretext that they were conspiring . . . , there developed a wicked persecution of a multitude of Indians who surely for the most part were innocent."[93] State alarm and desperation were evident in the statements of officials like Governor Santiago Méndez, who not only suggested the hanging of rebels but also that all other males less than fourteen years of age be marked with an iron brand with an "S" for "sublevado," or rebel, and sold into servitude.[94] Governor Miguel Barbachano later reinforced this edict by insisting that "the stubbornness of the indigenous race gave no hope for true pacification."[95] Forcible removal from the peninsula was the only solution.

Hostilities took place "within and were conditioned by a geopolitical setting that included international as well as local factors," notably the relations of Yucatan to Spain, of Yucatan to Mexico, and of Yucatan and Mexico to Caribbean neighbors like Cuba.[96] The Yucatecan government sought, as it had in the late 1840s, to demobilize the Maya peasantry. Initial attempts to dissuade an increasingly dispossessed, disaffected, desperate, and armed peasantry through cooptation devolved to military solutions as the conflict spread and escalated. The government was persuaded by Yucatan governor

Barbachano to deport the captured Maya rebels just as their Spanish fore-bears had done. The Spanish crown, which earlier offered to provide mili-tary aid to Mexico, acceded to Barbachano's proposal and offered Cuba as the optimal site. Both the empire and the republic stood to gain.

By the mid-nineteenth century, Cuba had become a slave-based labor system and the leading producer of the world's supply of sugar. From the late eighteenth century to the mid-1840s, Cuba's sugar industry had undergone substantial growth: the number of sugar mills increased from 424 to 1,442; technology advanced swiftly, massive tracts of land were transformed for the cultivation of cane, and the *ingenios* (sugar mills) expanded into more massive *centrales* (mill complexes).[97] In turn, the more enormous produc-tion centers translated into even harsher working conditions for the slaves who predominated in the workforce of the plantation system. Though the slave trade was officially abolished by Spain in 1817 under British pressure, a contraband slave trade continued into the mid-nineteenth century.

Yet factors intervened to augment the pressures of abolition in Cuba, mo-tivating the colonial government and the creole planter class to consider al-ternative forms of labor. The growing slave population, though momentarily reduced by disease epidemics, grew to overshadow the white population at a time when slave revolts were on the rise; mechanisms such as *coartación* (gradual self-purchase) enabled the expansion of the freed-person popula-tion; and as the price of contraband slaves became too high, the planter class became more amenable to the idea of wage labor as a way to offset the costs of labor and of modernizing the mills. Politically, portents of rebellion also grew among incipient separatists, freed persons among them, agitating for independence, while creole elites openly contemplated annexation to the United States as an antidote to economic and political instability, potential grassroots revolution, and an ineffective colonial government.[98]

By the mid-nineteenth century, Cuba's incipient agrarian capitalism was demonstrating a profitability that Spain's imperial government moved to protect against the conversely growing instability fostered by the internal and external forces of slaves, freed persons, *independentistas,* planters, and the United States. It did so through a combination of repression and re-form—repression of slave and other rebels and reforms including facili-tation of wage labor, partly through the gradual emancipation of African slaves—but chiefly also through immigration. Voluntary and involuntary immigration to Cuba played a seminal role in strengthening the colonial labor supply as it did generally in fostering the development of the Cuban economy and society.[99]

With the demise of the legal slave trade, Cuba's labor needs became dire. Campaigns to import European laborers having failed, the colonial government turned to two major sources: Chinese and Maya indentured laborers. Though economic and political factors influenced Maya deportations to Cuba, so too did culture and ethnicity, or more accurately, racialism, particularly in the perceived need to "whiten" the insular population vis-à-vis the growing slave and free black and mulatto populations. From the perspective of Cuban planters, labor was a key concern, but so too was pedigree when it came to considering the importation of Mayas from the Yucatan, who were judged climatically and culturally the right kind of laborer.[100]

Though the first such shipment of Maya laborers and their families began in April 1848, approved by the Cuban Comisión de Población Blanca and coordinated by the Junto de Fomento, the official decree from Yucatecan governor Barbachano did not come until later that year, on November 6.[101] His decree coincided with the official approval by the Spanish colonial government, by way of the captain-general of Cuba, rationalizing the shipments as necessary for the progress of agricultural production in Cuba and the protection of white Yucatecans from the depredations of rebellious Mayas. Ironically, Barbachano rationalized indentured labor as a form of protection for the Mayas.[102]

Whatever the rationalization, the shipment of Maya prisoners of war to Cuba served the political purposes of the Yucatecan government at the same time that it was intended to help resolve the labor shortage and white immigration questions in Cuba. Maya immigration was to be processed in an orderly manner based on established protocol: Cuban planters and other employers submitted requests or petitions for indentured Maya labor to the colonial government, which then conveyed the same to the Mexican consul, who in turn communicated the petitions to the state government. Contracts were arranged and written up by the public notary of Yucatan, witnessed by three *vecinos* (residents), and authorized and certified by the Yucatecan government and the Spanish vice consul.[103] In addition to these steps, the captain-general of Cuba dictated a detailed policy for the management, control, and obligations of the "colonos," as Chinese and Maya laborers alike were categorized.[104] Despite debate over the enterprise in Mexico City, by the summer of 1849 the Yucatecan government received official approval from the president, satisfied that the government of Yucatan was motivated by "philanthropic and humane sentiments" in shipping Maya prisoners of war to Cuba.[105] Like the colonial encomienda system, however, actual practice proved to mean far less than such ideal conditions for Maya laborers in Cuba.

From the late 1840s to the early 1860s, Maya laborers were transported to Cuba as individuals, couples, and families, generally forced into eight- to ten-year contracts in occupations predominantly in the sugar industry in the island colony's western regions. Many came from pueblos like Chemax and Tixualahtun and other Maya tributary villages in *partidos* (districts), like Valladolid in the northeastern regions of the Yucatan peninsula.[106] Most came from the eastern Yucatan, arguably the region even by the mid-nineteenth century that remained the most Maya and least Spanish.[107] Mayas entered the Spanish colony and proceeded to work under their patrones, most of them sugar planters. Hundreds of Mayas worked in ingenios in the west on plantations that were the foundation of Cuba's sugar monoculture economy. Probably the first ingenio in Cuba to be worked by Maya laborers even before official sanction was the Progreso sugar mill in Cardenas, where 41 Mayas arrived in March 1848 under the authorization of the Spanish and Yucatecan governments.[108] A month later, 53 more Mayas disembarked in Cuba.[109] With official sanction later in 1848, the traffic of human labor increased significantly. In March 1849, the captain-general of Cuba authorized the arrival of 135 "indios yucatecos"; a second shipment of some 200 Yucatec Mayas arrived in Havana in May of that year.[110]

According to the labor contracts, Maya workers were to be provided with adequate food, clothing, and shelter, along with medical aid when needed.[111] As the traffic of Maya prisoners of war continued and the Yucatecan rebellion with it, resistance to the deportations grew from Mexico and the abolitionist British, who saw little difference between Maya indentured labor and African slavery. If the Cuban indentured labor system was not as brutal as the African slave system, this remained a question more of degree than of kind. It was no secret that forced labor was the reality for deported Mayas during this early period or that, as in the old encomienda system, patrones, who tended to adhere strictly to the provisions concerning corporal punishment of their charges for infractions, often ignored or neglected the regulations regarding the well-being of Maya workers and their families.

By 1854 the debate came to a head. While national pressure from the

Mexican government, influenced in turn by international pressure led by the British, did not force an end to the traffic in Maya prisoners to Cuba, it did result in some limited revision of the policy of deploying Mayas in Cuba. This amounted to the so-called reforms of January 1854, as the Mexican government of Antonio López de Santa Anna announced several clarifying provisions for the continued transportation of Yucatec Mayas to Cuba. The more important articles addressed the apparent voluntary nature of each transaction, the limited contractual period of five years, the approval of each transaction by all parties involved, assurance of the well-being of the workers, and retention of the laborers' Mexican citizenship.[112]

The new agreement and concomitant arrangements opened the way for a substantial increase in the numbers of Mayas transported to Cuba. According to the contracts, after 1854, Mayas were to be contracted explicitly as "indios libres."[113] If, as was often the case, they brought their spouses and families, the wives and children could also be "freely employed" along with their husbands.[114] Children could also be employed at the age of twelve. A portion of the workers' salaries was deducted to pay for regular rations of corn, salt, coffee, beans, meat, clothing, and other supplies. Medical attention also was to be made available; if, however, illness or injury kept a worker away from work for more than five days, his wages were suspended until he recovered.[115]

Yet, if 1854 officially heralded a kinder, gentler form of indentured labor, it remained indentured labor. The growing numbers of Mayas who chose or appeared to choose to go to Cuba suggests decisions made based on the growing precariousness of life in the war-torn Yucatan. Meanwhile, the gap remained between the rhetoric and practice of the new labor migration agreement as increasing numbers of Mayas made their way to the island colony.

As the mid-nineteenth century progressed, during a period when the sugar economy was expanding beyond the confines of Havana Province and across the province of Matanzas, Mayas played a larger and more diverse role in western Cuba's economy as it became dominated by sugar monocultural export production. Maya men worked as farm laborers, sugar mill workers, cane cutters, cattle herders, and factory, road, and railroad laborers, to name a few. Maya women worked "in the usual work of their sex," in rural areas as cooks, washerwomen, and nurses' aides and in the cities primarily as domestic servants.[116] Maya men and women worked in several sectors and industries, from tobacco vegas to public works, railroads, and manu-facturing.[117] Mayas were also contracted by the colonial Catholic Church; the Jesuit school in Havana, for one, contracted twelve "indios de Yucatan" for domestic service at the *colegio*.[118] Geographically, Mayas worked in re-gions throughout western Cuba including the partidos surrounding Havana such as Cardenas, Cienfuegos, Matanzas, Camarioca, Nueva Paz, Bejucal, Güines, Nueva Filipina, Guamutas, Catalina, and Guanabacoa.[119] By the mid-nineteenth century, it appears that a disproportionately high number of Yucatec Mayas were sent to work in the two western provinces where the sugar industry became concentrated.

Matanzas, described by Bergad as "little more than an appendage to the economic system that revolved around the port city of Havana," began to be transformed by the beginning of the nineteenth century.[120] Formerly a "strategic-reserve area" for the colonial capital that supplied Havana with livestock, timber, and other provisions, Matanzas was in all respects "an un-developed, lightly populated frontier."[121] Conditions began to change in the mid-nineteenth century as sugar, coffee, and tobacco cultivation expanded beyond the environs of Havana and as more entrepreneurs facilitated the expansion of commercial agriculture. The sugar-plantation economy that overtook small landholding in western Cuba and Matanzas in particular by the middle of the century retained a considerable amount of diversity.[122] Sugar mills needed cattle for food and for draft purposes; the timber of the western woodlands was also a necessary resource for sugar planters.[123] The occupations of Maya laborers in Cuba were reflective of this relative diver-sity within a sugar monoculture.

Though most appear to have been employed on ingenios, some, like José Hu, a Maya contracted to a *patrona* in the district of Catalina, worked as cattle herders and laborers on *potreros* (cattle pastures), for example.[124] Maya women appear overwhelmingly to have worked as domestic servants, as did three "indias yucatecas" contracted in January 1860.[125] Maya children also worked, as far as can be determined by the available documentation, alongside their families. Some children apprenticed in specific skills and trades; for example, one Maya boy began an apprenticeship as a cook on the plantation in Güines where his parents were contracted.[126]

Compared to the Chinese, who were reportedly less acclimatized cul-turally and otherwise and prone to escape, Yucatec Mayas were generally considered preferable by employers and the colonial government and even

Mayas are preferred workers

superior because of their "docility, aptitude, and Catholicism."[127] Though Chinese immigrant laborers eventually significantly outnumbered Yucatec Maya workers, it was certainly not for lack of interest or effort on the part of Cuban planters and government officials. Calls for substantially increased imports of Maya laborers to Cuba came from various corners. Cuban entrepreneurs in 1855 petitioned the colonial government and insisted on the urgency of bringing Yucatecan colonos to the island colony. One interest, the Zangronis family, requested permission to bring 18,000 to 20,000 Yucatec Mayas.[128] The houses of Goicuría and Zangronis made a number of similar requests, including another one from the latter in October 1855 to transport 4,000 to 6,000 Maya men and women to the island. Though it was apparently revoked and then granted again by the colonial government, the outcome is unclear.[129] Individual requests from planters and hacendados varied from several hundred to several thousand.[130] At one point, the colonial government had apparently prepared a plan for the immigration of 10,000 Mayas, and at another point, in the spring of 1862, it seriously considered a new policy for the introduction of 20,000 more Yucatecan colonos.[131]

In a separate proposal, Cuban lawyer and statesman Cosme de la Torriente even wrote to the captain-general urging the importation of a thousand Amerindians from all over Spanish America.[132] Mexican scholar Moisés González Navarro has attributed the continued shortfall in the numbers of Yucatec Maya laborers in the face of colonial government and private plans to boost Yucatecan immigration to several factors, one being the dispersal of many thousands of Mayas from the Yucatan to Belize, Guatemala, and Veracruz as well as Cuba. The limited supply also can be attributed to growth in the henequen industry in the latter 1850s and the official ending of the traffic by the Mexican government in 1861. Finally, it can be attributed to working conditions for Mayas in Cuba in the 1850s and early 1860s.

Still, between 1849 and the time in 1861 when the Mexican government under President Benito Juárez declared an official end to the Yucatec Maya labor traffic to Cuba, hundreds if not thousands of Mayas journeyed to and worked in the island colony. The exact number, to date, remains in search of resolution, an unlikely outcome, given the substantial contraband traffic that existed throughout this period. Contemporary estimates range wildly from the approximately 800 suggested by the nineteenth-century Cuban historian Jacobo de la Pezuela to the thousands asserted by General Juan Suárez y Navarro, appointed by the Juárez government to oversee the separation of

Campeche from the Yucatan and to investigate the Maya traffic to Cuba.[133] The official Cuban census of 1861 indicated 1,046 Yucatec Mayas, fewer than half of whom resided in Havana; the rest, with the exception of 7 in eastern Cuba, were distributed throughout western Cuba.[134] After the demise of Spanish colonialism in Cuba in 1898, U.S. census officials estimated that some 900 Yucatec Mayas were in Cuba in the early 1860s, but the source of this number is unclear.

By the time of the U.S. census in Cuba in 1899, U.S. government enumerators counted a total of 1 Maya in the Zapata swamp of Matanzas Province and more than 1,100 residents categorized as "Mexicans," about 76 percent of whom were in Havana.[135] However, as even the director of the census, Lieutenant Colonel J. P. Sanger, conceded with some frustration, neither the earlier Spanish nor later U.S. census was entirely reliable; in the Spanish census Yucatec Mayas and Chinese were "included in the white class," a practice not wholly abandoned by government enumerators in US-occupied Cuba.[136] The precious few studies since then that have addressed the Maya traffic to Cuba either ignore the demographic question or provide little to no detailed analysis. Studies by Duvon Corbitt and Moisés González Navarro settle on a nicely rounded two thousand.[137] In her work on urban labor in nineteenth-century Cuba, Joan Casanovas estimates that several thousand Mayas worked in Cuba.[138] Further research remains to be done.

Yet, as González Navarro has rightly noted, the fact of a widespread, illicit labor traffic, for one, may ultimately thwart efforts at establishing an accurate estimate. One may speculate, based on the contraband traffic and the numerous proposals, petitions, and plans of private and official interests to import many thousands of Mayas to Cuba, that at a minimum, by the late nineteenth century several thousand Yucatec Mayas had worked in Cuba. The other question, of how many who came remained, is also bedeviled by problematical factors that likewise include statistical masking but also undocumented immigrants. The numbers of undocumented migrants is especially significant in the short-term and potentially the long-term impacts on Mayas entering Cuba; while the Spanish census altered the identities of Mayas in the island colony, illicit, concealed entry precluded their existence— and logically, any accompanying rights—altogether. Considerable numbers of Maya workers and families who labored in Cuba were not included in the official registration books for Yucatecan immigration. Paradoxically, there is some documentation for these undocumented workers: on numerous occasions colonial officials reported that the entries of substantial numbers of Yucatecan colonos were not indicated in the registry and that these had therefore entered Cuba illegally.[139]

The problem of illegal entry appears to fall largely under the categories of bureaucratic complications, confusion, corruption, and patrón connivance. This is indicated principally through colonial government reports and, where there are no reports, the recorded testimonies of Maya workers who were affected. There were often moments of confusion about the processing of immigrants that can be attributed in no small part to the inability to harmonize Mexican and Spanish imperial immigration and labor laws. Lack of clarity about labor migration policy and regulations was merely one complaint among many from Mexican and Spanish officials.[140]

While some illegal entries were later discovered by the colonial government, many were not. The more difficult type of entry to detect for colonial government officials was the illegal traffic in Maya labor condoned and sometimes coordinated and conducted by employers themselves. Some patrones reportedly ignored contracting procedures and fee schedules and did not register the Yucatec Maya colonos they employed.[141] Others were charged with introducing various Yucatec colonos without official government permission.[142] Some of this illicit traffic in Maya labor was also exposed by the Mayas themselves, an action that carried significant risk and had considerable impact on the lives of laborers and their families. Some Maya workers testified to having been deceived into thinking that they had proper contracts when none existed, sometimes after years of labor.[143] The consequences of illegal or nonexistent contracts could be quite serious for Maya workers and their families. Questions of the duration and fulfillment of contracts were not infrequently manipulated by unscrupulous employers, making it difficult if not impossible for workers to secure their freedom.[144] Added to this complication was the problem of determining one's status as a contracted colono, as a domestic worker, an officially separate category with limited freedoms, or as a free worker bound to normal immigration laws.[145]

Contraband labor trafficking was not the only issue afflicting Maya workers in Cuba. Patrón misdeeds extended into other types of abuse and worker maltreatment such as lack or absence of payment, harsh punishment, prolonged working hours, illegal renewal of contracts, and sometimes separation of families.[146] As did Amerindian slaves in the early colonial period and black slaves later, Maya workers and their families demonstrated a array of defense mechanisms ranging from subtle forms of everyday resistance to more overt and extreme means bred of desperation. Still others confronted their employers by petitioning Mexican and colonial officials.[147]

As for Maya demographics in colonial Cuba, if the number of Yucatec indígenas who ultimately came to Cuba remains in question, the fact of their roles in the development of the Cuban economy and society, despite fragmentary evidence for certain periods, is nonetheless relatively clear. From their initial arrival in Cuba as slaves under Spanish colonization through the centuries to the end of Spanish colonialism in the late nineteenth century, Mayas maintained a significant presence in Cuba as workers engaged, directly and indirectly, in the Cuban economy and society—in the founding stages of the colonial capital of Havana, the building and maintenance of defensive Spanish fortifications, roads, and other infrastructure, and at various levels of the growing sugar industry in western Cuba. Although proportionally few in number relative to their African and Chinese counterparts, they nonetheless played a significant, facilitating role in the rise of the world's foremost producer of sugar. If various factors such as working conditions, the Mexican polity and henequen economy, and the first Cuban independence wars ultimately prevented the number of Maya workers from reaching and overshadowing that of Chinese indentured laborers, this was by no means through lack of interest by employers and the colonial government in Cuba, who favored Mayas as laborers and attempted to bring in several tens of thousands of them from the Yucatan peninsula. Where employer abuses occurred, Mayas were by no means passive in their responses and acted in their interests and those of their families.

Notably, for the greater part of the period under study, although most Mayas came involuntarily as forced labor as a consequence of rebellion in the Yucatan peninsula, they did not stop coming to Cuba after the Mexican government officially prohibited the traffic in 1861. As the war waxed and waned but did not cease in the Yucatan for a half century and as dispossession advanced in the peninsula, Mayas continued to go voluntarily with their families to Cuba in search of work and perhaps new lives. The Maya presence endured, as is demonstrated in the existence of Maya descendants dispersed and scattered throughout western Cuba after the independence wars and those presently living in communities like Madruga in the Sierra del Grillo in western Cuba.

5

YUCATEC MAYAS, TRANSNATIONAL
RESISTANCE, AND THE QUOTIDIAN
STRUGGLES OF INDENTURED LABOR
IN CUBA, 1848-1864

In 1923 conservative Mexican journalist Carlos R. Menéndez published his *Historia del infame y vergonzoso comercio de indios,* a scathing indictment, albeit belated, of the Yucatecan and central Mexican governments' collusion in exporting Maya rebels and peasants for indentured labor in Cuba during the mid- to late nineteenth century.[1] The emphasis of Menéndez's documentary account lay in the political machinations, debates, and policies surrounding the forced exportation and effective enslavement of Mayas destined for the island colony. Less evident is a sense of conditions for Mayas in Cuba beyond the repeated charges of enslavement, which were entirely valid if not the whole story. Menéndez, himself the son of Cuban parents, both teachers, is also one more example of the Cuba-Yucatan connection. His *Historia* was "the first real broadside" against Mexican liberalism and liberal politicians complicit in the enslavement and trafficking of Mayas to Cuba.[2]

Menéndez's work remains an invaluable resource. It became an important reference in the handful of studies on the forced importation of Mayas to nineteenth-century Cuba written since Menéndez's tome that tend toward an emphasis on the political and diplomatic dynamic behind the Maya labor traffic.[3] The ground-breaking research of Duvon Corbitt and Moisés González Navarro on the 1847 Yucatecan rebellion and traffic of Mayas to Cuba focuses largely on the political-administrative dynamic behind the decision to ship Yucatec Mayas to the Spanish colony. More recent studies by Izaskun Álvarez Cuartero, by Jorge Victoria Ojeda, an important work on Maya domestic service in Cuba, and by Javier Rodríguez Piña tend toward a similar emphasis.[4] Relatively little is known of the conditions for and the role of the Mayas en route to and within Cuba and even less of the period after the Mexican government's supposed cessation of that traffic in 1861. In this chapter I use these studies as the departure point to examine in greater depth the struggles faced by Yucatec Mayas en route to and within late colonial Cuba, their responses to the forces arrayed against them, and the influence on the conditions of their exile that they had or attempted to exercise on the island colony.

As indentured workers, Mayas faced a number of opposing forces in Cuba, among the most formidable being their patrones. The patrón or patrona had considerable power to impose his or her authority on the laborer both within and outside the legal framework established by Mexican and Spanish governments. Yet, no less so than in their peninsular homeland, Mayas used a range of indigenous forms of adaptation, negotiation, and opposition to offset the tactics of the patrones. Through a complex of covert and overt forms of resistance, protest, petitions, litigation, flight, and, as a last resort, violence, Mayas in Cuba "sought to resist or strategically adapt to" their new conditions.[5] As such, Jeffrey Brannon and Gilbert Joseph contend, they "played an active role in shaping the terms of their oppression."[6] Maya workers played a significant part in determining the practice—versus the theory or policy—of working and living conditions in Cuba, asserted their interests and rights in the context of violations of these by patrones, and generally engaged in various and subtle, quotidian forms of opposition and resistance in defense of themselves and their families.

Maya negotiation and resistance in Cuba conceivably would have amounted to little more than repression and bloodshed were it not for a process facilitated by existing laws, Maya invocation of these laws, and their implementation by colonial government authorities. Cuban society, even in the autumn of the colonial period, remained in no small way the product of what Brian Owensby calls "a system of laws imposed by an empire that sought both to exploit and protect its most vulnerable subjects."[7] The Mayas of Yucatan had long possessed their own legal system, one that, centuries later, became integrated within Spanish imperial and colonial laws in a dynamic, evolving process that offered some measure of protection and endured until Mexican independence and liberalism challenged these ancient, corporatist precepts. Hence, the Caste War.

In Cuba, the imperial and colonial legal framework grounded in las Siete Partidas (Law of the Seven Parts) was comprised further of the slave or black code, a system of laws that upheld the legality of slavery and sanctioned the rule of the slave owner while also providing for the well-being of slaves against their masters' abuses. In this context, I argue in this chapter, Mayas in Cuba had a historical duality of precedents on which to base their negotiations with and resistance toward the recalcitrant patrón. As with their African and African-descended counterparts in the island colony, Mayas' initiative played an important role in prompting the implementation of existing laws and regulations that might otherwise have remained dead letters. That Mayas in Cuba were to a significant degree able to influence and even to some extent improve their working conditions in the island colony is further suggested by the evidence that after 1861 they continued to come and that after the expiration of their contracts, many remained in Cuba.

For importers and planters, meanwhile, the entire enterprise remained relatively constrained until the Mexican government under President Antonio López de Santa Anna calmed, at least momentarily, opponents in Mexico City and the British government with the concessionary, "protective" legislation of 1854.[8] Such an ostensibly charitable act substantially increased the potential for more transports of Mayas to Cuba; considerable numbers of Mayas continued to be shipped forcibly and illicitly.

The most immediate and enduring problem for all parties including Maya workers and their families was that of the status of Maya labor in Cuba. This dilemma found expression in and exacerbated problems of illegal acquisition, transportation, and entry of Mayas, all orchestrated by various colluding interests, from Mexican merchants and government agents to Cuban planters and other employers. Status of workers was an understandably sensitive question in a system dominated by slave labor. As the Maya rebellion raged on in the Yucatan after 1848, then captain-general of Cuba Federico Roncali, the count of Alcoy, agreed with the Spanish crown that the greatest challenge faced by the colonial and imperial governments was ensuring the subordination of and maintaining control over hundreds of thousands of African and creole slaves in the island colony.[9] Their conclusion was that "no group of workers of whatever status or race could be allowed to disrupt the slave regime," least of all Maya combatants sent to work in Cuba.[10]

Maya prisoners of war shipped to Cuba as contracted laborers were regarded in effect as having the same status as slaves. In agreement with the Yucatecan government, the Mayas in Cuba were to work under contractual conditions similar to those in Yucatan while at the same time being subject to the "tools of slavery"—binding and whipping—when control and punishment were deemed necessary. Something akin to a theoretical compromise between provisions for slaves and those for Maya contract workers in Yucatan appears to have been conceived by the Yucatecan and Spanish states wherein the line between voluntary and coerced colonos became blurred.[11] The potential for obfuscation and circumvention was not long in being realized.

By the early 1850s, it had become clear that the war in the Yucatan and receptivity of the Spanish colonial and imperial governments had provided an impetus for a growing traffic in Mayas, driven by Mexicans, including some government and military officials, merchants in Cuba, and later enterprising Spanish interests. Among the earliest and most active firms were the Havana merchant houses of Zangronis and Goicouria, to name but two. It also became clear that with or without contracts, the traffic and treatment of Mayas after 1848 from the peninsula to the island colony were pervaded by deception, exploitation, and brutality that, if quantitatively inferior, possessed qualities often resembling those of the African slave trade.[12]

In this context, one of the earliest and perhaps best-documented cases was brought before Havana authorities in 1853 concerning a certain Francisco Martí y Torrens, also known as "Pancho Marty," a peninsular slave trader, fishing industry magnate, and sometime purveyor of Yucatec Mayas, among various other interests.[13] Martí y Torrens was emblematic of a labor system in Cuba in which various labor forms—slave, free, and indentured—coexisted sometimes literally side by side. As a slave owner who also contracted indentured laborers, his was not an unusual state of affairs. According to colonial government reports, Martí y Torrens had acquired and introduced into the island colony "large numbers" of Yucatec Mayas at various times.[14] He vehemently defended the acquisition of "his" forty Mayas and fervently denied their having been treated like slaves. The prosecution ultimately found otherwise,[15] but the colonial government's interest in Martí y Torrens centered on those "indios yucatecos" for whom the patrón could not adequately account: those without contracts. The Spanish government eventually settled for a compromise whereby it compelled Martí y Torrens to return to Mexico "stolen" Mayas, that is, without proper contracts, while those who had contracts legally obtained from the governor of Yucatan remained with their patrón in Cuba.[16] Notably, the crown's ruling would foreshadow later decisions made under similar circumstances.

Mayas did come to Cuba voluntarily as contracted colonos, although the circumstances of their transport and labor were somewhat messier. Even in the postreform era, many came involuntarily, as prisoners of a lingering war in the peninsula, as captives of Spanish and other raiding parties, and as commodities of a rising, despicable trade, the profits of which continued to find their way into the pockets of Mexican government officials and military officers, Spanish merchants, and Cuban entrepreneurs. The observations of Karen Caplan regarding Maya *presentados* in the Yucatan expose more than a faint resemblance to the situation of Mayas in Cuba: "Technically, the new laws made distinctions among prisoners of war, noncombatants who were forcibly taken in by government troops, noncombatants who presented themselves willingly, and those who surrendered. And, technically, the government was in charge of their distribution. But, in practice, all of these people became part of a largely undistinguished pool of labor available to private individuals."[17]

Within the next two decades and even after the official cessation of the trade, Martí y Torrens, for one, "remained known" to the British and certainly the colonial government as an affluent planter and slave holder residing on the finca Pena Blanca.[18] He probably continued to employ Maya laborers and perhaps, with the help of the fleet of his "immense fishery business" that also plied Yucatecan waters, may even have continued to facilitate the transport of Mayas to Cuba.[19] Whether legally contracted or the victims of *el enganche* ("the hook" of deception) as perpetrated by slave raiders and other unscrupulous agents, Mayas who found themselves in Cuba were not entirely without recourse.

Even under the status of colonos, in which Mayas were officially assured of a body of rights declared after 1854, more problems emerged; some of them, like those based in conflicts between the immigration policies of the Mexican republic and colonial Cuba, were almost inevitable.[20] Paradoxically, these kinds of bureaucratic questions proved problematic for governments and advantageous for employers; they were problematic for governments as they attempted to regulate and profit from the growing traffic of Mayas to Cuba and advantageous for employers and other beneficiaries who were enabled in circumventing the regulatory framework, such as it was, for monitoring transports of Mayas to Cuba. Maya workers and their families, too, could be alternately beneficiaries and victims of the perplexity and consequences of the seemingly labyrinthine bureaucracies of the Mexican and Spanish governments and of the schemes of conniving traders and colluding patrones.

An example of the bureaucratic confusion and its potential outcome is the case of the Maya contractees Demetria Villalobos and her daughter. Colonial officials apparently agonized over their inability to reconcile republican with imperial laws in order to establish the status of the two yucatecas.[21] Villalobos and her daughter, meanwhile, at the mercy of the officials' ruling, likely nervously awaited their decision. Were they, in this instance, colonos with all the official rights and freedoms appertaining thereto or domestic servants without any such rights and therefore legally more vulnerable? One administrator, perhaps alluding to his opinion, captured some of the irony of the moment and recalled the remonstrance given Columbus by Queen Isabella: "Who has made slaves of my vassals the Indians?"[22] The case was later resolved in favor of Villalobos, who was declared "libre," free, although her daughter's status is less evident. Still the confusion persisted and extended to Spanish officials who repeatedly requested clarification about the process and therefore the status of Mayas sent to Cuba.[23]

Administrative lack of clarity over Maya importation inadvertently abetted contraband or illegal Maya transportation and created openings for Mayas in Cuba that could also entrap them. Laws existed for the proper contracting, transport, and treatment of Maya workers in Cuba, but the laws were often evaded, ignored, or otherwise contravened by patrones, at times with the complicity of government agents. This was not so difficult to do; as the Caste War rocked the peninsula, it also created opportunities. Rugeley has noted how the depleted treasury of the Yucatecan state became open to various sources of war-related revenues. The sale of captured Mayas as slaves to Cuba was one such source. Furthermore, the state and individuals who proceeded to profit from both the licit and illicit trade were aided by the convenient coupling of war and the geography that Rugeley describes: "Yucatan's anarchy, its vast and desolate coastline (Mexico's longest), and the chronic need for slave labor in the nineteenth-century Spanish Caribbean made the peninsula an inviting place to cast anchor."[24]

Existing colono contracts were, for the most part, signed and processed in Merida and Valladolid, Yucatan. As for the illicit traffic of Mayas to Cuba, however, Cozumel, Carmen, and Isla Mujeres were common collection and departure points. According to Maya testimonies, Isla Mujeres appears to have been an active and favorite site for traffickers including Martí y Torrens.[25] Some, like Martí's associate Juan Bautista Anduze, conducted a trade of Maya captives that made runs from Carmen to Cuba.[26] Cozumel, the largest of the islands, was a haven and a way station for Caste War refugees. Though it is less apparent that this isle played a significant role in the trafficking of Maya, although that is entirely possible, given Anduze's eventual move to Cozumel, it did serve as a departure point for Mayas with enough money to buy passage and license to work in Cuba.[27]

The export of Mayas that began in February 1848, resumed under new, nominally protective laws after 1854, and officially ended thirteen years later attracted all manner of interested parties in an assortment of transactions, from legally contracted enterprise to unlawful schemes; many of the same people could be found partaking of both. The ones like Martí y Torrens were succeeded by a series of Cuban, Spanish, and Yucatecan players. Among the Yucatecans were the likes of Martin Francisco Peraza and Liborio Irigoyen Cárdenas, both of whom served terms as governor of Yucatan. The evidence is stronger in the case of Peraza, who became "deeply complicit in the trade"; Irigoyen was accused of collusion but more clearly facilitated the trafficking of Mayas through other means, such as legislation.[28] Characteristically, both men publicly condemned the trade at the same time that they privately aided, abetted, and profited from it.[29] Others, like the Spanish merchants and slave entrepreneurs Miguel Pou and José de Jesús Madrazo, aspired and actively strived to monopolize the trade to Cuba.[30] The war likewise provided many similar opportunities for members of the military and sundry others on both sides of the straits.

Employers like the patrón Bruno Egea attempted to circumvent the contracting procedures by illegally arranging for the shipment of Mayas, avoiding the obligatory fees and paperwork, and effectively smuggling laborers into the island colony.[31] In the case of Egea, as in others, colonial authorities ruled that the mayas yucatecos had been brought to Cuba without authorization of either Mexican or Spanish authorities.[32] This deception also potentially entangled the Mayas in myriad ways. Colonial records indicate that some Mayas were deceived into thinking that they were coming as free laborers; Egea, for instance, had reportedly falsified contracts.[33]

Upon discovery by colonial authorities, however, a decision had to be made about the status of the migrants. The available evidence renders it not at all clear that in these situations, Mayas were simply turned back and returned to Mexico; the likelihood of that happening was probably weak, given the ongoing rebellion in the Yucatan and the unrelenting need for labor in Cuba. In still other cases, Mayas not only entered Cuba without contracts or with inadequate documentation but also were illegally sold by employers or other agents to different patrones in Cuba.[34] Sometimes, however, Mayas benefited from the indecision of Spanish, Mexican, and colonial Cuban bureaucracies.[35]

The case of the patrón Bruno Egea was merely one in a series of attempts at illegal importation that implicated the employers and various independent agents and government officials. Some individuals made repeated attempts. In August 1859, Martí y Torrens of Matanzas was at it again, reported to have illegally contracted and illicitly introduced a number of *colonos yucatecos*; a government official observed that the Mayas independently contracted by him "were not evident in the register books" designated for monitoring importees.[36] In July 1860, another patrón was charged with introducing various colonos yucatecos without government sanction.[37] The Secretaria del Gobierno de la Habana reported in October 1861 that various Mayas had been illegally contracted, arrived in Cuba without binding contracts of any kind, and therefore were considered free.[38]

At yet another level, there were noncontracted and unregistered yucatecos who accompanied contracted Maya workers on transports to the island colony. In one such instance in Havana in December 1861, aboard the *Mejica*, a steamer hired specifically to transport contracted Yucatec Mayas to Cuba, colonial officials discovered additional passengers, all, they reported, "without apparent contracts."[39] These kinds of circumstances caused as much frustration for a colonial government attempting to classify and monitor its immigrant labor force as it does still for researchers attempting to determine the magnitude of Maya immigration in Cuba based on available official records. The status question was often confounded by illegal importation that employed enganche, the hook of deception, at several levels and in varying degrees. Such subterfuge became particularly invidious after 1854 with the growing numbers of Mayas who freely contracted to go to Cuba.

These various kinds of contraventions were especially hard on the many families that accompanied Maya workers to Cuba. While existing government contracts fairly clearly stipulate status and conditions for family members, including clauses concerning their well-being, neither the contracts nor the surrounding conditions were consistent with the official policies. Upon the newcomers' arrival in Cuba, hardships were many. Patrón transgressions against Maya workers and their families did not end upon arrival in Cuba. They faced an array of difficulties, before and after the reforms of 1854, that included abuses of various stripe. According to colonial Cuban and republican Mexican records, charges included unpaid wages, "excessive punishment," illegal sale to new employers, and even the separation of families, something of a commonplace in the African slave trade.[40] All of this was aggravated by some of the bureaucratic ambiguities and illegalities that formed part of the dynamic of the importation of Mayas into Cuba. The potential for abuses existed at every phase of Maya workers' journeys to Cuba, in the processing, transporting, and deployment of indentured workers. Maya responses are evident at all of these stages.

In spite of the forces arrayed against them, Mayas on the pointed end of this human trade were not entirely without their own resources. Paradoxically, the same laws that employers and others attempted to circumvent and profit from could be applied at any stage of the indenturing process by the primary subjects of these laws. Mayas, when it was necessary and practicable, could and did combat negligent and abusive patrones and agents of human trafficking with the laws and regulations available to them. According to the records of the Cuban colonial and Spanish imperial governments, Maya workers in Cuba provided testimonies concerning the questionable practices of patrones throughout the period under study, and whether before or after 1854, the weight of evidence offered by yucateco testimony appears to have counted for something.[41] Precedents for these indigenous interventions were both Yucatecan and Spanish in origin. In their peninsular homelands, Maya workers did not passively accept their conditions but instead undertook a complex range of responses.

So too in Cuba. In fact, a number of the illegalities perpetrated were brought to the attention of the colonial authorities by Mayas who were being victimized. On one hand, when conditions allowed (and records are extant), Maya workers and their families appear, for the most part, to have worked through their contracts with their patrones in relationships that entailed some level of conflict. In the voluntary renewal of contracts, even colonos yucatecos who had claims against their employers for lack of payment or other transgressions might still choose to continue to work under them if those disputes were more or less amicably resolved. Of course, not all, and probably not even a majority, of these laborer-patrón relations were so benign. Far from any notion of a monolithic, timid labor army of "indios mansos" (tame or domesticated Indians) that government authorities presumed would be the practical result of their monitored labor in Cuba, Mayas made ready use of a variety of available options for the defense and protection of themselves and their families in Cuba. No simple dichotomy existed: for Mayas, the laborer-patrón relations were not merely good or bad. There was historical precedent for acts of resistance. From the point of embarkation to the ingenio or other work site in Cuba, Mayas took actions against their oppressors no less assertively than had been the case in the Yucatan, where they protested informally and formally, through the use of petitions and other legal recourse and, failing that, extralegal resort.[42]

Perhaps not surprisingly, one of the earliest instances of Mayas responding to actionable transgressions preceded the 1854 reforms. In the 1853 case involving the incorrigibly enterprising Martí y Torrens, in which a "considerable number of Yucatecan Indians" were "violently snatched away" from their homes, forcibly transported, and forced to work "without rights" or proper recompense, the Mayas in question played a significant role in the claim against him.[43] These Mayas were quite aware of their rights, facilitating the prosecution of the *reclamación* (claim), accepting the invocation of government protection through *amparo* (a legal recourse of long standing), and providing evidence (in a *declaración*) against their victimizers.[44]

Maya actions against abuses pertaining to the initial stages of the indenturing process followed fairly soon after the promulgation of the 1854 reforms. After a harrowing experience of being coerced into signing what was likely a dubious contract and then forced onto a transport steamer for passage to Cuba, a Yucatecan colono known as Apolinar eventually found the means to remedy his plight by filing a complaint in the summer of 1859 through a testimony to an escribano against the patrón responsible.[45] Later that same year, nearly thirty Mayas from various areas throughout northern Yucatan provided *declaraciones* against Miguel Pou, a Spanish merchant, trader, and "leading financier of Maya slavery."[46] With the help of cronies and subordinates, he had engineered one more in a series of plots to forcibly transport Maya workers and their families to Havana. Pou was not alone in being fingered by the Mayas in the declaraciones; some of Pou's cronies were powerful men and part of a larger network of political corruption in the state government and armed forces that starred Governor Augustín Acereto (1859–61) and his son Colonel Pedro Acereto, who was directly implicated in rounding up and transporting Maya men, women, and children.[47]

Many of these Mayas, like Mateo Canche, his wife, María Eusebia Camal, and Isidoro Chi, came from pueblos near Valladolid. Each gave testimony to all manner of intimidation, degradation, and humiliation, beginning with being made offers they literally could not refuse, to work as laborers and servants in Cuba for the next eight years or more and, upon refusing such offers, being tied up, dragged off, and guarded by soldiers and other armed men while in transit to Sisal, the point of exit.[48] It was just off the coast and en route to Cuba where the steamer transporting the traffickers and their prey was intercepted and apprehended by the coast guard. In their testimonies, most of the Maya males identified themselves as farmers; some were accompanied by their wives and children. Though all were effectively abducted for servitude in Cuba, the circumstances were not the same for everyone. Some, like Mateo Canche and Isidoro Chi, were sold by their patrón to Pou.[49] More than half of the group, when factoring in family members, were debtors like Anselmo Chi, Pedro Poot, José Moo, and Hilario May, who, upon failing to pay their *contribuciones* (taxes) to their Maya batabs, were arrested and sentenced to labor for local military officers; when done with them, the officers then sold them to Pou.[50] The experience of Anselmo Chi was likely representative of his fellow yucatecos'; according to his wife, Cecilia Coyoc, one moment he was peacefully working on his milpa; the next, he was seized by local authorities and hauled off to jail, sentenced to two months' labor breaking rocks, and then hauled off in fetters for shipment to Havana.[51]

The most despicable of these acts victimized children; orphans, some under the care of their godparents, were gathered up in Merida and shipped to Sisal for transport to Cuba. Twin brothers Lorenzo and José Canul, eleven years of age, their parents having died, counted among these "unfortunate Indians"; Gregoria Chac, also eleven, was abducted while under the care of her godmother.[52] All testified to having been deceived and then taken away from their guardians. When asked how the children—and presumably their guardians—had been deceived, José Canul described what appeared to be a common pattern; he had been "tricked" by "a gentleman [he] did not know" who told them that "the Governor of Merida had given an order to collect all the orphans"; they were taken to Isamal and from there to Merida to the house of Miguel Pou, destined for labor in Cuba.[53] Not unlike the experiences of so many African and African-descended slaves, Maya families were also separated and children taken by force from parents and guardians. Florentina Canul testified that she "was separated from her parents and sent to Isamal to the house of Don Antonio Acereto," where she remained until conveyed to the coast.[54] Likewise, brothers Pablo and José May, orphans living with their uncle, were surprised "when some armed soldiers with rifles arrived and picked us up, taking us to Merida" for transport to Cuba from the port of Sisal.[55]

Despite almost laughable attempts by the perpetrators to paint these and other enslaved indígenas as "free workers," the testimonies of these Mayas, men, women, and children, are unquestionably clear, as José Chan testified: "I went by force . . . [and] my compañeros also went against their will."[56] Any attempts by the Mayas to question or resist their antagonists, at least at the point at which they were accosted, appeared to be futile. Most either witnessed or experienced the consequences of opposition or resistance; Isidoro Chi, Antonio Tul, and others who opposed their captors and resisted were beaten or whipped.[57] Miguel Pou and his subordinates were sent to jail the following year when the new state government under Colonel Lorenzo Vargas publicly condemned the trafficking of Mayas; privately, or perhaps not so privately, he also continued to use Mayas as forced labor in Valladolid and possibly elsewhere. A year later, when Augustín Acereto returned to rule, Pou, along with others incarcerated for slaving, was freed.[58] Acereto's adversary and successor Liborio Irigoyen would prove to be little different, tolerating and even condoning an enterprise, Rugeley notes, "that could only have existed during a time of civil war."[59]

Once Mayas were in Cuba and toiling as indentured workers, their claims and petitions marked and illuminated patrón transgressions. In some instances, Mayas filed claims, as did one in the spring of 1860, against uncooperative employers for compelling them to work without a contract.[60] That same year in Guanabacoa, near Havana, the maya yucateco Lorenzo Oile filed a claim against a patrón for the completion of a contract in order to assert his other claim to his right to work for a second patrón.[61] And the yucateca María Barriel filed a complaint for having been deceived (engañado) and therefore illegally contracted in Mexico.[62] Families of colonos yucatecos also brought their grievances to the government seeking redress from offending or transgressing patrones. The Chan family brought a claim before the Consejo de Administración de la Isla de Cuba against Miguel Rivera, charging that the patrón had illegally, that is, without their knowledge and consent, prolonged their contracts.[63]

In such instances where confusion about the nature and legality of the contracts reigned, the colonial government appears to have proceeded according to law and resolved the disputes by annulling the contracts and declaring the freedom of the Mayas in question.[64] In the case of Chan and his family, colonial officials concluded that because of "the impossibility of ascertaining with precision the circumstances that mediated in these contracts . . . the Council believes that it should declare said contracts null, and the colonos at complete liberty."[65] The precise extent and consistency with which the government made such rulings is less clear, although the available evidence suggests that it did so not infrequently.[66]

Mayas yucatecos in Cuba were also no less assertive in taking legal action when possible against patrones for physical and other forms of maltreatment in work sites. By the early 1850s, and probably earlier, reports of the ill treatment of Maya workers in Cuba surfaced and were brought to the attention of Mexican and Spanish authorities. Charges of brutal working conditions contradicted the humanitarian rhetoric of the Mexican government; nor did such conditions cease after the concessions of 1854. If patrones themselves were loath to acknowledge the grievances of the indios yucatecos, acquaintances and associates like Pedro José Crescencio Martínez of Santa Clara were not so reluctant, openly admitting "the more numerous complaint of abuse."[67] Importantly, we would likely know considerably less of these incidents were it not for the initiative of Maya workers themselves; many of the reports of abuse were generated based on their complaints.[68] While less clear, the scale of Maya complaints is at least suggested in a series of letters and investigative reports to the captain-general of Cuba that stretch across two decades, the 1850s through the 1860s, acknowledging and reporting on the claims and testimonies of victimized Mayas.[69] The perpetuation of abuses in some areas of Cuba after 1860 suggests the inefficacy of imperial oversight and the determination of employers to extract maximum labor from their charges under conditions parallel to that of Cuba's slave system, the backbone of the plantation economy.

Mayas on the receiving end of such practices responded with a range of defenses, not the least of which was the use of negotiation and legal means of redress. Several factors account for the dynamic of Maya dissent and government response. First, Mayas in Cuba brought with them a culture of negotiation and protest long developed and practiced among indígenas in New Spain and even republican Mexico, one that often, if not always, served them well in their struggles with hacendados and the state.[70] With the onslaught of the Caste War and concomitant forced migration, Mayas brought these traditions with them to Cuba. At the same time, the colonial government in Cuba had a dual interest in maintaining economic and political stability, including labor stability, while also avoiding entanglement in political controversy and international incidents with the host country, Mexico. Finally, in both Cuba and Mexico, laws had long functioned, albeit imperfectly and unevenly, whereby indigenous and other subaltern peoples stood a chance at a modicum of justice. While these laws were gradually being undermined in republican Mexico, Spanish dominion in Cuba ensured their continuance.

Maya initiative, precedent, and expectations along with Spanish and colonial Cuban legal tradition and custom under slavery weigh heavily both in Maya actions and government decisions or rulings concerning those actions. In Cuba, legal practices like coartación and *pedir papel* (to request the right to change masters) had deep roots in the island colony; though such practices did not exist as slave rights under the Castilian legal codes, Alejandro de la Fuente argues that they nevertheless became "a pragmatic response to the frequent litigation initiated by slaves themselves."[71] African and creole *coartados* and other slaves had gone a long way through their own initiative in socializing colonial authorities toward ruling in favor of those in servitude. Lawyers, justices, and government authorities in general came to regard such prerogatives as *derechos* (rights).[72] Cuba was not unique in this respect. The Castilian legal codes had long provided for at least some protections for slaves, and ordinances from the audiencia of Santo Domingo in the sixteenth century reinforced a foundation for the good treatment of slaves that would later be augmented by the Código Negro of 1784 and then the Reglamento de Esclavos of 1842, laws that were to be implemented by designated officials like the *síndico* (advocate). The three foundational principles of these laws were "that masters should not abuse their slaves, that slaves could complain to a judge, and that judges should hear these claims and proceed accordingly"; these were ratified in numerous existing and subsequent regulations.[73]

By the beginning of the nineteenth century, "colonial law encompassed well-established principles regarding acceptable treatment of slaves, as well as the authority of local officials to interfere when these principles were violated." An increasing range of colonial officials assumed the responsibility for upholding these principles, which was consistent with the fact that colonial ordinances and imperial law had shifted the initiative for the well-being of slaves from the slave to judges and local officials.[74] Nevertheless, slaves continued to take the initiative and use the courts to seek justice well into the nineteenth century.[75] Slave owners and planters resisted through litigation and other means, but the laws and accompanying rights and regulations prevailed and were upheld. The long and continued exercise of various practices claimed by slaves as rights became so widespread that by the middle of the nineteenth century, colonial authorities codified a number of them into law.[76] Though we know that the laws were indeed enforced, it remains unclear just how consistently they were. What is evident, however, and of particular importance for this study, as de la Fuente asserts, is that such ordinances "restricted the dominion of slave owners and ... expressed a legal philosophy that subordinated the rights of property owners to the stability and 'true interests' of the colony."[77] Thrust into such an environment, under some of the same slave-owning patrones, and armed with their own experiences and traditions of negotiation and resistance, Maya colonos encountered a society steeped in a system, even under slavery, of laws and rights that had long provided a significant degree of empowerment for those in servitude.

Reports of grievances, petitions, and formal protests by Maya laborers in western Cuba under this system took various forms. Many were complaints filed by Maya workers against abusive patrones for unjust or negligent practices. One case included the very common grievance of *maltrato*, which ignited a series of charges and countercharges that in this instance drew even the Mexican consul into the furor.[78] Arriving in Cuba at the age of fourteen, José de Jesús Cabrera was trained to work as a cook, but when of age, he was employed as a laborer in many capacities. Having apparently fulfilled his original contract, the young yucateco signed on with a new employer. The new patrón, however, was another story. In reporting José Julián González to the colonial authorities, which Cabrera did several times, he made reference to having received better treatment from previous employers. González reportedly physically abused the yucateco, favoring "excessive punishment" and dealing with the colono in a "violent way." Cabrera had taken flight to escape the abuse but, notably, returned to pursue the charges against his patrón. For his part, González dismissed the colono's "unfounded complaints" and accused Cabrera of calumny, calling him a liar.[79] As to the resolution of this particular conflict, both parties looked to the authorities in Cuba and Mexico.

Charges of maltreatment or abuse (maltrato) often represented a combination of physical and other forms of abuse and negligence; the most common form of negligence protested was lack of payment, though there are also a number of other complaints that included the illegal sale of Maya workers from one patrón to another and refusal to terminate a contract once fulfilled. Patrón transgressions and Maya charges over the living and working conditions in the island colony span the 1850s through the 1860s. In a report dated October 1864, a colono yucateco asserted that he had endured all manner of abuses from his patrón but had fulfilled his contract. As if such maltreatment had not been enough, the patrón prevented him from leaving and refused to terminate the contract. This Maya filed a complaint against the patrón, charging him with "abuse, excess of punishment, lack of payment," and other complaints.[80] While Mayas' struggles were "circumscribed by the colonial realities" of Cuba's slave society, this did not deter a substantial number of them from protesting and asserting their claims against the injustices they faced.[81] This is perhaps particularly well illustrated in the cases involving Maya women.

On one hand, the cases of the Yucatec Maya women are exemplary in the manner in which they represent the multitudinous protests, petitions, and complaints filed by Maya colonos in Cuba over two decades.[82] Many yucateca women worked as domestic servants in Cuba; some filed charges against their patrones for a range of offenses, including withholding wages and selling their contracts to other employers.[83] Maya women turned to colonial officials as the ones with the "power to resolve" the disputes.[84] As colonial authorities observed, that Maya women (and men) did "not know how to read" did not dampen their resolve to secure their freedom from abusive conditions; these Maya women were no less assertive in making pleas to the government for resolution of their claims, invoking the government's moral obligation to "protection of the poor."[85] Whether with their families or on their own, women like Antonia Valle filed complaints against their employers for various abuses such as withheld wages and abusive treatment that included the forced separation of some women from their children.[86]

To the extent that many such grievances were generated by women, these reports further illustrate the substantial role of Yucatec Maya women in Cuba, particularly in the context of labor and household politics. As Restall has pointed out in postconquest Yucatan, likewise Maya women in Cuba were no less assertive or resourceful than men in defending their interests and those of their families.[87] These, too, Restall observes, had precedents in pre-independence Mexico: "In the postconquest Maya cah [community] the domestic sphere was female-dominated."[88] This implies the part played by women within Maya households in Cuba. It is possible, further, to glean some sense of that role based in part on evidence of their contribution to Maya negotiation with and resistance to the dominant colonial structures in the island colony. Demetria Villalobos, mentioned earlier, had declared ful-fillment of her contractual obligations and demanded her and her daughter's "manumission" as "personas de su derecho."[89] In another instance, a Maya yucateca lodged a formal grievance to the colonial government against the patrón Joaquin Lara for "withholding of wages and a false contract."[90]

Yucatecas María Lucía Camara and Feliciana Buendia, of Campeche and Merida, respectively, leveled several charges against two perpetra-tors, Manuel Mendiolea and Abdon Morales, who had deceived them in contracting them as free laborers (laundresses) in Mexico, and against the patrón Manuel Alcalde for a number of abuses that reportedly amounted to enslavement.[91] According to their declarations, Buendia and Camara were deceived from the moment they were contracted and boarded the Span-ish vessel *Mexico* to Havana. Buendia testified that other Yucatecan women were rounded up to be forcibly transported but that some "managed to es-cape."[92] Both women described how they were shifted from house to house for months at a time. Camara equated her working conditions with slav-ery, stating "that in the house of Alcalde they have given bad treatment to her, since they neither fed nor clothed her, and made her weigh the baskets of clothes of the family . . . that her husband had to feed her and clothe her . . . that her husband worked outside and Alcalde extracted an ounce and a half from the monthly wage, circumstances that she cannot prove because only the negros of the house are aware and [it is] not possible for them to be able to tell the truth."[93]

Patrones, already hostile to the complaints and protests of male Maya

workers, could only have resented with even greater antipathy the assertive actions of Maya women who evidently did not know their "place." One
patrón who took exception to Villalobos's open dissidence characterized
her as one who "sets a bad example for others in her class."[94] Several years
later, through the 1860s, the "bad examples" persisted, in the likes of yucateca María del Carmen Rivas, who asserted her right to freedom against a
designing patrón after having fulfilled her contract; of Camara, who was be-
littled by her perpetrators as "a wretch"; and of other Yucatecan women who
spoke out against their exploiters.[95] As Restall and others have noted, taking such an independent, even confrontational and potentially dangerous
position was by no means entirely atypical for Maya women. Whether in
Mexico or Cuba, often against formidable odds, Yucatecan women pushed
beyond the domestic sphere into the public domain of men.

Maya workers in Cuba, men and women, took the legal initiative into
their own hands to defend themselves and their families against unscrupulous employers and government agents. When circumstances proved
overwhelming, as they must have when politico and patrón colluded, Yucatec Mayas employed other means; flight was one such recourse of long
standing. Not unlike African, African-descended, and earlier Amerindian
slaves, Maya workers and their families could employ a range of defense
mechanisms from the subtle to the overt, bred of desperation. A number of
Maya workers joined the ranks of runaways among African slaves. Colonial
authorities reacted to these at several levels, from mediation to the issuing
and processing of orders for the capture of cimarrones yucatecos, as officials
did in the Regla district of Havana in the case of the pursuit in 1859 of the
yucateco Apolonio González, who had fled from his patrón.[96] In another
instance in 1861, a maya yucateco identified as José who "had come to this
island without contract, deceived by Francisco Corrujedo" and then denied
a wage fled his servitude, eventually finding refuge in the Mexican consulate
until his case was resolved.[97] In another case, an entire yucateco family was
apparently reported (perhaps by a patrón) as having breached their contract
and fled, a false claim, as it turned out. Upon apprehending the family and
investigating further, the police determined that the colono Felipe Santiago
Rivera, his wife, Baltasara, and their children had actually honored their
contract and "were free."[98] Other Mayas appear to have left and procured
employment elsewhere in the island colony.[99]

As the case of the Maya José suggests, while flight obviously achieved the goal of escape from adverse conditions, it could also serve as a form of negotiation, an act undertaken in tandem with legal actions. The colono yucateco Jesús Cabrera, of age by 1862 and under contract to a patrón by whom he was "treated severely" and often unjustly punished, deployed an array of defenses that encompassed complaints, formal petition, and flight.[100] When his protests failed, Jesús Cabrera fled but then returned, like other colonos yucatecos, to pursue legal charges.[101] In very few instances did Mayas return to exact revenge on unjust and abusive patrones.[102]

Significantly, flight and violence as singular responses by Maya workers to living and working conditions in Cuba are not as well represented in the documentation as the various legal means adopted, either alone or in combination with other actions, flight appearing as more prevalent. The more consistent use of legal means by Maya colonos, men and women, to address and resolve conflicts and abuses and the government responses suggest that the substantial initiative taken by Mayas in Cuba was not ignored by colonial officials. Though it is unlikely that all formal Maya grievances were resolved in favor of the appellants, the evidence strongly suggests that at minimum, numerous such cases were addressed by the government and many, if not a majority, from the first imperial decree to investigate abuses in 1853 to colonial reports that conveyed such investigations through the early 1860s, were ruled in favor of the Maya workers.

In his seminal work *Raza y tierra*, González Navarro argues that government officials largely ignored or rejected Maya claims and petitions. Yet, there is significant evidence to suggest that numerous claims were at least reviewed, that the government made some effort to implement the principles of the labor policies as determined by Spain and Mexico—at the very least, colonial government officials had an interest in augmenting the number of Yucatecan migrant workers—but that ultimately they did so inconsistently.[103] If the implementation of regulations was inconsistent, it was also not always official. Government authorities sometimes chose informal solutions to Maya-patrón struggles. In one such incident in late 1859, yucatecos Toribio Bé and Juan Yam squared off with Domingo André, patrón of the finca Santa Rosalia, over their contracts. Bé and Yam asserted that they had completed their three-year terms; André insisted that they were in debt to him for goods and services (pigs, chickens, and medical services to their wives) supplied on credit and that therefore they had not yet fulfilled their contracts, conditions that amounted to debt peonage.[104] Government

intervention proved bittersweet for the two colonos. While colonial officials agreed with the Mayas that they had completed their three-year term,
they concluded that, one way or another (they omitted the cost of medical
services, which should have been included in the contract), the outstanding
debt had to be paid in cash or in labor.

The singular importance of these struggles in the context of this history
is not only that Mayas played a part in the development of colonial Cuba
but that they also played a significant role in launching and facilitating government investigation of patrón-colono relations. Those Maya workers who
asserted their rights under the noted agreements sought legal redress considerably more often than they resorted to violence. Further, they did so as
people socialized to a tradition rooted in Maya and also Spanish custom
and law, the latter of which, if inconsistently implemented, nevertheless remained in force in colonial Cuba. Like other indígenas elsewhere, they resorted to the law knowing there were no guarantees but that they might still
derive some benefit.[105] Finally, a point likely not lost on colonial officials at
a time when slave rebellions "reached ominous proportions," legal action on
the part of Maya workers prevailed over rebellion.[106]

Contracts between Maya colonos and their patrones appear to have
ended in conflict almost as often as they did amicably. Further, contracts did
not end with the 1861 cessation of the Maya traffic by the Juárez government
in Mexico. Those that endured beyond the official cessation of 1861 were of
two types: those from the pre-1861 period and those under colonial Cuba's
new policy of free labor importation. Maya workers continued to come to
the island colony, while others renewed their contracts with their employers
there or sought independent employment elsewhere on the island.[107] After
1861, various Mayas in Cuba who had been contracted earlier as domestic
servants and workers requested, or demanded, conversion of their status to
"colonos libres," a category that had existed more on paper than in practice
before 1861 and for which more rights were accorded, apparently including
the freedom to choose additional employment in Cuba.[108] By 1862 a new
policy emerged under the Consejo de Administración de la Isla de Cuba for
the introduction of twenty thousand more Yucatecan colonos.[109] Though
the volume of voluntary Maya traffic during the period is not clear, this was
nonetheless a new phase of labor migration for Mayas in Cuba but one that
was still fraught with some of the old problems and abuses.

In October 1864, a "colono yucateco" filed a complaint against his patrón for the usual offenses, including preventing the yucateco from leaving after he had fulfilled his contractual obligations.[110] That same year in Guanabacoa, a Maya *colona* fought with her patrón over, among other things, the completion of her contract, a case she appears to have successfully made, against the protests of her patrón.[111] In 1863, yucateca María Barriel filed a complaint against a patrón who had apparently illegally contracted and otherwise maltreated her.[112] Several other Maya colonos who had been illegally contracted were declared free by colonial authorities.[113]

Whatever the tenor of contract termination, Maya workers in Cuba became free to return to Yucatan, renew their contracts, or seek employment elsewhere on the island. Santiago Cab and Juan Nó (or Noh) were among those who successfully fulfilled their contractual obligations and ended their working relationships with their patrones more or less agreeably, although their whereabouts afterward is less clear.[114] Other Maya colonos in the early 1860s, like the notable Jesús Cabrera, not only celebrated the end of their contracts but signed new ones, in his case with a new patrón, and remained in Cuba beyond the official Mexican cessation of 1861.[115] This also appears to have been the case for a young Maya farmer, married and "devoted to agriculture," who began a new contract on the stock farm La Pepillita in the district of Catalina.[116] Mayas remained on the island; some migrated regionally from the countryside to the cities for employment.[117] Maya colonos Toribio Chan and his wife, Polonia, also chose to stay in Cuba after they fulfilled their contracts, settling in Havana and finding employment in a local bakery.[118] In Guanabacoa in the autumn of 1864, another Maya completed one contract and then began a new one under the new labor policy of the Sección de Agricultura, Industria y Comercio.[119] Mayas like Julián Tun, Pablo Canoh, Tomás Chan, and Santiago Kamil and their families all ended their respective contracts but continued to work in Cuba as laborers, domestic workers, and farmers.[120] Most appear to have remained in western Cuba, moving between rural and urban areas depending on the availability of work.

Importantly, employers were willing to provide the opportunities. The colonial government's move in 1862 to encourage continued Maya immigration into Cuba and on a larger scale was in no small part the result of the labor, economic, and racial concerns of economic and political elites, as labor shortages endured, the colonial sugar economy was booming, and racial balance between white creoles and the island's large slave and free African

Cuban population remained cardinal concerns. Elites' calls for the importation of more Mayas and other Amerindians into Cuba and state facilitation were a reflection of these factors.[121] Maya proficiency in agriculture and in other areas of labor influenced employers' preferences. Though the migration of Mayas to Cuba may have decreased after 1861, it did not end.

In their participation, voluntarily or involuntarily, in rebellion, migration, and indentured labor in Cuba, Maya workers and their families conformed to a considerable extent to James Scott's thesis of subaltern forms of resistance: "Given the power of landowning elites and officials, the struggle waged by the poor was necessarily circumspect." Scott contends that "quieter forms" of resistance, which may include overt but individual rather than collective protest and often have only minimal formal organization, "may well have been more successful in mitigating claims by the powerful on the peasantry."[122] Though the hegemony of the Mexican republican and Cuban colonial governments and economic elites like the patrones often prevailed, numerous Mayas persevered in their attempts to mitigate that hegemony to whatever degree they could through their own actions; they reverted to a complex of forms of opposition, negotiation, and resistance. In no small part a reflection of experiences and precedent in their ancestral Yucatan, these forms included a diverse, fluid array and were utilized separately and combined as circumstances merited.

Whenever feasible, Mayas worked the system, exercising resistance schemes within the framework of existing power relations and attempting to use existing laws to their advantage, as did African Cuban slaves who invoked coartación laws toward their self-purchase and freedom. Furthermore, the available evidence strongly suggests that Mayas in Cuba relied most consistently on existing legal means to demand their rights and defend their interests, substantially more so than they turned to violence such as sabotage and assault; violence appears to have been periodically employed as a last, desperate resort.

Mayas in Cuba could and did appeal to existing laws. While we have precious little evidence of the interaction of Mayas with African and African-descended slaves, it is clear that, like then-extant slavery laws that included coartación, Mayas in Cuba drew from custom and laws and from laws born from custom, rooted in Yucatec Maya, Spanish, and Mexican provenance, laws like that of the 1854 concessions that advocated the well-being of Maya workers. While certainly abused and resisted by patrón and official alike, the laws existed, and Mayas as well as African Cubans made active use of them; although it should not be overstated, laws nonetheless created some space for Maya actions. This space was malleable, influenced by authorities at several levels—national, international, imperial—and Mayas alike. The imperial state's inadvertent facilitation of Maya resistance and the relative success of that resistance in enabling Mayas to defend themselves and their families and strategically adapt to their new living conditions in Cuba shed light on this microcosm of the Maya diaspora. The multifaceted nature of Yucatec Maya resistance in Cuba in turn sheds light on interpretations of Menéndez's important 1923 treatise on Maya traffic to Cuba; although sympathetic, Menéndez characteristically views "los indios yucatecos" as helpless, passive objects more often acted upon than active. The evidence, including testimony from "los indios" themselves, strongly suggests otherwise.

Mayas and other indigenous immigrants in Cuba found themselves in a place where, not unlike their homelands, they were pitted against patrones resistant to change and determined to continue the exploitation of coerced labor. In spite of the conditions noted and also likely because of a sped-up latifundismo in the Yucatan, Mayas continued to come to Cuba after 1861, now voluntarily under a new policy, while others renewed their contracts. Perhaps not all employers were culpable for gross abuses of their charges and treated them humanely. And dispossession also offered opportunities. For the duration of the nineteenth century, war in the Yucatan, while factionalized, went on unabated, motivating many Mayas to disperse and many others to seek work and sanctuary for themselves and their families in other lands.[123]

Cuba, meanwhile, continued to experienced chronic labor shortages, especially with the diminution of black slave labor and in spite of the importation of Chinese indentured workers. Under the auspices of the Dirección de Administración, Sección de Agricultura, Industria y Comercio, new contracts were entered into by Maya colonos who chose to stay in Cuba beyond the fulfilment of their original contracts, as well as by newcomers.[124] For some Maya workers who were contracted in 1861 or later, the aftermath—whether they stayed or returned to Mexico—is less clear.[125] It is clear, however, that a significant number of Maya laborers renewed contracts or sought other employment in Cuba; still other Mayas continued to make the trek to the island for work and perhaps a new start in life.[126] Even those Mayas who had experienced conflict with their employers could be found after 1861 renewing their contracts for employment as farm workers or in the bakeries, butcher shops, factories, loading docks, and homes of urban centers like Havana, Matanzas, and elsewhere on the island.[127] As one more dimension to a long-standing history of Yucatecan migration, the Mayas of Yucatan became the Mayas of Cuba.

Yucatec Mayas embodied one more component of the larger indigenous diaspora in Cuba and the Caribbean, one more human dimension to the multicultural or multinational indigenous presence in colonial Cuba. At the same time, Yucatec Mayas inhabited another middle ground somewhere in between their counterparts from Florida and northern New Spain, neither as relatively unfettered as the Calusa, Tequesta, or Uchisi in their passages to and from the island nor so literally shackled and unremittingly subjugated as Apache prisoners of war, Guachinangos, or Nahua forzados. Mayas came as both, as prisoners of war simultaneously "freely" contracted as "colonos libres," a category at different times honored in the breach and sometimes in fact. When violated, as already demonstrated, while some Mayas acquiesced, others challenged their abusive patrón, even successfully, their courage rooted in autochthonous custom, the continued relevance of imperial Spanish laws and their often inconsistent implementation, actions similarly taken by indigenous descendants of the Arawak Taíno in Cuba but for which there is even less evidence after the eighteenth century, let alone for that of interaction between the two peoples.

From a different perspective, it is evident that the multifaceted labor system of Cuba was embodied in more than African, African-descended, Chinese, European, and mestizo coerced and free labor. This system and society were made even more complex by the presence and contributions of the many arrivals of an indigenous diaspora. Until the end of the nineteenth century and beyond, labor-hungry Cuba remained an eager recipient of immigrants. Unlike most other host territories and, ironically, at a time when the autochthons of Cuba were believed extinct, the welcome extended to the indigenous peoples of the continental Americas.

6

BLOOD CONTRACT

Continuity, Change, and Persistence in Colonial Indigenous
Labor Forms and Elite Strategies

In the first census conducted by the U.S. government in Cuba in 1899, the
director, Lieutenant Colonel J. P. Sanger, made a number of observations
about, among other things, the relationship between Cuba's historical immigration patterns and the role of race and ethnicity.

At one level, Cuba was by no means unique, as many if not most countries in the Americas, including the United States and Canada, exercised
restrictive immigration policies based on the needs of economic production and capital and on augmenting the population with the "right kind" of
immigrant, usually meaning of white European stock. Cuba had undertaken
campaigns to lure people of Spanish, Canary Island, and other origins from
Europe to its shores to help ameliorate the chronic labor shortage. When
these efforts fell woefully short, campaigns and policies were initiated to
tap alternative sources of labor. One of these potential sources was Chinese
indentured labor. The other was Amerindian labor. Cuba, therefore, represented somewhat of an anomaly. In spite of the substantial immigration
of Chinese between 1847 and the end of the traffic in 1874, for a number of
reasons, Cuban preferences became redirected away from Asian labor and
toward Amerindian workers.

Importantly, however, Chinese and indigenous laborers like Yucatec
Mayas also constituted part of the effort to "whiten" the population. As
Sanger noted in 1899, "Many wild schemes for fostering the white popula-
tion of the island have been proposed and much has been written on the

subject by publicists, too, of good repute."[1] Indicative of such schemes, censuses under colonial governments in Cuba "included in the white class the Chinamen and the Yucatan Indians."[2] The desperation of the colonial government in Cuba to meet the island colony's relentless demand for immigration and labor long predated the needs of Cuba's post-emancipation economy. By the early 1790s the Spanish crown began to more actively encourage white laborers' immigration through the establishment of the Real Sociedad Económica de Amigos del País and the Real Consulado de Agricultura y Comercio. The first reports of these bodies reflected concerns that would become thematic for the duration of the colonial period in Cuba: "[A]lthough for the general development of the island the introduction of slaves should be favored, it is necessary to proceed carefully with the census figures in hand, in order that the number of Negroes may not only be prevented from exceeding that of whites, but that it may not be permitted to equal that number."[3]

don't want large Black slave population

It was precisely because there was "no grand rush to Cuba" by willing white laborers,[4] coinciding after 1762 with a particularly vulnerable Spanish imperial government, that thousands of forzados, many indígenas among them, found themselves in Cuba. In the waning decades of the eighteenth century, these were reinforced by various indigenous loyalists from eastern Florida who accompanied Spanish colonists and soldiers to western Cuba following the cession of Florida to Britain.[5] Revolution in Saint Domingue and the rapid transformation of Cuba into the world's foremost producer of sugar sanctioned the importation of African slaves at the same time that it reinforced the perceived urgent need to balance the growing slave population on the island with white laborers. The apparent inability of the crown to import foreign white laborers led in no small part to an increasing willingness to define "white" more broadly. At the turn of the nineteenth century, when the Consulado de Agricultura y Comercio more actively promoted white colonization, interested parties like the Marqués de Casa Peñalver included Canary Islanders and Amerindians from New Spain in the same category. Casa Peñalver envisioned indigenous laborers contracted for extended periods.[6]

In the late eighteenth and early nineteenth centuries these workers arrived in diverse forms: some, like the Calusa, Tequesta, and Uchisi of east Florida, largely as refugees and free laborers; others, like the Nahua, Zapotec, and others of the Valley of Mexico region and Mayas of Yucatan, as convict labor; and still more, like the Lipan Apache, the so-called indios bárbaros of the northern provinces of New Spain, as indigenous prisoners of war. The category of prisoner of war was further augmented, in the mid-nineteenth century, by additional waves of Yucatec Mayas, although, as demonstrated, many ostensibly were freely contracted. Sanger pointedly observed at the end of the century that indigenous people like the Mayas in Cuba were often represented as part of the white population.

The combined influences of colonial indigenous labor in Spanish America, including Cuba, along with historically persistent labor needs, a dearth of European immigrant labor, and a booming plantation economy driven by a subjugated African and African-descended labor force that increasingly was influenced, in turn, by active, state-sanctioned, and international British abolitionism, accounts in no small part for the willingness and incidence of imperial and colonial governments to promote the recruitment of Amerindian labor immigration and colonization in the island colony. By the nineteenth century, as the colonial government and indigenous people like the Yucatec Mayas themselves knew, indigenous immigrant workers were no strangers to Cuba.[7] If uneven in the development, the Spanish crown and private interests had, nevertheless, directly and indirectly collaborated since the sixteenth century in transporting indigenous labor from other regions of the Americas to Cuba and the Caribbean. By the mid-nineteenth century, these interests still converged, this time to promote the shipment to Cuba of Yucatec Maya prisoners of war during the rebellion in the Yucatan.[8]

Throughout and even before the 1850s, numerous petitions were filed by various interests on the island intent on securing individuals or groups of indios yucatecos for their particular needs. The petitions, some coming soon after the Mexican labor concessions of 1854, reflected a variety of interests and a collective singularity of purpose. The contracting parties comprised an interesting range that included planters, entrepreneurs, professionals, and even diplomats. Most had their interests represented or brokered by merchant houses or other private agents as middlemen for such transactions.[9] Pleas were made of the "urgent necessity" of Cuba, "a province of much interest" to Spain, to which indigenous immigrant workers would contribute.[10]

In order to invoke the domestic and international implications of granting the petition, appeals were made to "the spirit of sincere and intimate friendship" between the empire, its colony, and the Mexican republic.

Ultimately, however, the bottom line was the benefit to be had by an empire struggling to sustain and retain one of its few remaining American colonies, its Antillean pearl. Especially at a time when Cuba was the world's foremost producer of sugar and a generator of revenues for the metropolis, appeals to "utilizing the emigration" toward "the conservation of her wealth" tended to be decisive in favorably influencing the crown.[11] Numerous petitions, some more vehement than others, for the importation of indigenous Yucatecan and other Amerindian workers into Cuba followed and, with them, the continued collective promotion of the benefits for all interested parties.

By December 1855, Agustin Morales Sotolongo and Julian de Zaldivar y Pedroso had succeeded in securing permission to bring in two hundred yucatecos; the merchant houses of Zangronis and others followed suit.[12] In May 1858 Gabriel Valdez Carranza of Havana filed a petition for the importation of some two thousand colonos yucatecos for the avowed purpose of meeting the needs of Cuba's agricultural economy.[13] María Fehl, a widow, "native of France," and resident of Havana, requested and received permission to import colonos yucatecos as laborers and domestic servants, the crown apparently acknowledging her arguments for "the necessity of augmenting the number of manual workers on the island."[14] By the end of the decade, the colonial government reported, there were a "multitude" of hacendados and merchants in Cuba who had applied for permission to import indigenous laborers from Mexico; colonial authorities concluded that the demand was attributable to the "good results . . . that the immigration of this class of colonos has produced."[15]

Neither colonial and imperial officials nor contractors saw any need to limit their search for indígena labor. As early as the 1850s, the imperial government issued a decree permitting the introduction into Cuba of colonos indios of whatever origin from wherever in the Mexican republic and beyond.[16] In the interest of ameliorating the labor shortage, facilitating agricultural production, and preventing further slave rebellions or imbalance in the race ratio in the island colony, planters, *fábrica* owners, merchants, and other Cubans responded accordingly.[17]

In February 1859, Francisco José Calderon y Kessel petitioned for permission to introduce "6000 Indians from the former Spanish Americas."[18] While the Junta de Fomento de Agricultura y Comercio and the Comisión de Población Blanca considered it, Calderon made his case. His arguments included the conventional ones on the urgent labor needs of Cuba, the debatable success of Asian immigrant labor, and the unstable political and demographic conditions of a colony under African slavery, adding further that "great damage" would come upon hacendados and the state if the labor crisis were not effectively addressed.[19] Less conventionally, Calderon asserted, somewhat nostalgically, the unique bonds that Amerindians in the former Spanish colonies possessed with Spain, a kind of fondness and nostalgia for colonial social relations that indigenous peoples of the former Spanish Americas harbored parallel to the growing resentment of and opposition to the classical liberal economies and elitist political systems that had emerged since independence in the former colonies. "The Indians of the former Spanish possessions," he claimed, "remember the governments of our kings with gratitude."[20] As workers in the fincas of the new republics, he added, indígenas and mestizos alike had lost the rights that they once enjoyed under colonialism.[21] As one of the last bastions of the Spanish empire in the Americas, Calderon argued, Cuba represented a veritable sanctuary for the dispossessed indigenous peoples of the newly independent, and oppressive, republics.[22]

The Junta de Fomento de Agricultura y Comercio and the Comisión de Población Blanca concurred: indigenous laborers "offered advantages over the Asians, because the Indians of the American republics have with the island an affinity of habits and customs, unity of religion, and conserve traditional affection toward the government of Spain."[23] The governor and captain-general of Cuba also supported and promoted the petition, adding that "the immigration of the Indians discussed is more suitable than all of the other races."[24] Although favorable, officials steered the petitioner toward their preference for "the indigenous race of the island's neighboring states" of former Spanish America, singling out indios yucatecos as Amerindian workers especially suited to Cuba's economic needs.[25] Still, hedging their bets, officials remained somewhat open to considering prospects from the rest of the indigenous Americas.

That same year, Gabriel Díaz y Granados petitioned the crown for authorization for the introduction of one thousand colonos indios "of both sexes" from the coastal regions of South America for work in the "factories, establishments, farms and private homes" of the island colony.[26] Once again, the Junta de Fomento and Comisión de Población Blanca appeared receptive. Practically and ideologically, imperial and colonial authorities appeared to accede to the arguments for importing Amerindians, a race that, the claims repeated, had more in common with Spanish values and culture than Chinese indentured workers had.[27] Díaz's arguments echoed those of Calderon in their emphasis on the great need for labor, the damage done by delaying, and the suitability and affinity of the indigenous of the former Spanish colonies with the inhabitants, customs, and traditions of the empire's largest remaining American colony.[28] Díaz also extolled other virtues of "colonos indios" (here, farmers and other indigenous migrant workers) that made them attractive to patrones: the "Indian race" of South America was "more robust and docile . . . inured to the hard tasks of the tropical regions, they needed neither apprenticeship nor acclimatization, and finally . . . born and raised in the mountains, they come free of the vices that bring with them the pauperism and agglomeration of inhabitants that exist in the ports of the Celestial Empire."[29] Confident and determined, Díaz even submitted a draft of the contract.[30]

As in other cases, imperial and colonial officials reassured Díaz that they looked favorably on his request, but this petition raised questions. As a labor source, the southern continent was new territory for colonial authorities in Cuba. Exactly where in South America were the indigenous groups in question to be recruited, and who were they? How many women were to be included?[31] The more crucial questions for the crown, however, were based in international concerns. The issue of locality and the specific nation to be dealt with (indigenous and republican) persisted in the exchange of correspondence between Díaz and governing authorities and among themselves, as "the establishment of rules with the end of preventing international questions" remained a palpable concern.[32] By December 1861, the absence of any forthcoming clarification on the part of Díaz appears to have disinclined the Spanish government from acquiescing to his request.[33] Petitions for indigenous labor, however, whether from Mexico or beyond, endured into the late nineteenth century.

The official Mexican government cessation of the traffic of Mayas in 1861 did not dampen interest in Cuba in indigenous laborers. On the contrary, it may even have been in reaction to the cessation that private and state interests stepped up campaigns for the importation of Amerindian workers. For the next two decades, the colonial government in Cuba continued to consider, endorse, and promote colonization or immigration that also favored indigenous immigrant laborers.[34] Campaigns for indigenous labor immigration intensified with the eruption of the Ten Years War (1868–1878) and the greater political, economic, and labor crisis into which Cuba fell. Next to the enduring preference for white colonization, the promotional campaigns of the colonial government continued to favor indigenous workers in general and the indios yucatecos in particular as the seemingly natural choice for the island colony.[35]

Among the various entrepreneurs to answer the call were Antanasio de la Cruz Garcia, Manuel Gonzalo Palomino, and José María Salineros, who petitioned for authorization to import yucatecos into Cuba in mid-1870.[36] Like their predecessors, they pitched many of the same arguments to secure authorization from the crown for bringing in the colonos indios. The partners wanted to import Yucatecans as well as "others from the Mexican republic" and cited not only the grave needs—in part due to a recent cholera epidemic—of augmenting agricultural production on the island but also industry and the arts, securing the "public wealth," and generally helping ensure the continued productivity and order of Spain's largest remaining colony in the Americas.[37] The indígenas of Mexico, went the familiar refrain in one memo, were "a pacific race, docile and honest; they speak our language; are of a recognized religiosity, and participate in none of the irascibility of other peoples, as the experiences with the Asians brought to the country has confirmed."[38] Though the laborers to be recruited are largely only identified as Mexican or Yucatecan, the entrepreneurs also cited the royal decrees of November 1855 that explicitly and specifically provided for the introduction of indigenous laborers from the Yucatan or "whatever province of Mexico."[39] This is reinforced by additional petitions and related documentation that clarify the identity of "Mexicans" from the perspective of the crown and interested parties. As Celestino Gómez and his partner eventually made clear in their petition, they were speaking "essentially of the class of Yucatecan Indians."[40] This petition, like a number of others, appears to have been granted.[41]

That the crown and colonial government in Cuba remained open to prospective indigenous migration flows from elsewhere in the Americas is further evidenced in the December 1875 petition of Dr. Juan Sechy for authorization to import six hundred "indios venezolanos" into Cuba. Citing the usual arguments, colonial authorities once again concurred, with the chief of the Sección de Fomento endorsing Sechy's proposed indigenous importation as "suitable and in the greatest interest" of the empire and island colony.[42] Sechy had also submitted for official consideration an additional argument grounded in unique circumstances with which Spanish authorities besieged by independence insurrectos could identify: the Amerindians to be imported were those "dispersed in the revolution of Venezuela,"[43] likely among the many indigenous dispossessed and also perhaps earlier indentured under the rapidly and violently modernizing regime of the new president General Antonio Guzmán Blanco.[44] This was a petition, a cause, and a people with which the imperial government could identify and support—presumably loyal indigenous escaping a formerly loyal, now liberal, republican, and antimonarchical regime. Colonial and imperial authorities agreed to grant the petition.[45]

From 1862 through the 1870s, Spanish and colonial authorities continued to support the promotion of an immigration program that included indigenous peoples as "white." The metropolitan government dedicated substantial time and resources in addressing the question.[46] After extensive analysis and deliberation of the experiences, successes, failures, and various other issues concerning indigenous Yucatecan labor immigration, to which hundreds of pages were dedicated in the form of testimonies, correspondence, and reports, the imperial government moved in September 1875 to commission a study probing the possibilities of more extensive colonization involving Yucatec Mayas and other indigenous peoples in Mexico. The study's objectives were to "examine, discuss, and report" on the question of standardizing indigenous Yucatecan labor immigration and colonization in Cuba "to facilitate the colonization attempted."[47] Former deputy of the cortes José Agustin Argüelles was commissioned by the crown in September 1875 to study the system of colonization established in the colony of San Rafael in Mexico as a model for potential application in Cuba.[48] After some five years, in May 1880 Argüelles brought his completed report before the imperial government. He concluded that "the indigenous Mexicans meet the conditions for the colonization of our Antilles through the medium of free contracts"; he recommended that the governor and captain-general of Cuba look into the appropriate principles and procedures for drawing up and processing the contracts.[49]

The responses of the imperial and colonial governments appear to have been generally favorable to the conclusions in Argüelles's report, save for some debate between imperial and colonial authorities over the extent to which the indios yucatecos should be considered free labor. Elements within the colonial government's Sección de Fomento, in the context of

African Cubans fighting for independence and Chinese increasingly doing likewise, strongly favored a more strictly European and even peninsular colonization, the lack of which, as the same author inadvertently pointed out, led to the consideration of alternative forms of immigrant labor in the first place.[50] Although Argüelles also importantly noted the potential for importation of indigenous workers from Mexico and other regions of the Americas, imperial and colonial officials maintained their gaze on potential colonos yucatecos, as they proceeded to discuss the administrative and political details of importing and overseeing them in Cuba. Various imperial and colonial officials spent years working on this project of indigenous colonization.

The outcome of this enterprise in late colonial Cuba remains unclear, very likely disrupted by the island colony's submersion in the "throes of depression" in the 1880s, when hundreds of planters became insolvent, followed by the chaos of the independence war in the final decade of the century.[51] Still, fragmentary evidence suggests an uneven yet continued migration of indigenous people to Cuba during the late colonial period that encompassed immigrant laborers from the Yucatan, northern Mexico, Venezuela, and possibly other regions of the Americas. Further, if there is a paucity of evidence for more substantive indigenous immigration during this period, we must consider a Cuba in the midst of economic depression, independence insurrections, and the concomitant propensity for their dispersal, not to mention, as imperial and colonial government reports certainly do, the problem of illicit, contraband, illegal labor traffic to Cuba.[52]

As I have attempted to demonstrate, the significance of this dynamic process is greater than mere statistics can convey. On the one hand, after the abolition of slavery in 1886 and by the end of the nineteenth century, the white, European immigration so coveted by colonial authorities finally materialized: tens of thousands of Spanish and other immigrants arrived through the late 1880s, 1890s, and, after the disruptions of Cuba's last independence war, again in the new century. From 1899 to 1905, some 150,000 Spaniards and thousands of other nationalities arrived and stayed.[53] Of the more than 125,000 Chinese indentured laborers imported until 1874 and whom patrones both needed and disparaged, particularly when many if not most of them joined the independence movement against Spain, some 15,000 Chinese workers remained.[54] On the other hand, it is also clear that the imperial government in Spain and colonial government in Cuba invested heavily in the interest of colonization generally and in indigenous, often Yucatec Maya, immigrant labor in particular. For much of the nineteenth century, in the face of sporadic, unreliable, and ultimately limited success in attracting adequate numbers of white, European immigrant labor and when many of those who did come migrated to the towns and cities, perpetuating and aggravating the need for rural labor, imperial and colonial authorities in Cuba reverted, perhaps in part instinctively, to Amerindian labor.

Slavery may have been abolished in Cuba by the mid-1880s, Bergad notes, "but transformations of the social psychology engendered by centuries of human bondage would be more difficult to eradicate."[55] African slavery had been in decline, and indigenous slavery had been abolished for centuries by the Spanish crown, as had the encomienda and repartimiento, as systems of labor evolved from these earlier forms to one in which African slavery predominated but also coexisted with free or wage labor. If Cuba represented an exception in this realm, it was in the persistence of African slavery through the nineteenth century at a time when almost all other newly constituted republics of the former Spanish American empire had abolished it. However, by the mid- to late nineteenth century, as a result of abolitionist and other pressures, Cuba increasingly, if grudgingly, moved forward. Yet, to limit the argument to this would constitute an oversimplification of the process and history as it evolved in the largest remaining island colony in the Caribbean. As scholars have argued in the cases of colonial Mexico and the Andes, supposedly obsolete indigenous labor forms such as the repartimiento and *mita* (slave labor), also appear to have persisted well into the nineteenth century in Cuba. In this context, Cuba appears as less of an exception: these labor forms, originating in and associated with the conquest and early colonial economy, employed and similarly exploited Amerindian peoples like the Maya, Apache, and Nahua in the island colony.

While the perpetuation of early colonial labor forms suggests an even greater diversity in labor, it also indicates a persistence and diversity in elite strategies of labor coercion. Available evidence suggests that the importation of Amerindian labor and its continued promotion through the nineteenth century were indicative of a strategy of replacing expensive manumitted or otherwise freed African and African-descended labor, toward sustaining the essence of a system of forced labor under the guise of "free labor" that was otherwise in decline. Planters saw the writing on the wall. Imported indigenous labor may have offered an antidote: first, to planters resistant to the inevitable transition from slave to wage labor, and second, to those more willing to make the very gradual transition away from a socialized need to dominate, discipline, and control labor.[56]

As indicated in the preceding chapters, with the exception of indigenous convict labor, the proponents of the immigrant labor regime in Cuba habitually and officially promoted the importation of indigenous workers as free laborers. While Yucatec Mayas and other indígenas may have expected treatment befitting their official status as "colonos libres" in Cuba's plantation economy, Rebecca Scott asserts that many prospective patrones were not yet "weaned from their felt need to control, dominate, and discipline" labor.[57] More than this, however, in nineteenth-century Cuba plantation slave labor coexisted not only alongside free labor but also with early colonial coercive labor forms that tended to be applied, as in a much earlier period, to indigenous workers. Arguably, and painfully for Amerindian laborers in Cuba, this dimension of history was repeating itself, no less so than in other parts of the Americas.

The perpetuation of early colonial labor systems and adaptive elite strategies of coercion therein was evident in the persistence of Amerindian slavery and encomienda in northeastern Mexico at least to the eighteenth century.[58] In New Spain, labor systems were believed to have evolved "in a sequential and overlapping progression from slavery to encomienda, to repartimiento, to free labor," based on declining indigenous labor pools and the transition from mercantilist or precapitalist to capitalist economies.[59] In fact, core regions like the Valley of Mexico developed toward wage labor systems, while in peripheral economic areas like Yucatan and northern Mexico, progress toward wage labor became "arrested." Such areas, therefore, "retained more coercive, servile labor systems, including modified encomienda and corvee forms"; ultimately, Susan Deeds contends, "coercion in some form is almost never completely absent."[60] Nor was the Andean region immune in the nineteenth century to "modernizing Indian servitude."[61] Republican liberal governments like Ecuador continued to depend on indigenous tribute as a source of state revenues until at least the mid-nineteenth century, Brooke Larson notes, "without granting the package of juridical rights and jurisdictions to Indian communities that accompanied tribute obligations under the colonial system of dual republics. Indians owed tribute (now called the *contribución personal de indígenas*) but were denied legal rights to corporate landholdings or hereditary chiefdoms."[62] By 1876, although Ecuador's first national census removed "Indians" from the record, the government still ordered enumerators to "collect information about Indians to facilitate tax collection and labor conscription."[63]

In Bourbon-era Yucatan, the expansion of the hacienda, while pushing out the "doddering *encomenderos*," Rugeley attests, also "became a feudal Hispanic umbrella underneath which many older features of the Maya village lived on in modified form."[64] This included the onerous head tax along with mita forms of labor. After independence, if the names changed, the substance was retained: the head tax remained, now in the form of a state contribución, as did conscription for public labor, through the *fagina*.[65] The fagina was officially prohibited by new legislation in the 1830s, which hacendados and other employers often ignored as they continued to exploit and abuse their charges under a nominally new system of labor laws, taxes, and regulations.[66] Those Mayas who did not flee to isolated settlements or across the border fought back. Those who fought back and were captured by government forces underwent a migration, by force or guile, to Cuba.

By the mid-nineteenth century, Cuba's labor system was already in transition from a predominantly slave-labor to a primarily wage-labor system, as the costs of maintaining slave-based production, along with the advantages of mechanization, began to outweigh the benefits of an effectively defunct system; sugar planters eventually acquiesced to and then facilitated the change. In addition to this, manumission and coartación, functioning since before the 1800s, contributed to a situation in which the population of freed persons came to dwarf the numbers of slaves by the latter part of the century, effectively making abolition in 1886 a foregone conclusion.[67] Until recently, in the case of Cuba, African and African-descended slavery was the principle focus when it came to discussions and studies of labor, race, and ethnicity, in the context, not always explicitly examined, of persistent and coercive colonial labor forms. Understandings of the role of indigenous labor in Cuba had for all intents and purposes been relegated to a much earlier period. If the ostensible end of indigenous labor in Cuba is marked by the devastation of the Arawak Taíno by the end of the seventeenth century, and recent research indicates that it is not, it does not by necessity mark the end of Amerindian labor in the colony per se. At the same time, if by the nineteenth century, labor in Cuba was undergoing a transition from slave to free wage forms, this was neither a linear development nor an accurate depiction for all who worked in the island colony.

Labor realities in Cuba, like the indigenous presence, were considerably more diverse. In Cuba, labor forms like slavery and repartimiento that had their origins in the colonial beginnings of the Spanish American empire endured through the eighteenth and nineteenth centuries. They did so under both early colonial categories such as repartimiento and in the context of new pretenses, contracted out, for example, as free labor when actual conditions revealed the older, tried and true ways consistent with the needs of colonial plantation society.[68] Indigenous "colonos libres" not infrequently found themselves immersed in a system that looked and felt suspiciously like the repartimiento of old.

Late colonial Cuba manifested a diversity not only in its multifaceted labor system but also in a multinational or multicultural indigenous presence within that system. Even by the nineteenth century, this diverse international indigenous presence remained significant both intrinsically and for colonial state and private interests in Cuba. Further, this remained true during the apex of the African slave system and in the course of its decline in the island colony. Planters and other employers demonstrated a keen interest in finding ways, Rebecca Scott notes, to "combine the economic flexibility of free labor with the coercion of slavery."[69] Indigenous and other immigrant workers, whether in the form of indentured or convict labor, remained alternatives of long standing.

Among indigenous laborers, Yucatec Mayas were disproportionately represented in that system, serving at various times during and well beyond the early colonial period in Cuba. As has been demonstrated, Mayas served as forced or slave labor in Cuba well into the late colonial period. However, Mayas were not alone among indigenous immigrant laborers in Cuba. They were accompanied by various Apaches and other so-called indios mecos, as the demand for forced labor and the system of repartimiento persisted in Cuba.[70] Amerindians, men and women, were in demand in various capacities of servitude, from laborers to domestic servants, largely, as noted, through petitions and requests from individuals, organizations, and institutions representing economic and political elites in Cuba. In an 1802 "Noticia de Repartimiento de Mecos y Mecas," an inventory listing the human cargo aboard the Spanish naval warship San Roman, a broad range of the elites of colonial Cuban society is represented.[71] Elites in Cuba appear to have supported, facilitated, and profited from the perpetuation of the repartimiento as it was manifested by the extreme end of the late colonial period. Whether

Mecos or other captive and indentured indigenous laborers, this practice continued well into the latter part of the nineteenth century and, over time, encompassed or absorbed diverse Amerindian cultures in Cuba.

By the mid-nineteenth century, the most numerically prominent Amerindian culture to be forcibly transported to Cuba in a manner reminiscent of slavery and, when in Cuba, treated in a manner that resembled the ancient encomienda system were the Mayas of Yucatan. The magnitude of this human traffic to Cuba, because so much of it was illicit, continues to be difficult to quantify. Estimates of the known cases range in the area of two thousand to three thousand Mayas, although, as the few scholars who have addressed this question have observed, this is probably an underestimation of a traffic, legal and illicit, that some believe may have reached ten thousand souls.[72] The working conditions for Mayas in Cuba, not unlike the theory and practice of encomienda in the early colonial period, betrayed any notion of humanitarian treatment; such conditions often were brought to light by Maya workers themselves.[73] While Mayas in Cuba appear to have been persistent in protesting and resisting patrones, the latter appear to have been just as determined to perpetuate the forced labor conditions of their charges. Bergad has noted in the context of patrón treatment of Chinese laborers that it could not have been otherwise:

> Slavery governed the psychology of labor relations, and it was nearly impossible for planters whose economic lives and social interactions had been defined by slavery for generations to adjust to a milieu in which attitudes toward labor required a completely different set of economic, social, and cultural criteria. In a socioeconomic environment where free people could survive through other means, the stubborn insistence on maintaining slave-like conditions foreclosed the possibility of any widespread development of a free labor market.[74]

While many sugar planters adapted to the changes imposed during an era of impending abolition, there remained a market for Amerindian labor, as many still clung to the ethos and practice of slavery in Cuba. In fact, many planters continued to exercise a dual approach to overseeing life in their mills and plantations, accepting the changes wrought by technology and specialization—the eventual division between mill owners and colono-planters—while still clinging to a slave-owner mentality.[75]

Adults were not the only victims of this remnant but lingering system.

Of those indígenas distributed among elites in Cuba and who were also pressed into service in this manner were orphaned children. These, according to colonial authorities and their associates, were the future of labor in Cuba. They were also the most vulnerable. During the mid-nineteenth century, under legal requirements and conditions that resembled the more ancient obligations of encomienda, numerous indigenous and mestizo orphans arrived in Cuba; many accompanied other families transported to Cuba. Among these children were "the orphans or the destitute or children of families given up or surrendered by their parents" to be cared for, socialized, and educated by white elite families like those in Cuba until they reached adulthood.[76] Just as colonial authorities distributed Apaches and Mayas destined for domestic service among white families who had submitted requests "by special order," orphaned boys and girls were distributed among many of the same affluent white families.[77] The responsibilities of such would-be Samaritans and ostensible guardians included the maintenance, feeding, clothing, and education, including Christian teachings, of their young wards until they reached adulthood.[78] The actual motivations of elites requesting and receiving indigena domestic servants is betrayed as suggested in earlier correspondence that indicates less than Samaritan motives.[79] Nevertheless, families were directed and instructed to care for the orphans as if they were the children's parents and teachers or, as one official put it, as "preceptors to their disciples."[80]

The larger objectives in overseeing and supervising the care and work of these children had not changed appreciably since the need decreed in the eighteenth century, Ondina González notes, "to train these children to be good subjects and thus benefit the empire."[81] Domestic service ostensibly served as an exercise in socialization training and discipline for orphaned and other indigenous and mestizo children. It was designated as compensation for the care provided by the family. The line between guardian and patrón, on the one hand, and between ward and exploited and forced child labor, on the other, was more often than not illusory. In numerous cases, the exploited were Yucatec Maya children who, according to some contemporary observers, had historically come to elites for work and protection.[82] González has noted in the context of early colonial Cuba that children "lived in a world where survival was dependent on adults who had vested interests in the success of those children. As a group, the young had no economic or political power with which to claim the rights declared to be theirs by various institutions and royal decrees. . . . Young children had rights only when adults or institutions acted on their behalf."[83]

Colonial elites considered and rationalized both categories of indentured indigenous labor, adults and children, as eminently exploitable.[84] Still, even while an elite consensus appeared to exist, the sentiment of the elite classes in Cuba was not monolithic. The attitudes of economic and political elites in Cuba toward the persistence of remnant coercive colonial labor practices in Cuba, whether slavery or repartimiento, were not absolute. Nonetheless, at least until the revolutionary era of the 1890s, the dynamic of labor relations in Cuba suggest a consensus favoring their perpetuation. This is, in turn, a function of the attitudes of economic and political elites in Cuba toward indigenous adult and children colonos. If, as Bergad has observed, slavery governed the psychology of labor relations in Cuba, it also facilitated and rationalized the perpetuation of ostensibly obsolete coercive labor forms still practiced or imposed on indigenous Maya and Asian indentured laborers.

In a report dated April 25, 1849, the captain-general of Cuba expounded on the merits and utility of Yucatecan Indians as laborers in Cuba relative to the "troublesome" and resistant Chinese. He compared the insolence of the Chinese to the malleable indolence of the Yucatecan Indians, calling the latter "indolent and lazy in character, humble and subordinated when dominated."[85] The captain-general further expounded on the earlier, pre- and postconquest history of Spanish-indigenous relations: "In the hands of their caciques who punished and beat them, they [the Indians] were useful, inoffensive men."[86] In addition to purportedly responding well to subjugation by hacendados in Cuba, Yucatecan Indians were supposedly "well-constituted" for the indentured labor and accustomed to working in a tropical climate.[87]

In the mid-nineteenth century, government policy and regulations decreed the procedures for the distribution of indentured laborers to Cuban hacendados and other agricultural and productive interests, including domestic service.[88] Royal government circulars, while outlining the obligations of hacendados to colonos, also further stipulated the specific regime of discipline and punishments to be administered to indigenous and other indentured laborers. Hacendados in Cuba had the power to punish "disobedient" colonos with twelve lashes if they faltered in their contractual obligations; those "who persist in the disobedience" could expect eighteen more lashes, while the most "resistant" workers could face up to two months in shackles and stocks. Indigenous indentured workers who took flight from their patrones, if captured, could be punished by an even greater number of whippings and longer time in the stocks.[89]

Significantly, therefore, it should be more explicitly noted that planters and other economic elites in nineteenth-century Cuba were not totally at cross purposes with a Spanish imperial government and latently modernizing state seeking to transcend older colonial labor and production frameworks. Somewhat paradoxically, the same regime arguably facilitated the perpetuation of these ostensibly obsolete coercive forms through decreeing the application of some of their harsher components, such as corporal punishment, thereby, in effect, legitimizing mita-like labor. Elites therefore shared some consensus with the crown after all.

Although most elites abided by and supported them, these policies and regulations, were not met by unanimity. Some colonial intellectuals, while not averse to indentured labor per se, protested the physical abuse engendered in lashings or whippings of indigenous workers. In an 1849 report, Francisco Duran acknowledged the laws governing the treatment of colonos indios but questioned their applicability to indentured workers from countries no longer under Spanish sovereignty; others reported on the "scandalous" treatment and abuse of indigenous servants by members of the Spanish aristocracy in Cuba.[90] In the debate that existed and in reference to the magnitude or extent of abuses, contracts of indigenous colonos like the Mayas were characterized not as contracts freely entered into but as "contratos de sangre," or blood contracts.[91] Critics of this labor regime hopefully anticipated that such "bloody" (*sangriento*) contracts would be disapproved by the Mexican government.[92] In response, the office of the governor and captain-general of the island colony replied vehemently that such descriptions were inaccurate and could not possibly be attributed to contracts freely celebrated by the colonos indios.[93]

Indentured indigenous labor had its detractors and defenders. It appears that most elites strongly defended the disciplinary regime of the colonial government and, when it came to questions of corporal punishment, argued vehemently against treating colonos indios any differently than African slaves.[94] Some saw these as no different from any other *castas* who were "capital enemies" of whites, and they therefore wholeheartedly supported laws that ensured the "obedience and subordination" of these laborers in accordance with "their nature."[95] Not without spite, one such proponent asserted that humanitarian arguments about humane treatment of foreign indigenous indentured laborers may have been useful for men of letters but was counterproductive for the practical running of a business enterprise.[96] To the arguments that Spain was obligated to end slavery according to the treaties of 1817 and 1835 with Britain, the same elites answered back vehemently that the abolition treaties applied exclusively to the African slave trade and had no bearing on the traffic of indigenous indentured workers.[97] The conclusions for such a position, as noted in earlier analysis, were that the government's policies therein were rational, considerate, and protective of the interests of the hacendados and other employers, of the colony, and even of the workers and therefore was "well justified."[98]

Any substantive differences in elite views of the treatment of Mayas and other indentured laborers did not necessarily reflect similarly substantive differences in attitudes toward or understanding of the purported natural character of colonos indios. If they tended to disagree on considerations such as incentives, both sides also tended toward an emphasis on the indolence of indigenous workers at the same time that they viewed them as more climatically and culturally suitable than Asian workers. Still, and significantly, the debate that ensued for a time during the mid-nineteenth century in Cuba was less whether indigenous indentured laborers like the Mayas were being treated like slaves than whether they should be treated in the same manner. Opponents like Duran made clear the distinctions between the "proper" treatment of African and creole slaves and those indigenous and other foreign indentured laborers who were not, strictly speaking, slaves, at the same time that they pointed to the treaties that had earlier abolished the slave trade as reference points for the cessation of a similar traffic in Amerindian indentured workers. Such a position was likely taken by some of the same proponents who, by the end of the century, favored an immigration and colonization policy that not only condoned and promoted Amerindian labor immigration but did so under the premise of colonos indios as representing a whitening of the population in Cuba.

In the end, in spite of some measure of ambivalence about the perpetuation of more draconian treatment of indigenous, mestizo, and other nonwhite workers in Cuba and in spite of the concerns of the Spanish crown and late colonial intellectuals who represented some of the first reformists in Cuba, hacendados, planters, and other employers continued to exercise an authority over their workers that closely resembled older colonial forms. As the century progressed and slavery declined, planter attitudes were further borne out in the substantial support given by many of these same elites as well as the Spanish crown toward importing even more indígenas into the island colony.

At a time when virtually all other American nations and fledgling nations in the Western Hemisphere sought to develop according to models based in Europe and North America, models of modern society that had no place for indigenous peoples except as fully assimilated—or exterminated—and, as part of this great project, ambitiously and uniformly moved to facilitate that process with massive white, European immigration, Cuba offered an exception. Though certainly not for lack of trying, the colonial and imperial governments of the island, unlike those of almost all other nations in the Americas, nevertheless imagined options inconceivable to other American countries. Ironically, the island colony where indigenous peoples had historically been considered extinct appeared to be attempting to rejuvenate such a population through the promotion and development of immigration policies that also promoted Amerindian labor immigration. This should not be overstated or misconstrued, however; cheap, docile labor was a cardinal consideration there. Yet, imperial and colonial discussions of immigrant labor in Cuba, and the private petitions that were both a cause and a reflection of these, put repeated emphasis on the cultural affinity of indios yucatecos with Hispanic culture, a recurring argument toward potential assimilation and permanence of residency in Cuba.

Again, metropolitan and colonial governments expended considerable time and resources over a span of decades on such issues. The case study of Cuba may offer a rare instance when a more nuanced and relatively flexible understanding of race and ethnicity was reflected or realized in immigration questions and policy, again, at a time when whiter and more restrictive immigration was the norm everywhere else. Though by no means absolute, and certainly qualified by time, circumstance, and other variables, government policies in Cuba stood in relative contrast to the more simplistic, rigid, and dominant views and policies concerning indigenous peoples, labor, and immigration; in Cuba, the equation was stood on its head. Though the fact of the promotions and policies are central here, the question of the extent to which they bore fruit, as noted, remains unclear. Yucatec Mayas represent at least one instance in which indigenous immigrant workers did indeed stay: as individuals, as families, and in at least one instance, as a cohesive community.[99]

At least until European immigration satisfied their declared need for white labor and racial balance, planters and other patrones bade them stay, also fulfilling a need for many planters to maintain some semblance of a status quo as slavery gradually disintegrated around them. A hybrid system comprised of remnant slave labor as well as encomienda and repartimiento labor drawn from indígenas recruited from Mexico and other parts of tierra firme, "indios" who purportedly appreciated what they had under the Spanish, served just such a need and time. The perpetuation of early colonial indigenous labor forms in Cuba, while on a smaller scale than in northern Mexico and the Andes, nonetheless still provide significant evidence of the legacies of the early colonial epoch in the Spanish Caribbean.

More than mere vestiges, repartimiento and slavery remained very palpable as labor forms even by the latter part of the nineteenth century, as much so to interested elites who promoted and profited from such coercive labor as to those on whom the labor forms were imposed. Yucatec Mayas and other Amerindians, the original victims of Spanish conquest, colonization, and the accompanying harshly exploitative labor regimes, relived conditions imposed several centuries earlier in a revived or perpetuated system of distributed forced labor. Put another way, several hundred years after the implementation of a system of labor that brutalized the original indigenous and other Amerindian inhabitants and immigrants of postconquest Cuba, many of their descendants still endured such labor regimes. Also and importantly, even with the protective Spanish imperial legislation in place, elites strived to circumvent it in an effort, consistent with those of their ancestors, to exploit indigenous peoples in Cuba through systems that were parallel to or variations of early colonial labor forms. A more direct chronological and regional comparison may be even more instructive.

While Yucatec Mayas and other indigenous workers in Cuba shared some common and harsh realities, conditions that endured as well in the Yucatan peninsula and contributed decisively to the Yucatecan war that ensued, Amerindian workers in Cuba, as in the Yucatan, also made use of whatever part of the legislative framework that, although sanctioning their exploitation, also included aspects that addressed the rights of such workers, even if poorly or inconsistently implemented by government authorities themselves. In fact, precisely because of the poor implementation of any existing protective laws, with their perpetuation in whatever degree much less likely than their elimination in the face of heightened and aggressively coercive exploitation, Amerindian laborers like the Mayas in Cuba took the initiative into their own hands, invoking the laws, petitioning against abuses, and taking action on behalf of themselves and their families. Although the outcomes of many of these kinds of cases are not always clear, it is evident that Maya laborers in Cuba, for one group, while descendants of the first peoples to be so harshly exploited under the early mita labor systems of the Spanish, were not going to readily endure such perpetuated forms several hundred years later. If Cuba stands out as a site where indigenous labor exploitation endured, a microcosm of elite strategies to retain and perpetuate more ancient and oppressive colonial labor forms, it also is representative of the limits of that exploitation and of Amerindian responses that suggest an effort to overcome and transcend the colonialist legacy at the same time that, even if a truism, elites, whether late colonial or republican, endeavored to sustain in whatever guise.

CONCLUSION

Diaspora and the Enduring (and Diverse) Indigenous Presence in Cuba

If the Maya diaspora to Cuba faded in intensity by the end of the nineteenth century, it by no means ended. As is suggested by Cuban immigration records for the late 1880s and early 1890s, the Mayas of Yucatan continued to come to Cuba until at least the end of the nineteenth century.[1] In fact, according to ship manifests, Mayas also continued to arrive in Havana harbor into the early twentieth century, merely the latest in a series of journeys, indigenous passages stretching back a half millennium and more.[2]

The focus of this work has been the mobility, migration, and diaspora of indigenous peoples in colonial Cuba, including, where possible, the origins, identities, experiences, and struggles of the Yucatec Mayas and the Nahuas, Calusas, Timucuas, Uchises, Apaches, and other indígenas who arrived, worked, and lived in Cuba, involuntarily and voluntarily. The analytical focal point, furthermore, examines not only the presence but the diversity of this small but significant population of indigenous peoples, a varied autochthonous presence well beyond the early colonial period in Cuba. Not only did this diversity flow into and complement an already exceptionally diverse labor system; it also represented an intrinsically diverse world on its own. Further, the analytical emphasis has necessarily been on these indigenous visitors and immigrants and their relations with nonindigenous agents of the state—Spanish imperial, Cuban colonial, and Mexican republic—as well as the various employers or patrones and others.

Implicit in this analysis is the question of the relations among the indigenous peoples themselves, immigrant and indigenous host cultures, the indigenous Arawak Taíno, and other subaltern peoples in Cuba like African and African-descended slaves and freed persons and Chinese laborers. To what extent did these various peoples interact, mix, marry, and have impacts on one another? To what extent did these indigenous foreigners interact with others at all? These are questions of transculturation on which I have attempted to shed some light with the very limited evidence at hand. Questions of the evolution of ethnicity, identity, including the retention and persistence of indigeneity, and identity formation remain important considerations for further research. The extent of adequate historical evidence with which this story can be told remains, at this writing, unclear. This is important work that has yet to be done.

Even amid the paucity of available evidence there are clues, fragments that suggest that there must have been a range of such interactions. Some of them have been noted here. The indigenous newcomers, even those Nahuas, Mayas, and others transported as convict or prison labor and who worked in the *cuadrillas* (work gangs), obviously had some interactions with people in their midst, even if fleeting and whatever the likelihood of its being recorded. The greater promise of mining evidence to excavate such stories may lie in the more sustained interactions like those mentioned: from labor to intermarriage and relationships in between the two. Yet even in the case of marriage, issues of masking race or ethnicity can conceal relations, as in the early colonial period, when indigenous women who married Spanish men legally became "Spanish," and especially by the late colonial period, when racial reporting became less consistent. Still, we do have some very fragmentary evidence that can furnish us with a window or at least a scuttle into the lives of some indigenous immigrants in Cuba. Offered here are a few examples of the possibilities for further research into the next chapter of this story, one in which, again, Mayas and other Mesoamerican peoples appear to predominate.

From the very beginnings of Cuba's colonization within the Spanish Empire, reports exist of an apparent wealth of Yucatec Mayas in the founding settlements and towns of the early sixteenth-century island colony,[3] among them one community that helped found Havana. In turn, these reports lead us to some of the earliest instances of interactions between indigenous immigrant and indigenous host cultures, as recorded, for example, by the cabildo of Havana. Brief passages in the actas de cabildos tell us that the "Indians of Campeche" worked with the "indios naturales" (native Indians), indigenous Arawak Taíno, likely literally side by side, on road and other public works in and around the capital.[4] Further, both Arawak and Maya also likely encountered some of the many indigenous peoples from the Central America region, thousands of whom were enslaved during this period and transported to the Greater Antilles for work in the Caribbean colonies.[5] This diverse indigenous labor force probably also encountered some of the first African and African-descended slaves sanctioned by the Spanish crown to labor on the defense and public works of the capital and island.[6]

Imperial Spain's seemingly perpetual defense needs and Cuba's enduring labor demands ensured a concomitant need for laborers that indigenous peoples both within and outside the island colony continued to meet. Through the seventeenth and eighteenth centuries, surviving populations of Arawak Taíno peoples, those known to the colonial and imperial governments, residing in and governing over "Indian Towns" like El Caney and Jiguaní continued to serve the Spanish crown through their participation in defense and other public works in exchange for the autonomy of their communities. To the extent that there is some evidence suggesting small, scattered populations of Yucatec Mayas in eastern Cuba, it is plausible if not probable that Maya and Arawak continued to encounter one another in the context of these labors. If we do not yet know the incidence by which the descendants of the various indigenous cultures continued to encounter one another amid the social relations of labor, we most certainly know that these relations sometimes progressed and surpassed the realm of labor, toward more intimate and presumably enduring relationships after the early colonial period and into the long nineteenth century.

That these relations between indigenous Arawaks and indigenous immigrants transcended the realm of labor, though they may have been forged there, is suggested at least as early as the mid-sixteenth century. Colonial government officials of the time were aware of many indigenous immigrant peoples who were "not native born" and who had intermarried with island's autochthons and "become so identified with the [Arawak]."[7] Traces of these conjugal relations are further evident, though too often vague, in the parish registers where the descriptor "indio" is relatively consistently indicated more often than natal location, fueling more speculation than concrete evidence. Nonetheless, fragments persist through the centuries and are at least suggestive of the continued connubial relationships between indigenous immigrants and the host indigenous peoples.

Such relations and ensuing relationships extended to other subaltern subjects of the empire. A marriage consecrated at Espíritu Santo church in the barrio of Campeche took place in the summer of 1679 between Juan Alonso de los Reyes, "native Indian" from Merida, New Spain, and Eufrasia de Coca, a "black slave" of Dona Luisa de Oporto.[8] If the scale remains unclear, the endurance of more intimate social relations between indigenous immigrants, Arawak Taíno, African and African-descended slaves, and other subaltern peoples in the island colony is evident or at least suggested. Acts of resistance, for example, certainly could have provided the context or generated conditions for the mutual encounters of indigenous immigrant and host indigenous or other subaltern cultures, actions that forged alliances against abusive patrones, the colonial government, and the imperial state and that conceivably could have led to deeper relationships such as marriage. As indicated, allied with the Arawak Taíno were Yucatec Mayas and other indigenous people among the combatants behind the earliest movements of indigenous resistance against Spanish settlers and settlements during the early colonial period.[9] Given the evidence for intermarriage between Arawak Taíno and Yucatec, some may even have led parties of Arawak insurrectos against Cuba's colonizers. Indigenous immigrants also fought alongside fugitive African and African-descended slaves, as did at least one Yucatec Maya, known as Guachinango Pablo, who in 1797 reportedly led a palenque in western Cuba.[10]

By the nineteenth century, neither the massive influx of African slaves nor its augmentation by Chinese indentured laborers slaked the colonial economy's need for labor. As I have demonstrated, labor performed by imported Maya and other Indigenous workers remained a small but significant staple of production in Cuban colonial society. The Mayas of Yucatan provided the bulk of this indigenous immigrant workforce on the island colony. At the same time, labor conditions continued to provide opportunities for intercultural interactions, as indigenous workers and African or African-descended slaves almost inevitably found themselves thrown together in the various work sites. This is not particularly surprising, as numerous agents and patrones behind the importation of Yucatec Mayas to Cuba were, like Francisco Martí y Torrens, planters and slave owners. In one such instance likely not untypical, María Lucia Camara, the yucateca from Campeche, worked as a laundress alongside domestic slaves.[11]

Considering the substantial demand for indigenous domestic servants in urban centers like Havana that absorbed deported Apaches in the eighteenth century as readily as Mayas in the nineteenth, *criadas* who both replaced and augmented African-descended slave labor in colonial Cuban households were in a position that very likely and at several levels put them into contact with their African and conceivably Chinese counterparts. This is no less probable among the many Yucatec Maya men assigned to labor in the fields and mills of colonial Cuba's plantation economy. We know less about these kinds of encounters among indigenous immigrants themselves or between them and surviving Arawak Taíno descendants during the colonial period.

For the ensuing centuries, fragments of evidence both suggestive and more substantial exist among the records of the island's churches, colonial government documents, oral histories, and even the reports of archaeologists. All are suggestive of the range, complexity, and depth of more intimate indigenous social relationships and their implications for understanding Cuba's historic cultural heterogeneity. Something of this can be discerned or at least inferred from the work (deliberately and inadvertently) of other disciplines, including evidence that strongly suggests that this relational dynamic has its descendants and endures through the nineteenth and twentieth and into the twenty-first centuries.

Half a millennium ago, many of the valleys, plains, and undulating hills in the present-day provinces of Havana, Artemisa, Mayabeque, and Matanzas provinces (formerly Havana and Matanzas) in western Cuba were covered by forests of mahogany, ebony, cedar, and pine.[12] They were also inhabited by populations of indigenous Arawak Taíno people living in villages and towns organized in cacicazgos (chiefdoms) like those encountered by the Spanish throughout the island. The chiefdoms that occupied the present-day western provinces included Havana, Sabana (Sabaneque), Cubanacán, Hanábana (Hanamana), and Jagua.[13] Five centuries later, colonization, shipbuilding, and sugar had registered their impacts through deforestation of the area and devastation of the indigenous inhabitants. Neither the natural environment nor the population, however, is without survivors. When archaeologist and engineer Juan Cosculluela penetrated the region in the 1910s as part of the national government's infrastructural development program, he encountered near the Finca Orbea a community whose members asserted their ancestral ties to the ancient cacicazgo of Hanabana. This moment turned out to be seminal at two levels, in broadening our understanding of the persistence of the indigenous Arawak Taíno from the precolonial through colonial and national periods in Cuba and in shedding light on an equally persistent multicultural indigenous presence.

Though it is tempting to label such an encounter with something like "Modernity Meets Antiquity," we must refrain from any such suggestions of the essentialism so ingrained and enduring among that era's social scientists. Cosculluela met Epifanio Díaz, "El Pajaro," one of the community leaders and, like other members of his pueblo, Hanabana Quemada, an employee of the local finca. Díaz volunteered knowledge of his indigenous roots, including his family's ancestral ties to one of the first caciques in the region, information that Cosculluela reportedly confirmed in a local "ancient cemetery."[14]

The twentieth-century "discovery" of descendants of indigenous Arawak Taíno in western Cuba was both momentous and microcosmic, but the pueblo of Hanabana Quemada was and is notable for another reason. The cacique's descendant Díaz was married to a woman of Yucatec Maya heritage.[15] We do not know the name of the woman. Was she the only Maya in the pueblo nestled in a former cacicazgo or one of a number of Mayas resident in a mixed community? Was she a descendant of the enslaved Mayas of the early colony or in any way related to the Mayas trafficked in the nineteenth century or those who came later and recorded by the 1899 U.S. census as "Yucatan Indian" or as "Mexican"? While these questions may remain unanswered, it is clear that Díaz and his wife had a large family with numerous children and immediate and extended family members described by Cosculluela as "indiana clara" (clearly Indian).[16] Recent studies have suggested the existence of several towns and villages in western Cuba with small populations of Yucatec Mayas resident in either insulated or mixed communities. The pueblo of Hanabana Quemada represents one instance, a microcosm of the diverse and dispersed indigenous presence in Cuba.

Archaeological expeditions headed by Cuban and Soviet scientists in the 1960s and 1970s lent further credence to this mixed Mesoamerican-indigenous presence. Yucatec Mayas were encountered at the foot of the hill Loma del Grillo, in the community of Madruga in Mayabeque (formerly Havana) province. The residents identified themselves as Yucatec Mayas and practiced milpa agriculture, and at least the elder members of the community still spoke the Yucatec language. This community, if isolated and insulated early on, became less so with time. According to local elders, as time progressed, many of the youth increasingly interacted and intermarried with outsiders.[17]

Another component to this dynamic is represented by Mayas resident in Guanabacoa, originally a settlement established by the Spanish for indigenous Arawak Taíno since the colonial period who may have surviving descendants in the Havana suburb of the contemporary period. Again, through early colonial records like the actas de cabildos we do know that these indigenous residents of Guanabacoa and the barrio of Campeche interacted, at minimum, through the social relations of labor. Further, reports of Yucatec Mayas in Cuba, in communities either integrated or insulated, persist through the early and mid-twentieth century, predominantly in Cuba's western regions. During the mid- to late twentieth century, various Cuban, Mexican, and North American scholars and scientists have commented on the Yucatec Mayas of Madruga, believed to be descendants of the nineteenth-century traffic of Maya laborers as exiles of the Caste War. These Mayas represent one of several similar communities scattered throughout predominantly western but also eastern Cuba, including Nueva Paz just south of Madruga as well as Los Palos and a number of other towns, some more or less isolated than others, stretching as far west as Cabo de San Antonio and east to Holguin.[18]

Among numerous such communities that persist in western Cuba, Madruga has in recent years received most of the attention of North American and Latin American observers. This may be so for several reasons. My informal discussions with Cuban friends and colleagues suggest the popular reluctance of Cubans to acknowledge the existence of descendants of indigenous Arawak Taíno on the island, as the historian Felipe Pichardo Moya encountered decades ago. They are more likely, however, to acknowledge the endurance of descendant Mayas. This interest has recently grown at popular and academic levels. Madruga may be under the spotlight in part because, although difficult to access, it is nonetheless among the more accessible. Finally, the Mayas of Madruga may also stand out because of the persistence of certain characteristics, both physical (as distinct from physiological) and cultural, that are quintessentially Maya, enduring for centuries, while also adaptive. In order to shed some light on these questions, social scientists like Mexican anthropologist Victoria Novelo and Cuban archaeologists Karen Mahé Lugo Romera and Sonia Menéndez Castro visited the pueblo, respectively, in the 1990s and the first decade of the new millennium. Their findings, through observation and interviews with residents, are instructive, throwing light on this case study of contemporary descendants of indigenous immigrants in Cuba.

Founded through the gradual gathering of Yucatec Maya families at Loma del Grillo at the turn of the century, by the beginning of the twentieth century and in the decades before the 1959 revolution, the pueblo existed on a precarious foundation—precarious in part because of rampant latifundism—of milpa agriculture and coal production.[19] For more than a half century, largely isolated and illiterate in the Spanish language, the Yucatec Mayas of Madruga interacted minimally with the rest of society.[20] Conditions of relative isolation tended to reinforce the endurance and persistence of Yucatec Maya identity, therefore, well into the twentieth century. Isolated as they were, however, the Mayas could not insulate themselves from the sea change generated by the social revolution of 1959. Characteristically, pueblo residents remember this as a time of both substantial change and continuity. Change came in the form of agricultural reforms and literacy movements in the countryside, the former resulting in relocation of the Mayas not far from their original locations to parcels of land designated by the revolutionaries and the latter in the form of education and health care, a clinic and a school.[21]

Change under the revolution offered opportunities but also new struggles for the Maya community that challenged the maintenance of Yucatec Maya identity, as Maya children and youth went off to school and returned, having been exposed to new ideas and people. The revolution appeared to introduce a duality to the existence of the formerly isolated Mayas. While the pueblo remained relatively physically isolated, the members of the community became increasingly divided in relation to the larger revolutionary society. An informant observed that "the old ones resisted . . . but these people, the young ones saw possibilities in change."[22] For the Mayas of Madruga, as, no doubt, for other Maya communities in western Cuba, the revolution transformed the lives of the youth as the sons and daughters of Maya farmers and coal burners became nurses and teachers, some remaining in the community, others moving to the cities.[23] Under such conditions, the ramifications for the maintenance of Maya identity appear potentially foreboding. Novelo observes several factors that conspired against the reproduction of the group, including the internal migration of youth to the cities, mixed marriages, and the disappearance of community elders and the ancient knowledge and language they possessed and traditionally transmitted to younger generations.[24]

Half a century of social revolution later and more than a decade after Novelo's encounter, the Mayas of Madruga endure, still struggling with many of the same forces that challenge the integrity of their community and, by extension, their identity. Mahé and Menéndez have observed that Mayas both persisted and adapted. Having received modern housing in urban areas, many chose to remain in their traditional dwellings on their land; if traditional dishes were no longer quotidian practice, they were reserved for special days of celebration; and if Yucatec Maya was slowly giving way to the Spanish language, the Mayas of Madruga and surrounding communities continued to identify themselves as Yucatec Maya.[25]

In a news article published in June 2014, the Mayas of Madruga were characterized by the Cuban state media as "the last Mayas in Cuba." Yet it is clear that they are no more the last than other long-lived indigenous community in the country, whether descendants of Maya or Arawak Taíno. The Arawak Taíno, not incidentally, have in recent years become more evident and active in educating the Cuban and international community on the persistence as well as diversity of the indigenous presence on the island nation.[26] It is also important and remarkable that over the centuries a sense of indigeneity has endured among indigenous and diasporic indigenous peoples in Cuba, technically and perhaps ironically including the Arawak Taíno. Though no doubt abated over time—despite almost universal observations of the appearance and practices of contemporary "Indians" being indistinguishable from the general population—the persistence of an indigenous identity still manifests itself in the endurance, in varying degrees, of autochthonous languages, traditional forms of agriculture, and the relationship to the land, foods and food preparation, and even housing construction, combined with at least some of the modern amenities. As of the new millennium, therefore, descendants of indigenous immigrants like the Mayas of Madruga endure, as do some of the traditional practices maintained and adapted, a dynamic shared with their relations in Yucatan and Guatemala, as visiting Guatemalan Mayas recently observed.[27]

Though descendant Yucatec Maya and Arawak Taíno communities are becoming better known as distinct communities and peoples, it is likely that lesser-known contemporary mixed or hybrid communities also exist. Further, recent genetic studies have revealed the substantial indigenous make-up of Cuba's population, one considerably more diverse and substantively more indigenous at the roots than previously known.[28] In any event, the indigenous heritage of Cuba is possessed of substantially broader and deeper roots than has heretofore been understood, let alone recognized. Indigenous peoples, both insular and continental, have played significant roles in the historical development of Cuba and have made noteworthy contributions to the island's social, economic, and cultural development. Continental indigenous peoples, along with their African, Chinese, and indigenous Arawak Taíno counterparts, whether as voluntary immigrants or involuntary forced labor, made their mark, facilitating, in varying degrees, the evolution of Cuba's economy and society. With too few exceptions, their migrations, diasporas, and struggles remain shrouded, unlike the understandably more comprehensively documented diasporic experiences of African, African-descended, and Chinese peoples. Future research, which the present study hopes to encourage, should open more windows into the historic and contemporary multicultural or multinational indigenous presence in Cuba.

This ancient and enduring presence possesses dimensions that in turn broaden and deepen our understanding of indigenous peoples—and subaltern peoples generally—and Cuban history. Their presence reminds us of the adaptability and resourcefulness of indigenous peoples like the Yucatec Mayas who have, for the most part, not only been forced to contribute to Cuba's development but also have struggled through various regimes and generations, to the present day, to defend and protect their interests. That determination, negotiation, and resistance, again, along with that of their

Arawak Taíno counterparts and relations, account in no small part for the persistence of indigenous peoples and a multicultural indigenous presence in Cuba through the centuries to the current period. Their history, of its own accord and as a part of the larger history of Cuba, has barely begun to be told. When this multifaceted story is more completely and definitively related, it will tell us of a more diverse Cuba and Caribbean that include not one but a number of indigenous American cultures, then and now. It will also tell us that Cuba more closely represents a microcosm or, more accurately, a mirror of the continental cultural kaleidoscope than previously understood or appreciated.

NOTES

Introduction

1. David J. Robinson, ed., *Migration in Spanish America* (Cambridge: Cambridge University Press, 1990), 1.

2. Ibid.

3. Ibid., 2.

4. James Clifford, "Diasporas," *Cultural Anthropology* 9, no. 3 (1994): 309.

5. Ibid., 310.

6. Ibid., 308–10.

7. Ibid.

8. Matthew Restall, "Interculturation and the Indigenous Testament in Colonial Yucatan," in *Dead Giveaways: Indigenous Testaments of Colonial Mesoamerica and the Andes,* edited by Matthew Restall and Susan Kellogg (Salt Lake City: University of Utah Press, 1998), 141–42.

9. The one exception is the work of Florida anthropologist John Worth, who has done research on Florida Amerindians' travels to western Cuba; "A History of Southeastern Indians in Cuba, 1513–1823," paper presented at 61st Annual Meeting of the Southeastern Archaeological Conference, St. Louis, MO, October 22, 2004. See also Jason M. Yaremko, "Colonial Wars and Indigenous Geopolitics: Aboriginal Agency, the Cuba-Florida-Mexico Nexus, and the Other Diaspora," *Canadian Journal of Latin American and Caribbean Studies* 35, no. 70 (2011): 165–96.

10. Marcos A. Rodríguez Villamil, *Indios al este de La Habana* (Havana: Ediciones Extramuros, 2002).

11. Manuel Moreno Fraginals, *The Sugarmill: the Socioeconomic Complex of Sugar in Cuba, 1760-1860* (New York: Monthly Review Press, 1976); Rebecca Scott, *Slave Emancipation in Cuba: The Transition to Free Labor, 1860-1899* (Pittsburgh, PA: University of Pittsburgh Press, 2000); James C. Scott, *Weapons of the Weak: Everyday Forms of Peasant Resistance* (New Haven, CT: Yale University Press, 1985); Manuel

Barcia, *Seeds of Insurrection: Domination and Resistance on Western Cuban Plantations, 1808–1848* (Baton Rouge: Louisiana State University Press, 2008).

12. J. Scott, *Weapons of the Weak*. For a more recent application of Scott, see Barcia, *Seeds of Insurrection*.

13. See Charles Cutter, *The Legal Culture of Northern New Spain* (Albuquerque: University of New Mexico Press, 1995); Yanna Yannakakis, *The Art of Being In-Between: Native Intermediaries, Indian Identity, and Local Rule in Colonial Oaxaca* (Durham: Duke University Press, 2008); and Ethelia Ruiz Medrano and Susan Kellogg, eds., *Negotiation within Domination: New Spain's Indian Pueblos Confront the Spanish State* (Boulder: University Press of Colorado, 2010).

14. José Cuello, "The Persistence of Indian Slavery and Encomienda in the Northeast of Colonial Mexico, 1577-1723," *Journal of Social History* 21, no. 4 (1988): 683-700; Susan Deeds, "Rural Work in Nueva Vizcaya: Forms of Labor Coercion on the Periphery." *Hispanic American Historical Review* 69, no. 3 (1989): 425-49; Brooke Larson, *Trials of Nation Making: Liberalism, Race, and Ethnicity in the Andes, 1810-1910* (Cambridge: Cambridge University Press, 2004); and James C. Scott, *Domination and the Arts of Resistance: Hidden Transcripts* (New Haven, CT: Yale University Press, 1990).

Chapter 1. Imperial Geopolitics, the Florida-Cuba Nexus, and Amerindian Passages

1. Jerald T. Milanich, *Laboring in the Fields of the Lord: Spanish Missions and Southeastern Indians* (Washington, DC: Smithsonian Institution Press, 1999), 62.

2. Ibid.

3. Ibid., 66–67.

4. Ibid., 78.

5. Victor D. Thompson and John E. Worth, "Dwellers by the Sea: Native American Adaptations along the Southern Coasts of Eastern North America," *Journal of Archaeological Research* 19, no. 1 (March 2011): 80–82. See also Milanich, *Laboring in the Fields of the Lord*, 38–40.

6. Thompson and Worth, "Dwellers by the Sea," 81–82.

7. Amy Turner Bushnell, *Situado and Sabana: Spain's Support System for the Presidio and Mission Provinces of Florida*, Anthropological Papers, No. 74 (Athens, GA: American Museum of Natural History, September 21, 1994), 105.

8. Regarding the Calusa chief Carlos, see John H. Hann, *Indians of Central and South Florida, 1513–1763* (Gainesville: University Press of Florida, 2003), 13–16; John H. Hann, ed. and trans., *Missions to the Calusa* (Gainesville: University Press of Florida, 1991), 221.

9. George Lovell and William Swezey, "Indian Migration and Community

Formation," in *Migration in Colonial Spanish America*, edited by David J. Robinson (Cambridge: Cambridge University Press, 1990), 27–28.

10. Cited in ibid.

11. Ibid.

12. Pedro Menéndez de Avilés to Fray Francisco Borgia, March 1565, in *Monumenta antiquae Floridae, 1566–1572*, edited by Félix Zubillaga (Rome: Monumenta Historica Societatus Iesu, 1946), 1–3. Unless otherwise indicated, translations are mine.

13. Michael J. McNally, *Catholicism in South Florida* (Gainesville: University Presses of Florida, 1985), 2.

14. Ibid.

15. Pedro Menéndez de Avilés to Francisco Borgia, January 18, 1568, in *Monumenta antiquae Floridae*, 228–34.

16. Menéndez de Avilés to Francisco Borgia, January 18, 1568, in *Monumenta antiquae Floridae*, 231–32.

17. Ibid., 232. Juan Bautista de Segura to Francisco Borgia, November 18, 1568, in *Monumenta antiquae Floridae*, 358–70.

18. Father Juan Rogel to D. Avellaneda, Havana, November 1566–January 30, 1567, in *Monumenta antiquae Floridae*, 132–33. See also Hann, *Indians*, 155.

19. Rogel to Avellaneda, 134; Hann, *Indians*, 155.

20. Hann, 155.

21. Juan Rogel to Francisco Borgia, Havana, July 25, 1568, in *Monumenta antiquae Floridae*, 319.

22. Ibid.

23. Francisco Villareal to Juan Rogel, January 23, 1568, in *Monumenta antiquae Floridae*, 236–37.

24. Francisco Villareal to Francisco Borgia, March 5, 1570, in *Monumenta antiquae Floridae*, 415. See also the translation in Hann, *Indians*, 156.

25. Respectively, my and Hann's translations of Juan Rogel to Geronimo Ruiz del Portillo, April 25, 1568, in *Monumenta antiquae Floridae*, 290; in Hann, *Missions to the Calusa*, 221.

26. Juan Rogel to Francisco Borgia, November 10, 1568, doc. 91, in *Monumenta antiquae Floridae*, 272–311; Juan Rogel to Geronimo Ruiz del Portillo, April 25, 1568, doc. 85, in *Monumenta antiquae Floridae*, 330–43. "Father Juan Rogel to Father Jeronimo Ruiz del Portillo, April 25, 1568," in Hann, *Missions to the Calusa*, 230–78.

27. "Father Juan Rogel to Father Jeronimo Ruiz del Portillo, April 25, 1568," in Hann, *Missions to the Calusa*, 244–45.

28. "Account of the Florida Mission by Father Juan Rogel, Written Between the Years 1607–1611," doc. 139, in *Monumenta antiquae Floridae*, 606–7.

29. "Father Juan Rogel to Father Jeronimo Ruiz del Portillo, April 25, 1568," in Hann, *Missions to the Calusa*, 244–45.

30. This suggests that the woman was Calusa.

31. "Father Juan Rogel to Father Jeronimo Ruiz del Portillo, April 25, 1568," in Hann, *Missions to the Calusa*, 252–53.

32. Ibid.

33. Juan Bautista de Segura to Francisco Borgia, November 18, 1568, in *Monumenta antiquae Floridae*, 359–61.

34. Bautista de Segura to Borgia, November 18, 1568, in *Monumenta antiquae Floridae*, 360–62.

35. Ibid.

36. Milanich, *Laboring in the Fields of the Lord*, 97.

37. Menéndez de Avilés to Francisco Borgia, October 14, 1570, in *Monumenta antiquae Floridae*, 449–51.

38. Menéndez de Avilés to Francisco Borgia, January 10, 1571, in *Monumenta antiquae Floridae*, 480–85.

39. Ibid., 482.

40. This would include, by the late eighteenth century, the instruction of indigenous girls from Florida; James Brooks, *Captives and Cousins: Slavery, Kinship, and Community in the Southwest Borderlands* (Chapel Hill: University of North Carolina Press, 2002), 61.

41. "Relation of the Florida Mission," Father Juan Rogel, 1607–11, in *Monumenta antiquae Floridae*, 610. See also Worth, "History of Southeastern Indians in Cuba."

42. See correspondence in Francisco Javier Alegre, "Fundación del Colegio de Habana, 1656–1658," in his *Historia de la provincia de Jesús de Nueva España*, edited by Ernest Burrus and Felix Zubillaga (Rome: Institutum Historicum S.J., 1956–1960), 1:66–67.

43. Milanich, *Laboring in the Fields of the Lord*, 99.

44. McNally, *Catholicism in South Florida*, 2.

45. Worth, "History of Southeastern Indians in Cuba," 4–5.

46. See William Bartram, *Travels Through North & South Carolina, Georgia, East & West Florida, the Cherokee Country, the Extensive Territories of the Muscolges, or Creek Confederacy, and the Country of the Choctaws.* (Philadelphia: James and Johnson, 1791), 226; and James W. Covington, "Trade Relations between Southwestern Florida and Cuba, 1600–1840," *Florida Historical Quarterly* 38, no. 2 (1959): 116–17. For more on the ethnohistorical and archaeological evidence regarding indigenous navigation between Florida and the Greater Antilles and beyond during the colonial and precolonial periods, see Richard T. Callaghan, "Comments on the Mainland Origins of the Preceramic Cultures of the Greater Antilles," *Latin*

American Antiquity 14, no. 3 (2003): 323–38. See also Richard T. Callaghan, "Patterns of Contact between the Islands of the Caribbean and the Surrounding Mainland as a Navigational Problem," in *Islands at the Crossroads: Migration, Seafaring, and Interaction in the Caribbean*, edited by L. Antonio Curet and Mark W. Hauser (Tuscaloosa: University of Alabama Press, 2011), 59–72; and Mary Jane Berman, "Good as Gold: The Aesthetic Brilliance of the Lucayans," also in *Islands at the Crossroads*, edited by Curet and Hauser, 114–15.

47. Cited in Hann, *Missions to the Calusa*, 27–28.

48. Worth, "History of Southeastern Indians in Cuba," 6.

49. "Don Diego Ebelino de Compostela, Bishop of Santiago de Cuba, to the Dean and Chapter of Holy Cathedral Church of Santiago de Cuba," January 2, 1690, Santo Domingo, legajo (bundle)(hereafter leg.) 154, Archivo General de Indias, Seville (AGI), cited in Hann, *Missions to the Calusa*, 88.

50. Ibid., 89–90.

51. Ibid.

52. Ibid.

53. Ibid.

54. Ibid.

55. Ibid., 85.

56. Ibid., 85–86.

57. Testimony of Friars Relating to the Calusa Mission, February–March 1698, Santo Domingo, leg. 154, R.6, N.114a, AGI, in Hann, *Missions to the Calusa*, 162–80.

58. Ibid., 169–70.

59. Testimony of Lay Witnesses Relating to the Calusa Mission, February–March 1698, Santo Domingo, leg. 154, R.6, n.114a (AGI), in Hann, *Missions to the Calusa* 181–205. Several testimonies by friars and laypersons indicated that the Calusa consented to the baptizing and catechizing of their children but that "it would be difficult to withdraw the old peoples away from what their ancestors had observed"; Hann, *Missions to the Calusa*, 194.

60. Notes by the Council of the Indies, August 8, 1698, Santo Domingo, leg. 154, R.6, in Hann, *Missions to the Calusa*, 210.

61. According to one account, the old and ill cacique Carlos related to the friars that "he was dying with great unhappiness because priests were not coming"; Fray Feliciano Lopez to Fray Pedro Taybo, 1697, Santo Domingo, leg. 154, R.6, AGI, in Hann, *Missions to the Calusa*, 158. Arguably, the poor relations and expulsion may have been self-induced; the seven-year delay in coming to the Calusa potentially fueled or influenced dissent, disillusionment, and disaffection among the Calusa regarding the missionaries, sentiments aggravated in turn by the latter's separate residence and aggressive evangelizing, not to mention the Calusa's

(and European) association of Christian living with material culture, areas where the friars were judged deficient. Related to this last factor, one might consider the indigenous relationship between provisions, trade, and social factors of *confianza* (trust). Testimony of Friars Relating to the Calusa Mission, in Hann, *Missions to the Calusa*, 167, 170, 172, 174–75, and Testimony of Lay Witnesses Relating to the Calusa Mission, in Hann, *Missions to the Calusa*, 181–205.

62. Worth, "History of Southeastern Indians in Cuba," 6.

63. Robert C. Galgano, *Feast of Souls: Indians and Spaniards in the Seventeenth-Century Missions of Florida and New Mexico* (Albuquerque: University of New Mexico Press, 2005), 124.

64. Thompson and Worth, "Dwellers by the Sea," 82.

65. See John E. Worth, "Timucua and the Colonial System in Florida: The Rebellion of 1656," paper presented in the symposium "New Perspective on the Spanish Colonial Experience" at the 25th Conference of the Society for Historical Archaeology, Kingston, Jamaica, January 9, 1992, 12.

66. See Justin Blanton, "The Role of Cattle Ranching in the 1656 Timucuan Rebellion: A Struggle for Land, Labor, and Chiefly Power," *Florida Historical Quarterly* 92, no. 4 (2014): 667–84.

67. William C. Sturtevant, "Spanish-Indian Relations in Southeastern North America," *Ethnohistory* 9, no. 1 (1962): 68–69.

68. Hann, *Indians*, 98–103.

69. Worth, "History of Southeastern Indians in Cuba," 5–6; John E. Worth, "Pineland during the Spanish Period," in *The Archaeology of Pineland: A Coastal Southwest Florida Village Complex, AD 50–1700*, edited by Karen J. Walker and William H. Marquardt, 777–78, Monograph no. 4 (Gainesville: Institute of Archaeology and Paleoenvironmental Studies, 2013); Hann, *Indians*, 179.

70. Hann, *Indians*, 179–80.

71. Ibid.

72. Bishop Geronimo de Valdés to the King, December 9, 1711, Santo Domingo, leg. 860, AGI, in Hann, *Missions to the Calusa*, 335–36.

73. Ibid., 337.

74. Ibid. Governor Juan Francisco de Güemes y Horcasitas to the King, July 26, 1743, Santo Domingo, leg. 860, AGI, in Hann, *Missions to the Calusa*, 400–402; also cited in Hann, *Indians*, 180.

75. Bishop Geronimo de Valdés to the King, in Hann, *Missions to the Calusa*, 337. According to Hann, these numbers are not unreasonable when compared to population numbers several decades later; *Indians*, 180.

76. Hann, *Indians*.

77. Ibid., 180–81.

78. The King to Reverend in Christ, Father Bishop of the cathedral church of the city of Santiago and resident in that of Havana, February 23, 1716, Santo Domingo, leg. 860, AGI, in Hann, *Missions to the Calusa*, 343–44.

79. The King to the Governor Captain-General of the Island of Cuba and city of San Christobal of Havana, February 23, 1716, Santo Domingo, leg. 860, AGI, in Hann, *Missions to the Calusa*, 345–46.

80. Ibid., 344 margin note.

81. Governor Dionisio Martínez de la Vega to the King, July 7, 1732, Santo Domingo, leg. 860, AGI, in Hann, *Missions to the Calusa*, 382–83.

82. Ibid.

83. Ibid.

84. Governor Güemes y Horcasitas to the King, in Hann, *Missions to the Calusa*, 402–3.

85. Christóbal de Sayas Bazán, Letter and record of service, August 17, 1727, Santo Domingo, leg. 860, folio (hereafter fol.) 38–39, AGI.

86. Ibid.

87. Hann, *Indians*, 181.

88. Junta of Dionisio Martínez de la Vega, Gonzalo Menendez Valdés, Fray Melchor de Sotolongo, Juan Tomas de la Barrera Soto Mayor, Christóbal de Sayas Bazán, June 9, 1732, Santo Domingo, leg. 860, AGI.

89. Statement of the Captain Lucas Gomez, July 5, 1732, Santo Domingo, leg. 860, AGI, in Hann, *Missions to the Calusa*, 394–97. The statements of other crew members and participants corroborate the testimony of Gomez.

90. Ibid.

91. Hann, *Indians*, 181.

92. Milanich, *Laboring in the Fields of the Lord*, 191.

93. See notes by the Council of the Indies, Governor Dionisio Martínez de la Vega to the king, in Hann, *Missions to the Calusa*, 385–91.

94. Christóbal de Sayas Bazán, letter and record of service.

95. Worth, "History of Southeastern Indians in Cuba," 7.

96. Milanich, *Laboring in the Fields of the Lord*, 190.

97. Governor Güemes y Horcasitas to the King, in Hann, *Missions to the Calusa*, 403.

98. The basis for disagreement lay in the interpretations of the governor's reference to the Bay of Jagua. Hann argues that Güemes y Horcasitas reported that the Keys Indians ran away because the Amerindian envoys from Cuba had told them that when in Cuba, they would be moved to the Bay of Jagua (Xagua?), "once their children had been taken away from them"; Governor Güemes y Horcasitas to the King, in Hann, *Missions to the Calusa*, 403n5. Sturtevant has argued that the

Costas had fled from the keys, sending their children ahead of them to the Bay of Jagua in Cuba; "Last of the South Florida Aborigines," in *Tacachale: Essays on the Indians of Florida and Southeastern Georgia during the Historic Period*, edited by Jerald Milanich and Samuel Proctor (Gainesville: University Presses of Florida, 1978), 146–54.

99. Governor Güemes y Horcasitas to the King, in Hann, *Missions to the Calusa*, 400–401.

100. Hann, *Indians*, 183–84.

101. Testimony from the Autos concerning the principal Indian natives from the Keys of Florida having begged for holy baptism and from the rest that they set forth, left to the corresponding ministers and what measures His Lordship has provided on this subject, Memorial to the Governor of Havana, 1743, AGI, in Hann, *Missions to the Calusa*, 410–13.

102. Report on the Indians of Southern Florida and its Keys by José María Monaco and José Javier Alaña, Presented to Governor Juan Francisco Guemes y Horcasitas, 1760, Santo Domingo, leg. 1210, AGI, in Hann, *Missions to the Calusa*, 420. This is a revised version of the original 1743, report by José María Monaco and José Javier Alaña, Santo Domingo, found in leg. 860, AGI, and in Hann, *Missions to the Calusa*, 418–31.

103. Hann, *Missions to the Calusa*, 420.

104. Ibid., 421.

105. Hann, *Indians*, 184.

106. Governor Güemes y Horcasitas to the King, in Hann, *Missions to the Calusa*, 403–4.

107. Ibid.

108. Cited in Hann, *Indians*, 186.

109. Alegre, *Historia de la Provincia*, 4:397–98.

110. Milanich, *Laboring in the Fields of the Lord*, 193.

111. Ibid.

112. Worth, "History of Southeastern Indians in Cuba," 9.

113. Ibid.

114. Janet Landers, "Africans and Native Americans on the Spanish Florida Frontier," in *Beyond Black and Red: African-Native Relations in Colonial Latin America*, edited by Matthew Restall (Albuquerque: University of New Mexico Press, 2005), 63.

115. Robert L. Gold, "The East Florida Indians under Spanish and English Control: 1763–1765," *Florida Historical Quarterly* 44, nos. 1–2 (1965): 105–7. As Gold and others note, however, this process was not without incident. Regardless of promises of land rights, many local Indians reacted violently to news of the imperial

exchange: "the skeptical Indians brutally assaulted outposts and plantations on the Anglo-Spanish frontier. Indian barbarities continued to occur in Georgia and South Carolina even after presents were distributed," 107.

116. Ibid. "Listas de familias de Indios de Florida alojadas en Guanabacoa," 1764, Reales cédulas y órdenes de Florida, Cuba, leg. 416, folios 755–70, AGI.

117. Cited in Gold, "East Florida Indians," 107–8. Gold notes some inconsistencies in the numbers of Amerindian refugees reported for this period; one report indicates twenty or more Indian men, while another account reports fewer. See also Governor Feliu and Don Juan Eligio de la Puente to the governor of Cuba, St. Augustine and Havana, January 22, 1764; Don Juan Eligio de la Puente to the Governor of Cuba, Havana, September 22, 1766, Santo Domingo, leg. 2595, AGI.

118. Bernard Romans, *A Concise Natural History of East and West Florida* (New York: Printed for the author, 1775), 291–92.

119. Landers, "Africans and Native Americans," 63.

120. Ibid.

121. Gold, "East Florida Indians," 105–9; William Sturtevant, "Spanish-Indian Relations," 69–70; Milanich, *Laboring in the Fields of the Lord*, 193–95; Hann, *Indians*, 59–60, 103, 186.

122. Gold, "East Florida Indians," 108; Hann, *Indians*, 59.

123. Hann, *Indians*, 202.

124. "Listas de familias de Indios de Florida," AGI.

125. Hann, *Indians*, 59–60.

126. See Worth, "History of Southeastern Indians in Cuba, 1513–1823," 9.

127. Cited in ibid.

128. Mark F. Boyd and Jose N. Latorre, "Spanish Interest in British Florida," *Florida Historical Quarterly* 32, no. 2 (1953): 92.

129. Worth, "History of Southeastern Indians in Cuba," 9.

130. Sturtevant, "Spanish-Indian Relations," 72–73.

Chapter 2. The "Evil Designs" of "Frequent Intercourse": Havana, Empire, and Indigenous Geopolitics

1. Orders, Headquarters, New York, February 8, 1764, vol. 13, 1764, Thomas Gage Papers, American Series, William Clements Library, University of Michigan, Ann Arbor (hereafter cited as Gage Papers).

2. J. Harries to Thomas Gage, February 25, 1764, vol. 14, 1764, Gage Papers.

3. Ibid.

4. John Stuart to Gage, Charles Town, March 24, 1767, vol. 63, 1767; Gage to John Stuart, May 19, 1768, vol. 77, May-June 1768, Gage Papers.

5. John Stuart to Gage, Charles Town, July 2, 1768, vol. 78, 1768, Gage Papers.

6. John Stuart to Gage, Mobile, December 14, 1771, vol. 108, 1771–72; Charles Stuart to F. Haldimand, May 12, 1774, vol. 119, 1773–74, Gage Papers.

7. J. Leitch Wright Jr., *Creeks and Seminoles: Destruction and Regeneration of the Muscogulge People* (Lincoln: University of Nebraska Press, 1986), 101.

8. See J. Wright regarding the various indigenous communities represented under the umbrella term "Creeks"; *Creeks and Seminoles*, 1–36, 112–13.

9. Ibid., 101.

10. Olive P. Dickason, *Canada's First Nations: A History of Founding Peoples from Earliest Times*, 3rd ed. (Oxford: Oxford University Press, 2002), 155–56.

11. J. Wright, *Creeks and Seminoles*, 105.

12. Ibid., 107

13. Claudio Saunt, *A New Order of Things: Property, Power, and the Transformation of the Creek Indians, 1733–1816* (Cambridge: Cambridge University Press, 1999), 13–14.

14. While the origins of the name "Seminoles" are believed to be rooted in *cimarrones*, the Spanish word for "runaways," Saunt also notes that it may have originated from the Muscogee term *ishti semoli* meaning "wild men"; *New Order of Things*, 34–35.

15. Ibid., 5, 19.

16. Ibid., 38–63.

17. J. Wright, *Creeks and Seminoles*, 106.

18. Ibid.

19. Gold, "East Florida Indians."

20. Charles Fairbanks, *Florida Indians III: Ethnohistorical Report on the Florida Indians* (New York: Garland, 1974), 159.

21. Ventura Díaz to Count of Ricla, Apalache, January 19, 1764, AGI, in Mark F. Boyd, "From a Remote Frontier: Letters and Documents Pertaining to San Marcos de Apalache, 1763–1769," *Florida Historical Quarterly* 19, no. 3 (1941): 200.

22. Ibid.

23. J. Wright, *Creeks and Seminoles*, 111–12.

24. Cited in ibid.

25. John Stuart to Gage, Charles Town, March 24, 1767, vol. 63, 1767, Gage Papers.

26. "Abstract of a Letter from John Simpson, interpreter of the Creek Language at St. Marks, Apalache," February 4, 1767, in John Stuart to Gage, Charles Town, March 24, 1767, vol. 63, 1767, Gage Papers.

27. Ibid.

28. See John Stuart to Gage, Charles Town, September 7, 1772, vol. 114, September–October 1772, Gage Papers.

29. Pierce A. Sinnott to J. Stuart, March 2, 1768, Enclosure to John Stuart to Gage, May 17, 1768, vol. 77, May–June 1768, Gage Papers.

30. John Stuart to Gage, Charles Town, July 2, 1768, vol. 78, 1768; John Stuart to Gage, December 8, 1768, vol. 84, 1768, Gage Papers.

31. John Stuart to Gage, Charles Town, May 24, 1770, vol. 92, 1770; Gage to John Stuart, New York, June 25, 1770, vol. 93, 1770, Gage Papers.

32. "A Talk from the Headmen of Warriors of the Upper Creek Nation to Charles Stuart, Esq., n.d., 1770, in Stuart to Gage, December 13, 1770, vol. 98, 1770, Gage Papers.

33. John Stuart to Gage, Mobile, December 14, 1771, vol. 108, 1771–72, Gage Papers.

34. Gage to John Stuart, New York, February 17, 1772, vol. 109, January–March 1772, Gage Papers.

35. John Stuart to Gage, Charles Town, December 23, 1773, vol. 119, August 1773–June 1774, Gage Papers.

36. Charles Stuart to Haldimand, May 12, 1774, vol. 119, 1773–74, Gage Papers.

37. Ibid. Charles Stuart to Haldimand, May 13, 1774, vol. 119, 1773–74, Gage Papers.

38. John Stuart to Gage, Charles Town, May 26, 1775, vol. 129, May–June 1775, Gage Papers.

39. "Infrapolitics" is defined by James Scott as "the cultural and structural underpinning of the more visible political action"; *Domination and the Arts of Resistance*, 185.

40. Governor of Havana, Marquis de la Torre, to José de Galvéz, Havana, April 11, 1776, Cuba, leg. 1221, fol. 311, AGI, in "The Indian Frontier in British East Florida: Spanish Correspondence Concerning the Uchiz Indians, 1771-1783," translated by James Hill, in *Florida History Online*, University of North Florida (hereafter FHO-UNF), https://www.unf.edu/floridahistoryonline/Projects/uchize/index.html.

41. Quoted in Kathleen DuVal, "Choosing Enemies: The Prospects for an Anti-American Alliance in the Louisiana Territory," *Arkansas Historical Quarterly* 62, no. 3 (2003): 234.

42. Ibid.

43. See, Saunt, *New Order of Things*, 47.

44. In ibid., 49.

45. Ibid., 104.

46. Kathleen DuVal, *The Native Ground: Indians and Colonists in the Heart of the Continent* (Philadelphia: University of Pennsylvania Press, 2006), 158–61.

47. Saunt, *New Order of Things*, 46–63, 97–107.

48. Cuba, legajos (legs.) 1164, 1211–13, 1220–22, AGI, trans. Hill, FHO-UNF.

49. Report of Juan Josef Eligio de la Puente, Havana, May 16, 1777, Cuba, leg. 1222, fol. 748–49, AGI, trans. Hill, FHO-UNF.

50. Ibid.

51. Report of Juan Josef Eligio de la Puente, Havana, March 4, 1773, Cuba, leg. 1164, AGI, trans. Hill, FHO-UNF.

52. Report of Juan Josef Eligio de la Puente, Havana, January 28, 1781, Cuba, leg. 1300, fol. 427–30, AGI, trans. Hill, FHO-UNF.

53. John Stuart to Gage, Charles Town, March 24, 1767, vol. 63, 1767, Gage Papers.

54. Gage to John Stuart, May 19, 1768, vol. 77, May–June 1768, Gage Papers.

55. Abstract of a report from John Stuart, July 8, 1770, in "At a Council Held in the Council Chambers at Pensacola, the 3 of August 1771," no. 17, vol. 108, December 1771–January 1772, Gage Papers.

56. John Stuart to Gage, Charles Town, September 7, 1772, vol. 114, September–October 1772, Gage Papers.

57. [Marquis de la Torre] to Julián de Arriaga, Havana, April 1, 1774, Cuba, leg. 1218, fol. 618, AGI, trans. Hill, FHO-UNF.

58. [Marquis de la Torre] to Julián de Arriaga, Havana, September 28, 1775, Cuba, leg. 1220, fol. 491–92, AGI, trans. Hill, FHO-UNF.

59. "The Governor, Havana, April 11, 1776," Brief, Dealing with Various Communications from the Governor of Cuba on the Subject of Trade with the Uchise Indians, Extracted for the Council of the Indies, February 27, 1778, Archivo Histórico Nacional, Madrid (AHN), leg. 3884, expediente (exp.) 1, document (doc.) 9, trans. in Boyd and Latorre, "Spanish Interest in British Florida," 101.

60. Fairbanks, Florida Indians, 177–80. Among the myriad reasons, including diplomacy and trade, that Creeks and others went to Havana was to secure justice for crimes committed against indigenous individuals and communities. In one such case, a Spanish boat captain attacked and killed his indigenous passengers, apparently, and fortunately, a rare occurrence but another issue that the Spanish addressed; Declaration of the Captain Francisco Pelaez and the Indian Chanilla of the Uchiz Nation, Havana, May 5, 1777, leg. 1222, folios (fols.) 701–3, Cuba, AGI, trans. Hill, FHO-UNF.

61. "The Governor, Havana, February 16, 1773," Brief, Dealing with Various Communications from the Governor of Cuba on the Subject of Trade with the Uchise Indians, Extracted for the Council of the Indies, February 27, 1778, leg. 3884, exp. 1, doc. 9, AHN, trans. in Boyd and Latorre, "Spanish Interest in British Florida," 100.

62. Ibid.

63. See Fairbanks, Florida Indians.

64. Juan Josef Eligio de la Puente to the Governor of Havana, the Marquis de la Torre; Havana, March 6, 1773, leg. 1164, Cuba, AGI, trans. Hill, FHO-UNF.

65. Ibid.

66. [Marquis de la Torre] to Julián de Arriaga, Havana, September 28, 1775, Cuba, leg. 1220, fols. 491–92, AGI, trans. Hill, FHO-UNF.

67. Julián de Arriaga to the Marquis de la Torre, Governor of Havana, October 14, 1775, Cuba, leg. 1213, fol. 578, AGI, trans. Hill, FHO-UNF.

68. Saunt, *New Order of Things*, 22–26.

69. John Stuart to Gage, Charles Town, September 7, 1772, vol. 114, September–October 1772, Gage Papers.

70. John Stuart to Gage, Mobile, December 14, 1771, vol. 108, 1771–72, Gage Papers.

71. Juan Josef Eligio de la Puente to the Governor of Havana, March 6, 1773, AGI, trans. Hill, FHO-UNF.

72. John Stuart to Gage, Mobile, December 14, 1771, vol. 108, 1771–72, Gage Papers.

73. De la Puente to the Governor of Havana, March 6, 1773, AGI, trans. Hill, FHO-UNF.

74. Ibid. De la Puente concluded his report with an accounting of the expense of accommodating and supplying Estimslayche and his delegation while in Havana, noting that "as they are all important men, it was not possible to conduct [them/their stay] with less expense nor greater economy, in the purchase of effects and food."

75. Enclosure to John Stuart to Gage, January 18, 1775: Samuel Thomas, Interpreter, to Taitt, Creek Town on Flint River, December 10, 1774, vol. 125, December 1774–February 1775, Gage Papers.

76. Don Rafael de la Luz, Interim Senior Assistant to the Plaza of Havana, May 2, 1775, leg. 1220, Cuba, AGI, trans. Hill, FHO-UNF.

77. Ibid.

78. Ibid.

79. De la Puente to the Governor of Havana, March 6, 1773, AGI, trans. Hill, FHO-UNF.

80. Governor of Havana, Marquis de la Torre, to don Julián de Arriaga; Havana, May 4, 1775, leg. 1220, Cuba, AGI, trans. Hill, FHO-UNF.

81. [Governor of Havana, Marquis de la Torre] to don Julián de Arriaga; Havana, June 1, 1776, leg. 1220, Cuba, AGI, trans. Hill, FHO-UNF.

82. Ibid.

83. Don Rafael de la Luz, Interim Senior Assistant to the Plaza of Havana, January 14, 1776, leg. 1221, folios 316–17, Cuba, AGI, trans. Hill, FHO-UNF.

84. Don Rafael de la Luz, Interim Senior Assistant to the Plaza of Havana, May 2, 1775, leg. 1220, Cuba, AGI, trans. Hill, FHO-UNF.

85. "Declarations of the Master Joseph Bermudez and of the Cacique Tunape, Havana, December 22, 1777," related to and reported by Juan Joseph Eligio de la Puente, leg. 3884, exp. 1, doc. 6, AHN, trans. in Boyd and Latorre, "Spanish Interest in British Florida," 112–14.

86. Ibid.

87. "Don Juan Joseph Eligio de la Puente to Don Diego Joseph Navarro, January 12, 1778," Brief, Dealing with Various Communications from the Governor of Cuba on the Subject of Trade with the Uchise Indians, Extracted for the Council of the Indies, February 27, 1778, leg. 3884, exp. 1, doc. 9, AHN, trans. in Boyd and Latorre, "Spanish Interest in British Florida," 115–16.

88. Quoted in Fairbanks, *Florida Indians*, 178.

89. Ibid.

90. Anthropologist John Worth has been working on a more in-depth study of this dynamic; see his "History of Southeastern Indians in Cuba."

91. Covington, "Trade Relations," 116.

92. Ibid., 117.

93. Ibid.

94. Bartram, *Travels*, 226.

95. Ibid.

96. Don Rafael de la Luz, Interim Senior Assistant to the Plaza of Havana, May 2, 1775, leg. 1220, Cuba, AGI, trans. Hill, FHO-UNF.

97. Don Rafael de la Luz, Interim Senior Assistant to the Plaza of Havana, August 2, 1775, leg. 1220, Cuba, AGI, trans. Hill, FHO-UNF.

98. Ibid.

99. J. Wright, *Creeks and Seminoles*, 111.

100. [Marquis de la Torre] to don Julián de Arriaga; Havana, September 28, 1775, leg. 1220, Cuba, AGI, trans. Hill, FHO-UNF.

101. Don Rafael de la Luz, Interim Senior Assistant to the Plaza of Havana, January 14, 1776, leg. 1221, Cuba, AGI, trans. Hill, FHO-UNF.

102. Juan Josef Eligio de la Puente to Julián de Arriaga, Havana, July 2, 1771, leg. 1211, Cuba, AGI, trans. Hill, FHO-UNF.

103. Ibid.

104. Ibid.

105. Worth, "History of Southeastern Indians in Cuba," 9.

106. Ibid. See also Saunt, *New Order of Things,* and Alan Gallay, *The Indian Slave Trade* (New Haven, CT: Yale University Press, 2002).

107. Romans, *A Concise Natural History*, 198.

108. Milanich, *Laboring in the Fields of the Lord,* 193; see also Boyd and Latorre, "Spanish Interest in British Florida," 100–130.

109. Cited in J. Wright, *Creeks and Seminoles,* 272.

110. Worth, "History of Southeastern Indians in Cuba," 10.

111. Covington, "Trade Relations," 120. See also Margaret Stack, "An Archaeological and Archival Appraisal of 'Spanish Indians' on the West Coast of Florida in the Eighteenth and Nineteenth Centuries," master's thesis, Department of Applied Anthropology, University of South Florida, 2011.

112. Covington, "Trade Relations," 120.

113. Ibid., 119.

114. Ibid., 119–38. Also see James W. Covington, ed., "A Petition from Some Latin American Fishermen, 1838," *Tequesta* 14 (1954): 61–65; and Worth, "History of Southeastern Indians in Cuba," 10.

115. Quoted in Covington, "Petition," 62–63.

Chapter 3. "Barbarous Nations": Apaches, "Mecos," and Other "Indios Bárbaros" in Colonial Cuba

1. "Barbarous nations" is a common reference to Apache and other indigenous nations confronted by Spanish military authorities in New Spain's northern provinces; examples are found in reports of the Comandante General de las Provincias Internas de Nueva España, 1798–1799, leg. 7029, Archivo General de Simancas, Spain (AGS).

2. Quoted in David J. Weber, *Bárbaros: Spaniards and Their Savages in the Age of Enlightenment* (New Haven, CT: Yale University Press, 2005), 141.

3. Ibid., 142.

4. An abbreviated version of "Chichimecos," another collective, generic term, "mecos" is a Spanish term that once referred to the various nomadic and resistant Chichimecos peoples of northern New Spain. By the eighteenth century, it came to be applied to Apache and other Amerindians resistant to Spanish colonization. Further, the term "Apache" was also later similarly generalized to apply to groups that included the Pima, Yaqui, and marginalized "gente de razón" (people of reason). For further analyses of these terms and the corresponding and complex peoples, see Cecilia Sheridan Prieto, "Reflexiones en torno: A las identidades nativas en el noreste colonial," *Relaciones. Estudios de Historia y Sociedad* 23, no. 92 (2002): 77–106; Marie-Areti Hers and José Luis Mirafuente, eds., *Nómadas y sedentarios en el Norte de México* (Mexico City: Universidad Nacional Autónoma de México, 2000); Sara Ortelli, *Trama de una guerra conveniente: Nueva Vizcaya y la sombra de los apaches, 1748–1790* (Mexico City: Colegio de México, 2009), 85–93.

5. Max L. Moorhead, *The Apache Frontier: Jacobo Ugarte and Spanish-Indian*

Relations in Northern New Spain, 1769–1791 (Norman: University of Oklahoma Press, 1968), 170–75, 200–205.

6. See Julianna Barr, *Peace Came in the Form of a Woman: Indians and Spaniards in the Texas Borderlands* (Chapel Hill: University of North Carolina Press, 2007), 160–61.

7. Ibid., 160–64; Moorhead, *Apache Frontier*, 170–200.

8. William Griffen, *Apaches at War and Peace: The Janos Presidio, 1750–1858* (Norman: University of Oklahoma Press, 1998), 1–2.

9. Ibid. See also Martín González de la Vara, "Amigos, enemigos, o socios? El comercio con los 'indios bárbaros' en Nuevo México, siglo XVIII," *Relaciones* 23, no. 92 (2002): 109–34.

10. Brooks, *Captives and Cousins*, 33.

11. See Ortelli, *Trama de una guerra conveniente*, 26–51. For analysis of relations among the Spanish, Apache, and other indigenous groups, particularly the Comanche, see Joaquín Rivaya Martínez, "Diplomacia interétnica en la frontera norte de Nueva España: Un análisis de los tratados hispano-comanches de 1785 y 1786 y sus consecuencias desde una perspectiva etnohistórica," Débats, *Nuevo Mundo Mundos Nuevos*, November 30, 2011, https://nuevomundo.revues.org/62228.

12. Barr, *Peace Came in the Form of a Woman*, 160–64.

13. Ibid.

14. Ibid., 164.

15. Quoted in Cuauhtémoc Velasco Ávila, "Peace Agreements and War Signals: Negotiations With the Apaches and Comanches in the Interior Provinces of New Spain," in *Negotiation within Domination: New Spain's Indian Pueblos Confront the Spanish State*, edited by Ethelia Ruíz Medrano and Susan Kellogg (Boulder: University Press of Colorado, 2010), 184.

16. Weber, *Bárbaros*, 234.

17. Cited in ibid.

18. Ibid., 235.

19. Ibid., 235–37.

20. Velasco Ávila, "Peace Agreements and War Signals," 185–95.

21. Ibid., 195.

22. Max L. Moorhead, "Spanish Deportation of Hostile Apaches: The Policy and the Practice," *Arizona and the West* 17, no. 3 (1975): 206.

23. Barr, *Peace Came in the Form of a Woman*, 170. See also Brooks, *Captives and Cousins*, 61.

24. Barr, *Peace Came in the Form of a Woman*, 170.

25. Quoted in Moorhead, "Spanish Deportation," 206. Regarding Spanish colonial government distinctions between "external" enemies like the Apaches and

"internal," non-indigenous enemies, and the relationship between the two, see Sara Ortelli, "Enemigos internos y súbditos desleales: La infidencia en Nueva Vizcaya en tiempos de los Borbones," *Anuario de Estudios Americanos* 61, no. 2 (2004): 467–89.

26. Barr, 168-169.

27. Christon Archer, "The Deportation of Barbarian Indians from the Internal Provinces of New Spain, 1789–1810," *The Americas* 29, no. 3 (1973): 376.

28. Quoted in Moorhead, *Apache Frontier*, 29–30.

29. Ibid.

30. Archer, "Deportation of Barbarian Indians," 377.

31. Quoted in Moorhead, *Apache Frontier*, 50–51.

32. Ibid.

33. Diego Josef Navarro, Governor of Cuba, January 22, 1781; Diego Josef Navarro, Governor of Cuba, to Viceroy Martín de Mayorga, January 23, 1781, Havana, Gobierno Virreinal, Correspondencia de Diversas Autoridades (GVC) 035, exp. 5, vol. 21, Archivo General de la Nación, Mexico City (AGN).

34. [Unknown] to Matias de Galvez y Gallardo, Viveroy, June 14, 1784, Havana, Real Hacienda, Archivo Histórico de Hacienda (RHA) 008, exp. 8, vol. 1083, AGN.

35. Luis de Unzaga y Amezaga, Governor of Cuba, to Matias de Gálvez y Gallardo, Viceroy, September 20, 1783, Havana, RHA 008, exp. 38, vol. 1083, AGN; cited in Archer, "Deportation of Barbarian Indians," 381.

36. Ibid.

37. Archer, "Deportation of Barbarian Indians," 377.

38. Governor, Veracruz, December 13, 1785, GVC 035, exp. 5, vol. 21, AGN.

39. Archer, "Deportation of Barbarian Indians," 377, 381.

40. Mark Santiago, *The Jar of Severed Hands: Spanish Deportation of Apache Prisoners of War, 1770–1810* (Norman: University of Oklahoma Press, 2011), 135.

41. Correspondence and reports in Provincias Internas (PI) 092, exp. 13, vol. 208, AGN.

42. See report of Miguel Joseph de Azanza to Viceroy of New Spain, April 5, 1796, Gobierno Virreinal, Reales Cédulas Originales y Duplicados (GVRC) 100, exp. 242, vol. 163, AGN.

43. Pedro de Nava to Marques de Branciforte, Chihuahua, November 11, 1797, PI 092, exp. 13, vol. 208, AGN.

44. Report of Antonio Cordero to Viceroy of New Spain, August 27, 1798, PI 092, exp. 14, vol. 238, AGN.

45. [Unknown] to Antonio Cordero, September 19, 1798, PI 092, exp. 14, vol. 238, AGN.

46. Alvarez to Viceroy of New Spain, April 11, 1799, GVRC 100, exp. 233, vol. 172, AGN.

47. Report of Juan Antonio de Araujo, January 22, 1798, PI 092, exp. 13, v. 208, AGN. Mortality rates of individual colleras sometimes reached as high as 70 percent; Hernan Maximiliano Venegas Delgado, Carlos Manuel Valdes Davila, and Paloma Amanda Alvarado Cardenas, "Emigración forzosa de los indios de la frontera norte imperial española en américa y su envío a la Habana, Cuba, en calidad de esclavos (1763–1821)," paper presented at the 28th Simpósio Nacional de História, Associação Nacional dos Professores Universitários de História (ANPUH), Natal, Brazil, July 22–26, 2013, 19–21.

48. Santiago, *Severed Hands*, appendix, 201–2.

49. Ibid., 135.

50. Colonial government reports, 1800–1802, PI 092, exp. 14, vol. 238, AGN.

51. Bernardo Bonavia to Viceroy of New Spain, July 22, 1816, PI 092, exp. 12, vol. 227, AGN. "Piezas" was a term used by the Spanish in the accounting of various items including lands, animals, and slaves.

52. Correspondence and reports, August–December 1816, PI 092, exp. 12, vol. 227; PI 092, exp. 13, vol. 227; PI 092, exp. 14, vol. 238, AGN.

53. Ibid.

54. Antonio Cornel to Governor Captain-General, Havana, January 28, 1800, Reales Cédulas y Órdenes, leg. 37, no. 3, Archivo Nacional de la República de Cuba (ANC).

55. Evelyn Powell Jennings, "State Enslavement in Colonial Havana," in *Slavery without Sugar: Diversity in Caribbean Economy and Society since the 17th Century*, edited by Verene A. Shepherd (Gainesville: University Press of Florida, 2002), 157–59.

56. Ibid., 159–60.

57. Ibid.

58. Ibid., 152–53.

59. Ibid., 154, 156–62.

60. See "Extracto de Revista," 1765–68, Santo Domingo, legs. 1647 and 2122, AGI. See also Jennings, "State Enslavement in Colonial Havana," 162.

61. See Acordada and other colonial criminal records for the 1780s in exp. 019 (Criminal Caja 5723), Indiferente Virreinal, Instituciones Coloniales, AGN. Very little is known about these earlier groups, some of whom were Nahua, Mixtec, and Zapotec, people convicted of various offenses and sentenced to hard labor in Cuba. For some elaboration, see chapter 4.

62. Antonio Cornel to Governor Captain-General, Havana, January 28, 1800, Reales Cédulas y Órdenes, leg. 37, no. 3, ANC.

63. Crown to the Captain General of Cuba, Madrid, July 1803, leg. 6865, AGS. See also Griffen, *Apaches*, 106–7.

64. Duvon C. Corbitt, "Immigration in Cuba," *Hispanic American Historical Review* 22, no. 2 (1942): 282–86. See also Governor Captain-General to His Excellency, April 25, 1849, Ultramar 91, exp. 6, AHN; U.S. Government, Report on the Census of Cuba, 1899 (Washington: GPO, 1900), 734–35.

65. Noticia del Repartimiento de Mecos y Mecos, February 9, 1802, leg. 1716, Cuba, Archivo General de Indias, Seville (AGI).

66. Weber, *Bárbaros*, 238.

67. Antonio de la Ossa to Governor Captain-General, Havana, February 9, 1802, Cuba, leg. 1716, AGI.

68. Ibid.

69. Colonel Manuel Cavello to Governor Captain-General, Havana, February 9, 1802, Cuba, leg. 1716, AGI.

70. José Antonio de Abreu y Marques to Governor Captain-General, Havana, February 9, 1802, Cuba, leg. 1716, AGI.

71. Ana Gamonales to Governor Captain-General, Havana, February 9, 1802, Cuba, leg. 1716, AGI.

72. Juan Díaz to Governor Captain-General, Casablanca, February 10, 1802, Cuba, leg. 1716, AGI.

73. Mario Lazo de la Vega to Governor Captain-General, Havana, February 10, 1802, Cuba, leg. 1716, AGI.

74. Anselmo de Gamón to Governor Captain-General, Havana, February 10, 1802, Cuba, leg. 1716, AGI.

75. Rosalia Peñalver to Governor Captain-General, Havana, February 20, 1802, Cuba, leg. 1716, AGI.

76. Gregoria Puebla to Governor Captain-General, Havana, February 20, 1802, Cuba, leg. 1716, AGI.

77. Francisco de Rus to Governor Captain-General, Havana, February 20, 1802, Cuba, leg. 1716, AGI.

78. Francisco Mendieta to Governor Captain-General, Havana, February 11, 1802, Cuba, leg. 1716, AGI.

79. Josefa de Castro to Governor Captain-General, Havana, February 11, 1802, Cuba, leg. 1716, AGI.

80. María del Rosario de Acosta to Governor Captain-General, Havana, February, 1802, Cuba, leg. 1716, AGI.

81. Clara Cortes to Governor Captain-General, Havana, February 12, 1802, Cuba, leg. 1716, AGI.

82. María Josefa de Velasco to Governor Captain-General, Havana, February, 1802, Cuba, leg. 1716, AGI.

83. María Magdalena Lazo to Governor Captain-General, Havana, March 3, 1802, Cuba, leg. 1716, AGI.

84. María Loreto de Castro to Governor Captain-General, Havana, August 3, 1802, Cuba, leg. 1716, AGI.

85. Ana María Gamonales to Governor Captain-General, Havana, August 4, 1802, Cuba, leg. 1716, AGI.

86. María de Africa Albuquerque to Governor Captain-General, Havana, March 4, 1802, Cuba, leg. 1716, AGI.

87. An example is Maximo de Buchet to Governor Captain-General, Havana, August 4, 1802, Cuba, leg. 1716, AGI.

88. Gaspar Calbo to Governor Captain-General, Havana, March 31, 1802; Valentin Moralejo to Governor Captain-General, Havana, April 1, 1802; María Loreto de Castro to Governor Captain-General, Havana, August 3, 1802; Maximo de Bouchet to Governor Captain-General, Havana, August 4, 1802; Ana Subeniq to Governor Captain-General, Havana, August 4, 1802; Lorenzo de Avila to Governor Captain-General, Havana, August, 1802; Josefa Martely to Governor Captain-General, Havana, August 6, 1802; Rosa de Tenia to Governor Captain-General, Havana, August 5, 1802; Valentin Moralejo to Governor Captain-General, Havana, August 13, 1802; Juan Rengil to Governor Captain-General, Havana, August, 1802; Joaquin de Zalba to Governor Captain-General, Havana, August 29, 1802; [Francisca] to Governor Captain-General, Havana, August 29, 1802; Miguel de la Vega to Governor Captain-General, Havana, November 15, 1802; Maximo du Bouchet to Juan Ibanez, Havana, November 16, 1802; Maximo du Bouchet to Governor Captain-General, Havana, November 16, 1802; Wenceslao del Cristo to Governor Captain-General, Havana, n.d. [1802–3]; all are found in Cuba, leg. 1716, AGI.

89. Wenceslao del Cristo to Governor Captain-General, Havana, n.d. [1802–3], Cuba, leg. 1716, AGI.

90. Melchor Lugo to Governor Captain-General, Havana, June 14, 1803, Cuba, leg. 1716, AGI.

91. Weber, *Bárbaros*, 236.

92. See Lorenzo de Avila to Governor Captain-General, Havana, August, 1802, Cuba, leg. 1716, AGI.

93. Report to the Viceroy of New Spain, Durango, July 29, 1816, PI 092, exp.12, vol. 227, AGN.

94. [Unknown] to Matias de Galvez, Havana, September 20, 1783, RHA 008, exp. 38, vol. 1083, AGN.

95. Ibid.

96. Diego Josef Navarro, Governor of Cuba, to Juan Ignacio de Urriza, Havana, January 22, 1781, GVC 035, exp. 5, vol. 21, AGN; Luis Unzaga y Amezaga to Matias de Galvez, Havana, June 14, 1784, RHA 008, exp. 8, vol. 1083, AGN; Mexico, September 26, 1800, PI 092, exp. 14, vol. 238, AGN.

97. Robert W. Patch, *Maya Revolt and Revolution in the Eighteenth Century* (New York: M. E. Sharpe, 2002), 177.

98. See reports ca. 1816 in PI 092, exp. 13, vol. 227, AGN. See also Santiago, *Severed Hands*.

99. Weber, *Bárbaros*, 238.

100. Ibid.

101. Ibid., 239.

102. Ibid.

103. Antonio Cornel to Governor Captain-General, Havana, January 28, 1800, Reales Cédulas y Órdenes, leg. 37, no. 3, ANC; ca. 1800, PI 092, exp. 14, vol. 238, AGN.

104. Archer, "Deportation of Barbarian Indians," 383.

105. The evidence for this is more extensive for Mayas and other Mesoamerican exiles in Cuba; see chapter 5 of this volume.

106. Statement, January 18, 1804, Cuba, leg. 1716, AGI. See also Archer, "Deportation of Barbarian Indians," 383–84, and Gabino La Rosa Corzo, *Runaway Slave Settlements in Cuba: Resistance and Repression*, (Chapel Hill: University of North Carolina Press, 1988), 88.

107. Ibid.

108. Cited in Archer, "Deportation of Barbarian Indians," 384.

109. Reports, October–December, 1802, PI 092, exp. 14, vol. 238, AGN.

110. Ibid. See also Venegas Delgado, Valdes Davila, and Alvarado Cardenas, "Emigración forzosa de los indios," 29–32. Both earlier and more recent archaeological evidence also provides some elaboration on the possible if not probable dynamic of the survival of Apache and other Meco individuals and groups living outside of colonial society in Cuba, with respect to their means as well as their supposed ends. See, for example, Mark Harrington, *Cuba before Columbus: Indian Notes and Monographs*, part 1, vol. 1 (New York: Museum of the American Indian, Heye Foundation, 1921), 324, 352–53; and Divaldo Gutiérrez Calvache, Racso Fernández Ortega, and José B. González Tendero, "Notas sobre le presencia de figuras antropomorfas de arqueros en el arte rupestre cubano," *Rupestreweb: Arte Rupestre en América Latina*, 2008, http://rupestreweb.info/arqueros.html.

111. Velasco Ávila, "Peace Agreements and War Signals," 186.

112. Laird Bergad, *Cuban Rural Society in the Nineteenth Century* (Princeton, NJ: Princeton University Press, 1990), 255–59.

113. [Unknown] to Miguel Josef Azanza, Viceroy of New Spain, July 27, 1799, leg. 6980, no. 13, Secretaria del Despacho de Guerra, AGS.

114. Venegas Delgado, Valdes Davila, and Alvarado Cardenas, "Emigración forzosa de los indios," 33–35.

115. Barr, *Peace Came in the Form of a Woman*, 247.

116. Ibid., 164–69, 270–78.

117. Cited in Brooks, *Captives and Cousins*, 61.

118. Ibid.

119. Manuel Cabello, "Noticia que demuestra las Indias Mecas que de Veracruz vinieron en el navio de guerra San Ramón y hoy día de la fecha las he desembarcado y depositado en la Casa Blanca de orden del Señor Gobernador y Capitan General," Havana, February 9, 1802, Cuba, leg. 1716, AGI.

120. Ibid.

121. La Rosa Corzo, *Runaway Slave Settlements*, 88–89.

122. Ibid., 89–90.

123. Reports, October–December, 1802, PI 092, exp. 14, vol. 238, AGN.

124. Someruelos to the Fiscal Protector de Indios, Havana, October 6, 1802, PI 092, exp. 14, vol. 238, AGN.

125. Correspondence, November 1802–January 1803, PI 092, exp. 14, vol. 238, AGN.

126. La Rosa Corzo, *Runaway Slave Settlements*, 88–89. See also Antonio Santamaría García and Sigfrido Vázquez, "Indios foráneos en Cuba a principios del siglo XIX: Historia de un suceso en el contexto de la movilidad poblacional y la geostrategia del imperio español," *Colonial Latin American Historical Review* 1, no. 1 (2013): 27–30; and Juan Torres Lasqueti, *Colección de datos históricos-geográficos y estadísticas de Puerto del Príncipe y su jurisdicción* (Havana: El Retiro, 1888), 111, 116–17.

127. La Rosa Corzo, *Runaway Slave Settlements*, 87–90.

128. Francisco Pérez de la Riva, "Cuban Palenques," in *Maroon Societies: Rebel Slave Communities in the Americas*, edited by Richard Price, 2nd ed. (Baltimore, MD: Johns Hopkins University Press, 1979), 50–57.

129. Ibid.

130. Ibid., 58–59.

131. Twentieth-century studies on surviving indigenous peoples in Cuba include Harrington, *Cuba before Columbus*, and Manuel Rivero de la Calle, *Las culturas aborígenes de Cuba* (Havana: Editora Universitaria, 1966). For recent challenges to concepts of mestizaje and cultural homogeneity (versus indigeneity), see Maximilian C. Forte, ed., *Indigenous Resurgence in the Contemporary Caribbean: Amerindian Survival and Revival* (New York: Peter Lang, 2006); Virginia Tilley,

Seeing Indians: Race, Nation, and Power in El Salvador (Albuquerque: University of New Mexico Press, 2005); and Jeffrey Gould, *To Die in This Way: Nicaraguan Indians and the Myth of Mestizaje* (Durham, NC: Duke University Press, 2007). Spanish-aligned Apaches in the northern provinces also made requests for the return of deported kin; while documentation exists to support the view that at least some of these were granted in the case of deportees in Mexico City, evidence addressing deported Apaches in Cuba was not located; Griffen, *Apaches*, 106–7.

132. See Francisco Javier Sánchez Moreno, "Los indios bárbaros en la frontera noreste de Nueva España entre 1810 y 1821," *Temas Americanistas*, no. 26 (2011): 20–47.

133. Griffen, *Apaches*, 123–24.

Chapter 4. Mayas and the Mesoamerican Presence in Cuba

1. Alejo Carpentier, *Obras completas de Alejo Carpentier XII: ese músico que llevo dentro* (Mexico City: Siglo ventiuno editores, 1987), 355–56.

2. Christopher H. Lutz and W. George Lovell, "Survivors on the Move: Maya Migration in Time and Space," in *The Maya Diaspora: Guatemalan Roots, New American Lives*, edited by James Loucky and Marilyn M. Moors (Philadelphia: Temple University Press, 2000), 11–12.

3. Ibid.

4. Ibid.

5. Ibid.

6. For a synopsis see Jason M. Yaremko, "De Campeche a la Guerra de Castas: La presencia maya en Cuba, siglos XVI al XIX," *Chacmool: Cuadernos de Trabajo Cubano-Mexicanos* 6 (2010): 85–114.

7. See William F. Keegan, "West Indian Archaeology. [Part] 3. Ceramic Age," *Journal of Archaeological Research* 8, no. 2 (June 2000): 136–37. See also Samuel Wilson, Harry B. Iceland, and Thomas R. Hester, "Preceramic Connections between Yucatan and the Caribbean," *Latin American Antiquity* 9, no. 4 (1998): 342–52; Callaghan, "Comments"; Jaime R. Pagán-Jiménez, "Early Phytocultural Processes in the Pre-Colonial Antilles," in *Communities in Contact: Essays in Archaeology, Ethnohistory, and Ethnography of the Amerindian Circum-Caribbean*, edited by Corinne L. Hofman and Anne van Duijvenbode (Leiden, Netherlands: Sidestone Press, 2010), 87–116; and Reniel Rodríguez Ramos, "Close Encounters of the Caribbean Kind," in *Islands at the Crossroads: Migration, Seafaring, and Interaction in the Caribbean*, edited by L. Antonio Curet and Mark Hauser (Tuscaloosa: University of Alabama Press, 2011), 164–92.

8. Robin Blackburn, *The Making of New World Slavery: From the Baroque to the Modern, 1492–1800* (London: Verso, 1998), 133. See also Joaquin García Icazbalceta,

Don Fray Juan de Zumárraga, primer obispo y arzobispo de México: Estudio biográfico y bibliográfico (Mexico City: Antigua Libreria de Andrade y Morales, 1881), 16–76, and "Carta á Su Majestad Electo Obispo de México, D. Fr. Juan de Zumárraga," August 27, 1529, also in García Icazbalceta, "Documents," 1–42; Donald Chipman, "The Traffic in Indian Slaves in the Province of Panuco, New Spain, 1523–1533," *The Americas* 23, no. 2 (1966): 142–55; Murdo MacLeod, *Spanish Central America,* 50.

9. Don E. Dumond, *The Machete and the Cross: Campesino Rebellion in Yucatan* (Lincoln: University of Nebraska Press, 1996), 13; Nancy M. Farriss, "Persistent Maya Resistance and Cultural Retention in Yucatan," in *The Indian in Latin American History: Resistance, Resilience, and Acculturation,* edited by John E. Kicza (Wilmington, DE: Scholarly Resources, 1993), 51–53.

10. Dumond, *The Machete and the Cross,* 13–15.

11. Louis A. Pérez Jr., *Cuba: Between Reform and Revolution,* 2nd ed. (New York: Oxford University Press, 1995), 32–38.

12. Cabildo de 10 abril de 1564, Actas Capitulares del Ayuntamiento de La Habana, April 10, 1564, Archivo del Museo de la Ciudad de La Habana, Havana (AMCH).

13. I. A. Wright, *The Early History of Cuba: 1492–1586* (New York: Macmillan, 1916), 193, 317.

14. Ibid., 79–80.

15. See Marcos Arriaga Mesa, *La Habana, 1550–1600: Tierra, hombres y mercado* (Madrid: Silex Ediciones, 2014), 68–69, 214–18.

16. Ibid.

17. Ibid., 80; Gonzalo Fernández de Oviedo, *Historia general y natural de las Indias,* part I, edited by José Amador de los Rios (Madrid: Imprenta de la Real Academia de la Historia, 1851), 504–15. See also Juan de Grijalva, *The Discovery of New Spain in 1518,* edited and translated by Henry Wagner (New York: Cortes Society, Kraus Reprint, 1942), 20, 90–106.

18. Ibid.

19. I. Wright, *Early History of Cuba,* 185–86.

20. Carlos E. Bojórquez Urzaiz, "El barrio de Campeche en La Habana, "*Cuadernos Culturales* 5 (1994): 30.

21. Cabildo de 12 junio de 1554, Actas Capitulares del Ayuntamiento de La Habana, April 10, 1564, AMCH. Notably, although Guanabacoa began as a reduced settlement for the "free" remaining or surviving indigenous inhabitants of the island colony, the Taíno, it acquired an increasingly diverse Amerindian population that included among its ranks Timucua, Calusa, and other indigenous peoples from Florida and Maya from Yucatan.

22. José María de la Torre, *Lo que fuimos y lo que somos: La Habana antigua y*

moderna (Havana: Imprenta Spencer, 1857), 49–50. See also Bojórquez Urzaiz, "El barrio de Campeche," 31.

23. Ibid.

24. Fernando Ortiz, *Nuevo Catauro de cubanismo* (Havana: Ciencias Sociales, 1985), 196. See also Bojórquez Urzaiz, "El barrio de Campeche," 31–32.

25. Pérez, *Cuba*, 32–34.

26. Ibid.

27. For more on Maya material culture in colonial Cuba's western and eastern regions, see the important work by Cuban archaeologists Karen Mahé Lugo Romera and Sonia Menéndez Castro, *Barrio de Campeche: Tres estudios arqueológicos* (Havana: Fundación Fernando Ortiz, 2003), and Roberto Valcarcel Rojas et al., "El Chorro de Maíta: A Diverse Approach to a Context of Diversity," in *Communities in Contact: Essays in Archaeology, Ethnohistory, and Ethnography of the Amerindian Circum-Caribbean*, edited by Corinne Hofman and Anne van Duijvenbode (Leiden, Netherlands: Sidestone Press, 2011), 236–42.

28. Cabildo de 14 de febrero 1575, Actas Capitulares del Ayuntamiento de La Habana, February 14, 1575, AMCH.

29. Cited in I. Wright, *Early History of Cuba*, 282.

30. Cabildo de 14 de febrero 1575, AMCH.

31. Jacobo de la Pezuela y Lobo, *Historia de la isla de Cuba*, vol. 2 (Madrid: Bally-Bailliere, 1868), 189. Also cited in Bojórquez Urzaiz, "El barrio de Campeche," 32.

32. See Santamaría García and Vázquez, "Indios foráneos en Cuba."

33. I. Wright, *Early History of Cuba*, 186.

34. Cited in Enrique Sosa Rodríguez, "Aproximadamente al studio de la presencia yucateca en La Habana a partir de algunos libros en archivos parroquiales," in *Habanero campechano*, by Carlos E. Bojórquez Urzaiz, Enrique Sosa Rodríguez, and Luis Millet Camara (Merida, Mexico: Ediciones de la Universidad Autónoma de Yucatán, 1991), 35-36.

35. Sosa Rodríguez, 34–38, 48–60. See also the Libros de Bautismos de Pardos y Morenos for the years 1721-1765, Iglesia de Santo Cristo de Buen Viaje (SCBV), and also February 1787 and April 1788, Iglesia Espiritu Santo (ES), Havana, Cuba. Available online at Ecclesiastical and Secular Sources for Slave Societies (ESSSS). http://diglib.library.vanderbilt.edu/esss-processquery.pl?SID=20160111151306152&VolumeName=Libro%202,%20Baut%20PM,%201721-1730&ArchiveName=Santo%20Cristo%20del%20Buen%20Viaje. Accessed 2008.

36. Ibid.

37. Cited in Bojórquez Urzaiz, "El barrio de Campeche," 31.

38. Ibid. See also Pérez, *Cuba*, 33.

39. Peréz de la Riva, "Cuban Palenques," 57.

40. The provenance of the term *guachinango* has been debated; although some argue in favor of the Canary Islands, evidence points more convincingly to Nahuatl origins in the Valley of Mexico. The understanding of *guachinango*, aside from its common definition as a type of fish (red snapper is *guachinango* in Mexico, *pargo* in Cuba), is more complex and appears to depend at least in part upon geography. While used in colonial Mexico as a referent for that underclass of peoples dominated by indigenous and mestizo Mexicans, in Cuba "guachinangos," if not excluding mestizos altogether, was used predominantly in reference to indigenous peoples in Cuba, those having migrated voluntarily and involuntarily "from Mexico and all of the territory comprising New Spain" and was used with this understanding by colonial officials and Cubans generally. Eighteenth- and nineteenth-century references, at least, were along these lines; Esteban Pichardo y Tapia, *Diccionario provincial casi razonado de vozes y frases cubanas* (Havana: Imprenta el Trabajo, 1875), 219. See also Pezuela y Lobo, *Historia de la isla de Cuba*, 16; ; Sergio Valdés Bernal and Yohanis Balga Rodríguez, "El legado indoamericano en el español del Caribe insular hispánico," *Convergencia* 32 (2003): 17, 23; Sergio Valdés Bernal, "Las inquietudes lingüísticas de Antonio Bachiller y Morales," paper presented at the conference "Tres lunes, tres bicentenarios: Antonio Bachiller y Morales, Ramon de Palma y Cirilo Villaverde," May 21, 2012, Aula Magna del Colegio Universitario San Geronimo de la Habana" Havana, 7; Santamaria García and Vázquez, "Indios foráneos en Cuba," 1, 13–14, 19–20, 27–28, 32; Victoria Novelo, "Migraciones mayas y yucatecas a Cuba," *Dimensión Antropológica* 59 (2013): 130.

41. Colin M. MacLachlan, *Criminal Justice in Eighteenth Century Mexico* (Berkeley: University of California Press, 1974), 80–81.

42. Allan J. Kuethe, *Cuba, 1753–1815: Crown, Military, and Society* (Knoxville: University of Tennessee Press, 1986), ix–xi.

43. Patch, *Maya Revolt*, 155.

44. Ibid., 178–80.

45. Autos criminales seguidos de oficio de la Real Justicia sobre la sublevacion que los Yndios del Pueblo de Cisteil y los demas que convocaron hicieron contra Ambas Magistrades el de 19 de Noviembre de 1761, Mexico, leg. 3050, microfilm reels C-7595–97, AGI; also cited in Patch, *Maya Revolt*, 178–79.

46. Archer, "Deportation of Barbarian Indians," 376–85.

47. Patch, *Maya Revolt*, 178.

48. For the various classifications of Guachinangos, see "Estado de Revista" records for the years 1764, 1765, and 1768, Havana, Santo Domingo, legs. 1647, 1212, and 2122, AGI, and "Relación de Revista" records for the years 1771, 1772, 1775, and 1777, Havana, Cuba, legs. 1139, 1151 and 1208, AGI.

49. An example with such designations is Report, Don Francisco Xavier de

Ripalda, Conde de Ripalda, Capitan del Regimento Infanteria de Lombardia Teniente de Governador, y Capitan de Guerra de esta Ciudad de la Trinidad y villas anexas Juez Subdelegado de la Intendencia General de Ejercito y Real Hacienda por Su Magestia de España, to Captain-General of Cuba, Marquis de la Torre, [1772], Cuba, leg. 1174, AGI.

50. Acordada and other colonial criminal records for the 1780s in Indiferente Virreinal (IV), Instituciones Coloniales, exp. 019 (Criminal Caja 5723), AGN.

51. See sentencing reports for October 23, 26, and 31, 1780, and December 2, 22, 23, 1780, IV, exp. 019, AGN.

52. Report, December 2, 1780, IV, exp. 019, AGN.

53. Report, October 23, 1780, IV, exp. 019, AGN.

54. "Estado de Revista," April 17, 1768; "Estado de Revista," May 19, 1768; "Estado de Revista," June 19, 1768; "Estado de Revista," July 24, 1768, Santo Domingo, leg. 2122, AGI.

55. Miguel de Altarriba to [Unknown], Havana, October 7, 1765, Santo Domingo, leg. 1647, AGI.

56. "Extracto de Revista," 1765–68, Santo Domingo, legs. 1647 and 2122, AGI; Jennings, "State Enslavement in Colonial Havana," 162.

57. "Extracto de Revista," 1765–68, Santo Domingo, legs. 1647 and 2122, AGI.

58. [Unknown] to Governor Captain-General Marques de la Torre, Havana, June 20, 1772, Cuba, leg. 1151, AGI.

59. Table, "Estado que comprehende el numero de forzados," Havana, June 29–July 30, 1780, Cuba, leg. 1240, AGI.

60. Sentencing reports for August 27 and 29, 1774, exp. 015; October 23, 26, and 31, 1780, and December 2, 22, 23, 1780, exp. 019; January 27, 1787, exp. 009; and September 26, 1811, exp. 005, AGN.

61. Examples are found, for instance, in the actas of Havana and Matanzas, for the period 1500–1700, Havana.

62. Cited in Bojórquez Urzaiz, "El barrio de Campeche," 31.

63. Actas Capitulares de Matanzas, 1770–1773, vol. 6, 112–20, Archivo Histórico Provincial de Matanzas, Cuba (AHPM); also cited in Pedro A. Alfonso, *Memorias de un Matancero. Apuntes para la historia de la isla de Cuba con relación de la ciudad de San Carlos y San Severino de Matanzas* (Matanzas, Cuba: Ediciones de la Imprenta de Marsal, adjunta a la de la Aurora, 1854), 118–20.

64. Actas Capitulares de Matanzas, 1770–1773, vol. 6, 112–20, AHPM.

65. Ibid.

66. Matthew Restall, *The Maya World: Yucatec Culture and Society, 1550–1850* (Stanford, CA: Stanford University Press, 1997), 87–88.

67. Ibid.

68. See Wolfgang Gabbert, *Becoming Maya: Ethnicity and Social Inequality in Yucatan since 1500* (Tucson: University of Arizona Press, 2004); and Terry Rugeley, *Rebellion Now and Forever: Maya, Hispanics, and Caste War Violence in Yucatan, 1800–1880* (Stanford, CA: Stanford University Press, 2009).

69. "Don Agustín Vicente Chan contra el Sr. D. Antonio María de Cardenas de Monte Hermoso en cobro de pesos," January 18, 1861, Escribanias, leg. 14, no. 6, ANC.

70. "Doña Polonia May y Cab," October 5–10, 1874, Archivo de J. N. Ortega, Escribanias, leg. 308, no. 4, ANC.

71. Ibid.

72. Ibid.

73. Ibid.

74. Ibid.

75. Ibid. Since the early postconquest period, Maya elites tended toward greater identification with the Spanish than with the macehual of their own culture. By the nineteenth-century in Yucatan, their descendants' use of the status category "indio" in reference to Maya peasants would not have been at all unusual, nor would their exploitation of Maya servants. For further examples of these and other social class distinctions, see Gabbert, *Becoming Maya*, 33–36, and Laura Machuca Gallegos, "Los hacendados y rancheros mayas de Yucatán en al siglo XIX," *Estudios de Cultura Maya* 36 (2010): 173–200.

76. "Antonio Can," November 5, 1891-April 14, 1892, Archivo de Galleti, Escribanias, leg. 545, no. 4, ANC. Doctors eventually determined that Can suffered from both mania and dementia, diagnoses common for the era, and admitted him to the city asylum.

77. See Jason M. Yaremko, "'Frontier Indians': 'Indios Mansos,' 'Indios Bravos,' and the Layers of Indigenous Existence in the Caribbean Borderlands," in *Borderlands in World History, 1700–1914*, edited by Paul Readman, Cynthia Radding, and Chad Bryant (London: Palgrave Macmillan, 2014), 227–30.

78. Victoria Reifler Bricker, *The Indian Christ, the Indian King: The Historical Substrate of Maya Myth and Ritual* (Austin: University of Texas Press, 1981), 87–89. See also Moisés González Navarro, *Raza y Tierra: La guerra de castas y el henequén*, Nueva serie 10 (Mexico City: Colegio de México, Centro de Estudios Históricos, 1970).

79. Ibid.

80. Bricker, *Indian Christ*, 89.

81. Terry Rugeley, *Yucatan's Maya Peasantry and the Origins of the Caste War* (Austin: University of Texas Press, 1996), xiv.

82. Ibid., xv–xvii.

83. Ibid.; Rugeley provides a more detailed discussion of the political role of taxation and the Maya.

84. Ibid., xvi–xvii.

85. Ibid.

86. Arturo Güémez Pineda, *Mayas: Gobierno y tierras frentea la acometida liberal en Yucatán, 1812–1847* (Merida, Mexico: Universidad Autónoma de Yucatán, 2005), 251–301.

87. Ibid.

88. Dumond, *The Machete and the Cross*, 2–3.

89. Ibid.

90. Karen Caplan, *Indigenous Citizens: Local Liberalism in Early National Oaxaca and Yucatán* (Stanford, CA: Stanford University Press, 2010), 183–84.

91. Quoted in ibid., 184.

92. Ibid.

93. Quoted in ibid., 185.

94. Ibid., 187.

95. Quoted in ibid.

96. Dumond, *The Machete and the Cross*, 1–2. For a broader economic and geopolitical analysis that considers Maya relations with the British in Belize during this period, see Martha Herminia Villalobos González, *El bosque sitiado: Asaltos armados, concesiones forestales, y estrategias de resistencia durante la Guerra de Castas* (Mexico City: Miguel Angel Porrua, 2006).

97. Pérez, *Cuba*, 76–81.

98. Ibid., 98–103. See also Laird Bergad, Fe Iglesias García, and María del Carmen Barcia, *The Cuban Slave Market, 1790–1880* (Cambridge: Cambridge University Press, 1995), 28–35.

99. See Franklin Knight, *Slave Society in Cuba during the Nineteenth Century* (Madison: University of Wisconsin Press, 1970); José Luciano Franco, *Comercio clandestino de esclavos* (Havana: Editorial de Ciencias Sociales, 1985); David R. Murray, *Odious Commerce; Britain, Spain, and the Abolition of the Cuban Slave Trade* (Cambridge: University of Cambridge Press, 1980); Herbert Klein, *African Slavery in Latin America and the Caribbean* (Oxford: Oxford University Press, 1986); R. Scott, *Slave Emancipation in Cuba*; Barcia, *Seeds of Insurrection*; Michele Reid-Vazquez, *The Year of the Lash: Free People of Color in Cuba and the Nineteenth-Century Atlantic World* (Athens: University of Georgia Press, 2011).

100. See "Ayuda a la población blanca de Yucatán," 1848–50, Ultramar, leg. 22, exp. 43, AHN. See also Duvon C. Corbitt, "Los colonos yucatecos," *Revista Bimestre Cubana* 39, no. 1 (1937): 64–70; González Navarro, *Raza y tierra*, 108–12; Carlos R. Menéndez, *Historia del infame y vergonzoso comercio de indios vendidos a*

los esclavistas de Cuba por los políticos yucatecos desde 1848 hasta 1861, justificación de la revolución de 1847, documentos irrefutables que lo comprueban (Merida, Mexico: Talleres Gráficos de la Revista de Mérida, 1923), 22.

101. González Navarro, *Raza y tierra*, 112, 128–34. The regional Secciones de Fomento reported to the captain-general.

102. Dirección de Gobierno Ultramar to Ministerio de la Gobernación del Reino, October 9, 1848, Ultramar 22, exp. 43, AHN.

103. González Navarro, *Raza y tierra*, 116.

104. Cited in Corbitt, "Los colonos yucatecos," 76–80.

105. Buenaventura Vivó, *Las memorias de D. Buenaventura Vivó y la venta de indios yucatecos en Cuba*, edited by Carlos Menéndez (Merida, Mexico: Talleres de la Compañia Tipgráfica Yucateca, 1932), 14–15.

106. See, for example, "Empresa de colonización de autorización del supremeogobierno de la república mejicana," May 28, 1855, Gobierno Superior Civil, leg. 641, no. 20248, ANC.

107. Bricker, *Indian Christ*, 87–89; Rugeley. *Yucatan's Maya Peasantry*, xiii–xviii, 8–15, 86; Dumond, *The Machete and the Cross*, 38–45.

108. Teniente Gobernador to Capitan General, Cardenas, March 13, 1848, Junta de Fomento, leg. 195, no. 8754, ANC; also cited in Corbitt, "Los colonos yucatecos," 67.

109. Ibid.

110. Vivó, *Las memorias*, 14–15

111. González Navarro, *Raza y tierra*, 125.

112. Ibid., 132–33.

113. "Empresa de colonización de autorización del supremo gobierno de la república mejicana," May 28, 1855, Gobierno Superior Civil, leg. 641, no. 20248, ANC.

114. Ibid.

115. Ibid.

116. Ibid.

117. See the labor obligations outlined in "Contrata de Hombres Solos," 1859, Gobierno Superior Civil, leg. 640, ANC.

118. Señor Rector del Colegio de Jesuitas to Governor Captain-General, 1860, Gobierno Superior Civil, leg. 640, no. 20221, ANC.

119. See examples in legajos in Fondos Gobierno Superior Civil, Gobierno Civil, and Junta de Fomento, ANC.

120. Bergad, *Cuban Rural Society*, 334–35.

121. Ibid.

122. Ibid.

123. Ibid.

124. Office of the Lieutenant Governor, Sección de Fomento, Güines, April 13, 1861, Gobierno Superior Civil, leg. 641, no. 20248, ANC.

125. Sección de Fomento, La Habana, to Governor Captain-General, January 29, 1860, Gobierno Superior Civil, leg. 640, no. 20224, ANC.

126. Consulado mexicano de La Habana to Teniente de Gobernador, Güines, October 26, 1858, Gobierno Superior Civil, leg. 640, no. 20247, ANC.

127. González-Navarro, *Raza y tierra*, 138.

128. Ibid., 138–42.

129. Ibid.

130. Ibid., 138–44.

131. Nelson Reed, *The Caste War of Yucatan* (Stanford, CA: Stanford University Press, 1964), 105; Secretaria General, Gobernador de Administración, Habana, to Gobierno Superior Civil, March 12, 1862, Gobierno Superior Civil, leg. 641, no. 20248, ANC; Consejo de Administración de la Isla de Cuba to Gobierno Superior Civil, March 21, 1862, Gobierno Superior Civil, leg. 641, no. 20248, ANC.

132. Cosme de la Torriente to Gobierno-Capitan General, April 7, 1859, Gobierno General, leg. 341, no. 16498, ANC.

133. See Jacobo de la Pezuela y Lobo, *Diccionario geográfico, estadístico e histórico de la Isla de Cuba*, vol. 4 (Madrid: Mellado, 1866); Juan Suárez y Navarro, *Informe de Yucatán* (Mexico City: Publicación Oficial, 1861), 45.

134. *Noticias Cuba* 1862, cited in González-Navarro, *Raza y tierra*, 148–49.

135. See U.S. Government, Report on the Census of Cuba, 1899 (Washington: GOP, 1900), 67.

136. Ibid., 67, 734.

137. González-Navarro, *Raza y tierra*, 148–50.

138. Joan Casanovas, *Bread or Bullets! Urban Labor and Spanish Colonialism in Cuba, 1850–1898* (Pittsburgh, PA: University of Pittsburgh Press, 1998), 72.

139. F. Fernando del Pino to Governor Captain-General, January 29, 1860, and July 28, 1860, Gobierno Superior Civil, leg. 640, no. 20215, ANC; Manuel Arroyas to Governor Captain-General, August 20, 1859, Gobierno Superior Civil, leg. 640, no. 20224, ANC; Secretaria Politica to Governor Captain-General, Matanzas, July 20, 1859, Gobierno Superior Civil, leg. 640, no. 20224, ANC.

140. See Vicente Perron, Vice Consul, España, Isla de Carmen to Governor Captain-General, February 24, 1860, Gobierno Superior Civil, leg. 640, no. 20215, ANC.

141. F. Fernando del Pino to Governor Captain-General, January 29, 1860, Gobierno Superior Civil, leg. 640, no. 20215, ANC.

142. Manuel Arroyas to Governor Captain-General, August 20, 1859, Gobierno Superior Civil, leg. 640, no. 20225, ANC; F. Fernando del Pino to Governor Captain-General, July 28, 1860, Gobierno Superior Civil, leg. 640, no. 20222, ANC.

143. Sección de Fomento to Governor Captain-General, April 23, 1860, Gobierno Superior Civil, leg. 640, no. 20220, ANC. See also [Unknown] to Capitan-General, November 11, 1859, and Francisco Valdez to Governor Captain-General, November 22, 1859, Gobierno Superior Civil, leg. 640, no. 20215, ANC.

144. Ibid.

145. F. Fernandino del Pino to Governor Captain-General, January 4, 1860, Gobierno Superior Civil, leg. 640, no. 20225; Felipe Arango to Governor Captain-General, February 3, 1860, Gobierno Superior Civil, leg. 640, no. 20225, ANC.

146. For examples from the period under study (1849–61), see Gobierno Superior Civil, leg. 638, no. 20151, leg. 640, no. 20215, leg. 642, no. 20297, and leg. 643, no. 20318, ANC.

147. See the cases in Gobierno Superior Civil, leg. 640, nos. 20215, 20222, and 20225, ANC.

Chapter 5. Yucatec Mayas, Transnational Resistance, and the Quotidian Struggles of Indentured Labor in Cuba, 1848–1864

1. Menéndez, *Historia del infame y vergonzoso comercio.*"

2. Allen Wells, "Forgotten Chapters of Yucatan's Past: Nineteenth-Century Politics in Historiographical Perspective," *Mexican Studies/Estudios Mexicanos* 12, no. 2 (1996): 205–6.

3. See Corbitt, "Los colonos yucatecos," 64–69. Moisés González Navarro, "La guerra de castas en Yucatán y la venta de mayas a Cuba," *Historia Mexicana* 18, no. 1 (1968): 1–34; González Navarro, *Raza y tierra*; Alejandro García Alvarez, "Traficante en el golfo," *Revista Historia Social* 17 (1993): 33–46; Izaskun Álvarez Cuartero, "De Tihosuco a la Habana: La venta de indios Yucatecos a Cuba durante la guerra de castas," *Studia Historica. Historia Antigua* 25 (2007): 559–76.

4. Álvarez Cuartero, "De Tihosuco a la Habana"; Jorge Victoria Ojeda, "Los indígenas mayas del servicio doméstico en Cuba, 1847–1853," *Chacmool: Cuadernos de Trabajo Cubano-Mexicanos* 1 (2003): 335–65; Javier Rodríguez Piña, *Guerra de castas: la venta d elos indios mayas a Cuba, 1848–1861* (Mexico City: Consejo Nacional para la Cultura y las Artes, Dirección General de Publicaciones, 1990).

5. Jeffrey T. Brannon and Gilbert M. Joseph, "The Erosion of Traditional Society: The Early Expansion of Commercial Agriculture and the Mayan Response," in *Land, Labour, and Capital in Modern Yucatan: Essays in Regional History and Political Economy*, edited by Jeffrey T. Brannon and Gilbert M. Joseph (Tuscaloosa: University of Alabama Press, 1991), 13.

6. Ibid.

7. Brian P. Owensby, *Empire of Law and Indian Justice in Colonial Mexico* (Stanford, CA: Stanford University Press, 2008), 1.

8. González Navarro, *Raza y tierra*, 132–33.

9. "Expediente sobre la introducción de indios de Yucatan en Cuba para trabajos agricolas," March 2, 1850, MSS 13857, fol. 33, Biblioteca Nacional de España, Madrid (BNE). See also González Navarro, "La guerra de castas," 21–22; and Evelyn Powell Jennings, "'Some Unhappy Indians Trafficked by Force': Race, Status, and Work Discipline in Mid-Nineteenth-Century Cuba," in *Human Bondage in the Cultural Contact Zone*, edited by Raphael Hormann and Gesa Mackenthun (Munich: Waxmann, 2010), 219–20.

10. Jennings, "'Some Unhappy Indians,'" 220.

11. Ibid. Also see González Navarro, "La guerra de castas," 21–22.

12. Jennings, "'Some Unhappy Indians,'" 221.

13. Thomas Savage, Vice Consul General to William Seward, United States Consul General, Havana, November 4, 1865, in U.S. Government, Papers Relating to Foreign Affairs Accompanying the Annual Message of the President to the First Session Thirty-Ninth Congress, Part 1 (Washington: GPO, 1866), 666.

14. "Expediente sobre la introducción de indios," fols. 76, 81, BNE.

15. The Yucatec Mayas in question were characterized as those "in power and outside of the power" ("en poder y fuera del poder") of Martí y Torrens and presumably other patrones. See "Expediente sobre la introducción de indios," fol. 52, BNE.

16. "Expediente sobre la introducción de indios," fols. 36–37, 55, BNE. See also Jennings, "'Some Unhappy Indians,'" 221–23 and González Navarro, "La guerra de castas," 21–26.

17. Caplan, *Indigenous Citizens*, 207.

18. "Statement of the Number of Slaves Landed and Proportion Captured in the Island of Cuba during 1859," in Britain, *Correspondence with the British Commissioners at Sierra Leone, Havana, the Cape of Good hope, and Loanda, and Reports from British Admiralty Courts and from British Naval Officers Relating to the Slave Trade, from April 1, 1859, to March 31, 1860* (London: Harrison and Sons, 1860), 18.

19. In the 1860s until his death, Martí y Torrens was one of a number of illegal slave traders pursued by British and then United States officials; Thomas Savage, Vice Consul General to William Seward, Havana, November 4, 1865. United States. Papers Relating to Foreign Affairs Accompanying the Annual Message of the President to the First Session Thirty-Ninth Congress, Pt.1 (Washington, DC: GPO, 1866), 666.

20. See correspondence and reports in Fondo Gobierno Superior Civil, leg. 638, no. 20149, leg. 640, nos. 20215 and 20225, and leg. 641, no. 20248, and in Reales Cédulas y Órdenes, leg. 55, no. 189, ANC.

21. Contrata a Colona Yucateca Demetria Villalobos al patrón Don José I. Madrazon, May 31, 1859; [Unknown] to Governor Captain-General of Cuba,

January 29, 1860; F. Fernando del Pino to Governor Captain-General, May 30 1860, Gobierno Superior Civil, leg. 638, no. 20149, ANC.

22. [Unknown] to Governor Captain-General of Cuba, January 29, 1860, Gobierno Superior Civil, leg. 638, no. 20149, ANC.

23. Presidencia del Consejo de Ministerios, Ultramar, to Governor Captain-General of Cuba, December 12, 1853, Reales Cédulas y Órdenes, leg. 55, no. 189, ANC; [Unknown] to Governor Captain-General of Cuba, November 11, 1859; Vice Consul of Spain to Governor Captain-General of Cuba, February 24, 1860; [Unknown] to Governor Captain-General of Cuba, July 18, 1860, Gobierno Superior Civil, leg. 640, no. 20215, ANC.

24. Rugeley, *Rebellion Now and Forever*, 98–99.

25. "Expediente sobre la introducción de indios," fols. 55, 76–77, BNE.

26. Rugeley, *Rebellion Now and Forever*, 311.

27. Ibid., 138–39.

28. Ibid., 180.

29. Ibid.

30. Reports, March 1860–March 1867, Relaciones Exteriores, fols. 1–51, exp. 6, caja 92, AGN.

31. F. Fernandez del Pino to Governor Captain-General of Cuba, January 29, 1860, Gobierno Superior Civil, leg. 640, no. 20215, ANC.

32. Ibid. See also González Navarro, *Raza y tierra*, 160–61.

33. F. Fernandez del Pino to Governor Captain-General of Cuba, January 29, 1860.

34. Examples include Victoriana Acosta to Governor Captain-General, October 21, 1859; F. Fernando de Pino to Governor Captain-General, November 17, 1859; and Rafael Morales to Governor Capitan-General, March 26, 1860, Havana, Gobierno Superior Civil, leg. 640, no. 20215, ANC.

35. Victoriana Acosta to Governor Captain-General, October 21, 1859, and January 27, 1860, Gobierno Superior Civil, leg. 640, no. 20215. See also F. Fernando de Pino to Governor Captain-General, June 19, 1860, and Sección de Fomento to Governor Captain-General, September 6, 1860, Gobierno Superior Civil, leg. 640, no. 20224, ANC.

36. Manuel Arroyas to Governor Captain-General of Cuba, August 20, 1859, Gobierno Superior Civil, leg. 640, no. 20225, ANC. See also González Navarro, *Raza y tierra*, 127–29.

37. F. Fernandez del Pino to Governor Captain-General of Cuba, July 28, 1860, Gobierno Superior Civil, leg. 640, no. 20222, ANC.

38. Secretaria del Gobierno de la Habana to Governor Captain-General of Cuba, October 12, 1861, Gobierno Superior Civil, leg. 641, no. 20248, ANC.

39. [Sindicatura] to the Secretary of the Gobierno Superior Civil, December 11, 1861, Gobierno Superior Civil, leg. 641, no. 20248, ANC.

40. [Unknown] to Gobierno Superior Civil, January 20, 1862; Fernando de Lavanco to Gobierno Superior Civil, Gobierno Superior Civil, leg. 643, no. 20318, ANC.

41. An example is found in "Expediente sobre la introducción de indios," fols. 55, 76–77, BNE.

42. Rugeley, *Yucatan's Maya Peasantry*, 72–78.

43. "Expediente sobre la introducción de indios," fols. 76–79, BNE.

44. Ibid., fols. 80–81.

45. Apolinar Gonzalez to Governor Captain-General, August 1859, Gobierno Superior Civil, leg. 640, no. 20224, ANC.

46. Rugeley, *Rebellion Now and Forever*, 189.

47. "Testimonio," 1860, Justicia, exp.118, vol. 649, AGN.

48. Ibid.

49. Ibid.

50. Ibid.

51. Ibid.

52. Ibid. The expression was directed at Mayas destined for labor in Cuba; Miguel de los Santos Albanez, Primera Secretaria de Estado, Ultramar, to Ministro de Estado Encargado del Despacho de los Negocios de Ultramar, October 27, 1855, Ultramar 93, exp. 45, AHN. Documents from the AHN cited in this chapter and chapter 6 are in digitized format available online through Portal de Archivos Españoles (PARES). http://pares.mcu.es/ParesBusquedas/servlets/Control_servlet. accessed 2010.

53. "Testimonio," 1860, Justicia, exp.118, vol. 649, AGN.

54. Ibid.

55. Ibid.

56. Ibid.

57. Ibid.

58. Rugeley, *Rebellion Now and Forever*, 188–90.

59. Ibid., 200.

60. Sección de Fomento to Governor Captain-General of Cuba, April 23, 1860, Gobierno Superior Civil, leg. 640, no. 20220, ANC.

61. F. Fernandez del Pino to Governor Captain-General, June 19, 1860; Sección de Fomento to Governor Captain-General, September 6, 1860, Gobierno Superior Civil, leg. 640, no. 20247, ANC.

62. Secretaria, Sección de Fomento, to Gobierno Superior Civil, April 29, 1863, Gobierno Superior Civil, leg. 641, no. 20248, ANC.

63. Consejo de Administración de la Isla de Cuba, la Habana, to Gobierno Superior Civil, September 12, 1863, Gobierno Superior Civil, leg. 641, no. 20248, ANC.

64. Ibid.

65. Ibid.

66. Specific cases can be found in Gobierno Superior Civil, leg. 640, nos. 20215, 20222, and 20225, ANC.

67. Declaración de D. Pedro José Crescencio Martínez, Havana, July 14, 1861, Gobierno Superior Civil, leg. 640, ANC.

68. Ultramar, Presidencia del Consejo de Ministros to Governor Captain-General, November 11, 1853, Reales Cédulas y Órdenes, leg. 172, no. 327, ANC; [Sección de Fomento] to Gobierno Politico, [1860], Gobierno Superior Civil, leg. 641, no. 20249, ANC.

69. Ibid.

70. For further discussion of indigenous negotiation of colonial law, see Owensby, *Empire of Law and Indian Justice*; Ethelia Ruíz Medrano, *Mexico's Indigenous Communities: Their Lands and Histories, 1500–2010* (Boulder: University Press of Colorado, 2010); and José Manuel A. Chávez-Gómez, "Waterways, Legal Ways, and Ethnic Interactions: The Rios District of Tabasco during the Seventeenth and Eighteenth Centuries," in Ruiz Medrano and Kellogg, *Negotiation within Domination*, 205–28.

71. Alejandro de la Fuente, "Slaves and the Creation of Legal Rights in Cuba: Coartación and Papel," *Hispanic American Historical Review* 87, no. 4 (2007): 661.

72. Ibid.

73. Ibid., 670.

74. Ibid., 672.

75. Ibid., 672–84.

76. Ibid., 692.

77. Ibid., 691.

78. See case file for José de Jesús Cabrera, Gobierno Superior Civil, leg. 640, no. 20247, ANC; also cited in González Navarro, *Raza y tierra*, 154–55.

79. Ibid.

80. [Juan G.] to Gobierno Superior Civil, October 28, 1864, Gobierno Superior Civil, leg. 642, no. 20297, ANC.

81. Owensby, *Empire of Law and Indian Justice*, 147.

82. Victoriana Acosta to Governor Captain-General, October 21, 1859; Victoriana Acosta to Governor Captain-General, January 27, 1860, Gobierno Superior Civil, leg. 640, no. 20215; F. Fernandez del Pino to Governor Captain-General, September 13, 1860, Gobierno Superior Civil, leg. 640, no. 20225; [Unknown] to

Governor Captain-General, January 20, 1862; Fernando de Levanco to Governor Captain-General, November 2, 1862, Gobierno Superior Civil, leg. 643, no. 20318, ANC.

83. Victoriana Acosta to Governor Captain-General of Cuba, October 21, 1859; F. Fernando del Pino to Governor Captain-General of Cuba, November 17, 1859, Gobierno Superior Civil, leg. 640, no. 20215, ANC.

84. F. Fernando del Pino to Governor Captain-General of Cuba, January 26, 1860, Gobierno Superior Civil, leg. 640, no. 20215, ANC.

85. Victoriana Acosta to Governor Captain-General of Cuba, October 21, 1859; Francisco Valdez to Governor Captain-General of Cuba, November 22, 1859; Victoriana Acosta to Governor Captain-General of Cuba, January 27, 1860, Gobierno Superior Civil, leg. 640, no. 20215, ANC.

86. [Unknown] to Gobierno Superior Civil, January 20, 1862; [Fernando de Levan] to Gobierno Superior Civil, November 2, 1862, Gobierno Superior Civil, leg. 643, no. 20318, ANC.

87. See Matthew Restall, "'He Wished It in Vein': Subordination and Resistance among Maya Women in Post-Conquest Yucatan," *Ethnohistory* 42, no. 4 (1995): 577–94.

88. Restall, *Maya World*, 139.

89. Antonio Aranjo to Gobierno Superior Civil, May 21, 1860, Gobierno Superior Civil, leg. 638, no. 20149, ANC.

90. Sección de Fomento to Governor Captain-General of Cuba, June 2, 1862, Gobierno Superior Civil, leg. 641, no. 20248, ANC.

91. "Sobre validez de las contratas de unos colonos yucatecos," 1870, Ultramar 90, exp. 20, AHN.

92. "Declaración de Fabiana Buendia," July 29, 1861, Ultramar 90, exp. 20, AHN.

93. "Declaración de Da. María Lucia Camara," July 13, 1861, Gobierno Superior Civil, leg. 640, no. 20224, ANC.

94. Carlos Barreiro to Governor Captain-General of Cuba, September 15, 1859, Gobierno Superior Civil, leg. 638, no. 20149, ANC; "Declaración de Manuel Alcalde," Ultramar 90, exp. 20, AHN.

95. Secretaria, Gobierno Superior Civil to Gobierno Superior Civil, May 12, 1863, Gobierno Superior Civil, leg. 641, no. 20248, ANC.

96. [Unknown] to [Manuel], Comisario de Policia, Distrito Regla, September 10, 1859, Gobierno Superior Civil, leg. 640, no. 20215, ANC.

97. Sección de Fomento to Gobierno Superior Civil, October 12, 1861, Gobierno Superior Civil, leg. 641, no. 20248, ANC.

98. F. Fernando del Pino to Governor Captain-General of Cuba, January 4,

1860; Felipe Arango to Governor Captain-General of Cuba, February 3, 1860, Gobierno Superior Civil, leg. 640, no. 20225, ANC.

99. Secretaria Politica to Governor Captain-General, Matanzas, July 20, 1859; Jefatura Superior de Policia to Governor Captain-General, November 28, 1859, Gobierno Superior, Civil, leg. 640, no. 20225, ANC.

100. Case file, José de Jesús Cabrera, Gobierno Superior Civil, leg., 640, no. 20247, ANC. Also see González Navarro, *Raza y tierra*, 154.

101. Ibid.

102. Such cases are found in Gobierno Superior Civil, leg. 640, no. 20215, ANC.

103. Gobierno Superior Civil, legs. 638, 640, 641, ANC.

104. We have considerably little evidence of debt peonage among Maya workers in Cuba; Secretaria de Gobierno to Governor Captain-General, Havana, September 19, 1860, Gobierno Superior Civil, leg. 638, no. 20151, ANC.

105. See Owensby, *Empire of Law and Indian Justice*, 130–66.

106. Pérez, *Cuba*, 100.

107. For examples, see Jefatura Superior de Policia to Governor Captain-General, Havana, September 22, 1864, leg. 640, no. 20225; Tenencia de Gobierno, Sección de Fomento, Cienfuegos, April 11, 1863; Tenencia de Gobierno, Sección de Fomento, Bejucal, May 18, 1863, leg. 640, no. 20248; Manuel Perecho to Governor Captain-General, February 25, 1864, Gobierno Superior Civil, leg. 642, no. 20300, ANC.

108. Juan Jimenez to Governor Captain-General, August 19, 1861; Jefatura Superior de Policia to Governor Captain-General, September 22, 1864, Gobierno Superior Civil, leg. 640, no. 20225, ANC.

109. Consejo de Administración de la Isla de Cuba to March 21, 1862, Gobierno Superior Civil, leg. 641, no. 20248, ANC.

110. [Juan G.] to Gobierno Superior Civil, October 28, 1864, Gobierno Superior Civil, leg. 642, no. 20297, ANC.

111. Juan Gerez, Secretaria de Agricultura, to Gobierno Superior Civil, September 9, 1864, Gobierno Superior Civil, leg. 642, no. 20296, ANC.

112. Secretaria, Sección de Fomento, to Gobierno Superior Civil, April 29, 1863, Gobierno Superior Civil, leg. 641, no. 20248, ANC.

113. Secretaria del Gobierno Político de la Habana to Governor Captain-General of Cuba, October 12, 1861, Gobierno Superior Civil, leg. 641, no. 20248, ANC.

114. Dirección del Ramo de Aprendizaje y Administración del Depósito Judicial de Esclavos to Gobierno Superior Civil, October 15, 1863, leg. 641, no. 20248; [Juan G?] to Gobierno Superior Civil, July 19, 1864, Gobierno Superior Civil, leg. 642, no. 20300, ANC.

115. Tenencia de Gobierno, Sección de Fomento, to Governor Captain-General of Cuba, March 6, 1863, Gobierno Superior Civil, leg. 641, no. 20248, ANC.

116. Tenencia de Gobierno to Governor Captain-General, Güines, April 13, 1861, Gobierno Superior Civil, leg. 641, no. 20248, ANC.

117. Sección de Fomento to Governor Captain-General, July 28, 1860, Gobierno Superior Civil, leg. 640, no. 20215, ANC.

118. Secretaria Politica to Governor Captain-General of Cuba, July 20, 1859; Jefatura Superior de Policia to Governor Captain-General, November 23, 1859, Gobierno Superior Civil, leg. 640, no. 20225, ANC. See also the series of correspondence and reports in Gobierno Superior Civil, leg. 641, no. 20248, ANC.

119. Tenencia de Gobierno, Sección de Fomento, to Gobierno Superior Civil, September 6, 1864, Gobierno Superior Civil, leg. 642, no. 20296, ANC.

120. See Relación de los colonos yucatecos que pasan a la capital para ingresar en el Depósito de su clases, Cardenas, September 25, 1863, Gobierno Superior Civil, leg. 641, no. 20248, ANC.

121. See Cosme de la Torriente to Governor Captain-General of Cuba, April 7, 1859; [Unknown] to Governor Captain-General of Cuba, May 11, 1859, Gobierno Superior Civil, leg. 341, no. 16498; F. Fernandes del Pino to Governor Captain-General, February 19, 1861; [Unknown] to Governor Captain-General, March 17, 1862, Gobierno Superior Civil, leg. 641, no. 20248, ANC.

122. J. Scott, *Domination and the Arts of Resistance*, 17. See also J. Scott, *Weapons of the Weak*, 29–36; José Arturo Güémez Pineda, "Everyday Forms of Maya Resistance: Cattle Rustling in Northwestern Yucatan," in *Land, Labor, and Capital in Modern Yucatan: Essays in Regional History and Political Economy*, edited by Jeffrey T. Brannon and Gilbert M. Joseph, 18–19 (Tuscaloosa: University of Alabama Press, 1991).

123. For more on the Caste War in the later period, see Inés de Castro, *Cantones y comandantes: Una visión diferente de la Guerra de Castas desde la región de los Pacíficos del Sur* (Campeche, Mexico: Universidad Autónoma de Campeche, 2007), and Lean Sweeney, *La supervivencia de los bandidos: Los mayas icaichés y la política fronteriza del sureste de la península de Yucatán, 1847–1904* (Merida, Mexico: Universidad Nacional Autónoma de México, 2006).

124. Dirección de Administración, Sección de Agricultura, Industria y Comercio to [Unknown], July 19, 1864, Gobierno Superior Civil, leg. 642, no. 20, ANC; Tenencia de Gobierno, Sección de Agricultura, Industria y Comercio, Guanabacoa, to Gobierno Superior Civil, September 6, 1864, Gobierno Superior Civil, leg. 642, no. 20296, ANC.

125. [Juan] to Gobierno Superior Civil, July 19, 1864, Gobierno Superior Civil, leg. 642, no. 20300, ANC.

126. Tenencia de Gobierno, Sección de Agricultura, Industria y Comercio, Guanabacoa, to Gobierno Superior Civil, September 6, 1864, Gobierno Superior Civil, leg. 642, no. 20296, ANC. There are also numerous cases documented for the years 1861–65 in Gobierno Superior Civil, leg. 641, no. 20248, ANC.

127. See Tenencia de Gobierno, Sección de Fomento, to Governor Captain-General, March 6, 1863, Gobierno Superior Civil, leg. 641, no. 20248, ANC. See also Tenencia de Gobierno, Sección de Fomento, Güines, to Governor Captain-General, April 13, 1861, Secretaria Politica to Governor Captain-General, July 20, 1859, Matanzas, and Jefatura Superior de Policia to Governor Captain-General, Havana, November 28, 1859, Gobierno Superior Civil, leg. 640, no. 20225, ANC.

Chapter 6. Blood Contract: Continuity, Change, and Persistence in Colonial Indigenous Labor Forms and Elite Strategies

1. In U.S. Government, Report on the Census of Cuba, 734–35.

2. Ibid.

3. Cited in Corbitt, "Immigration in Cuba," 283–84.

4. Ibid., 280–81. See also Knight, "Migration and Culture: A Case Study of Cuba, 1750–1900," paper presented at the Historical Society Conference on Migration, Diaspora, Ethnicity, and Nationalism, June 5–7, 2008, Johns Hopkins University, Baltimore, 7.

5. Corbitt, 280-281.

6. Ibid., 284.

7. Ibid.

8. "Sobre el reglamento de trato de asiáticos y yucatecas," 1847–50, Ultramar 91, exp. 6, and "Sobre circular de reglas de trato de asiáticos y yucatecas," 1849–53, Ultramar 91, exp. 7, AHN.

9. Antonio Caballero, First Secretary of State, to President, Council of Ministers, March 31, 1854, Ultramar 91, exp. 8, AHN; Note, First Secretary of State, January 23, 1854, Ultramar 91, exp. 8, AHN.

10. First Secretary of State, March 20, 1854, Ultramar 91, exp. 8, AHN.

11. Ibid.

12. Governor Captain-General of Cuba to the Minister of War and Overseas, December 2, 1858, Ultramar 91, exp. 9, AHN.

13. Gabriel V. Carranza to Her Excellency, March 13, 1858, Ultramar 91, exp. 8, AHN.

14. Secretaria de Gobierno, Sección de Fomento to Ministro de la Guerra y de Ultramar, June 12, 1860, Ultramar 91, exp. 9, AHN.

15. Governor Captain-General of Cuba to the Minister of War and Overseas, December 2, 1858, Ultramar 91, exp. 9, AHN.

16. Primera Secretaria de Estado, Ultramar, to Governor Captain-General, November 7, 1855, Reales Cédulas y Órdenes, leg. 188, no. 136, ANC.

17. Among examples are the proposals for the importation into Cuba of a thousand Amerindians from across Spanish America; [Unknown] to the Governor Captain-General, April 7, 1859; [Unknown] to Governor Captain-General, May 11, 1859, Gobierno Superior Civil, leg. 341, no. 16498, ANC.

18. Consejo de Estado to Ministerio de la Guerra y Ultramar, April 1859, Ultramar 90, exp. 17, AHN.

19. Secretaria de Gobierno, Sección de Fomento to [Unknown], December 28, 1858, Ultramar 90, exp. 17, AHN.

20. Ibid.

21. Ibid.

22. Ibid.

23. J. F. Pacheco, Sección de Fomento to Ministro de la Guerra y Ultramar, June 17, 1859, Ultramar 90, exp. 17, AHN.

24. Cited in ibid.

25. Ibid.

26. [Unknown] to Díaz Mendoza, Havana, September 10, 1860, Ultramar 90, exp. 19, AHN.

27. Díaz Mendoza, "Note," December 5, 1860, Ultramar 90, exp. 19, AHN.

28. Gabriel Díaz Granados to Gobierno Superior Civil, May 9, 1859; Gabriel Díaz Granados to Gobernador Civil, January 31, 1860, Ultramar 90, exp. 19, AHN.

29. Gabriel Díaz Granados to Gobernador Civil, January 31, 1860, Ultramar 90, exp. 19, AHN.

30. Ibid.

31. "Dictamen de la Comisión de población blanca," April 30, 1860, Ultramar 90, exp. 19, AHN.

32. "Al President del Consejo de Estado," Madrid, December 20, 1860, Ultramar, 90, exp. 19, AHN.

33. "Al Gobernador Capitan General de la Isla de Cuba," July 9, 1861, Ultramar, 90, exp. 19, AHN.

34. See reports and studies commissioned during the 1862–73 period, in "Expediente sobre promoción de colonización [blanco y yucateco] en Cuba, 1862–1873," Ultramar 91, exp. 1, and "Expediente sobre promoción de colonización [blanco y yucateco] en Cuba, 1862–1873," Ultramar 91, exp. 2, AHN.

35. Ibid.

36. Report, Governor Captain-General of Cuba, November 27, 1870, Ultramar, 90, exp. 16, AHN.

37. "Note," January 18, 1871; exp. promovido por Don Atanasio de la Cruz

Garcia, Don Manuel Gonzalo Palomino y Don José M. Salinero, en solicitud de permiso para introducir colonos Mejicanos, November 24, 1870, Ultramar 90, exp. 16, AHN.

38. Expediente promovido por Don Atanasio de la Cruz Garcia, Don Manuel Gonzalo Palomino y Don José M. Salinero, ensolicitud de permiso para introducir colonos Mejicanos, November 24, 1870, Ultramar, 90, exp. 16, AHN.

39. Ibid.

40. Sección de Fomento to Ministro de Ultramar, April 26, 1871, Ultramar 90, exp. 16, AHN. Additional documentation that makes several references to "Mexicans" also includes a reference to "indios yucatecos" in parentheses; Indices, Ultramar 90, exp. 16, AHN.

41. Sección de Fomento to Ministro de Ultramar, April 26, 1871, Ultramar 90, exp. 16, AHN.

42. Report, Sección de Fomento, March 24, 1876, Ultramar, 102, exp. 38, AHN.

43. Cited in Ministerio de Ultramar to [Unknown], ca. 1876, Ultramar 102, exp. 38, AHN.

44. See Winthrop R. Wright, chapter 3, "Whitening the Population, 1850–1900," in his *Café con leche: Race, Class, and National Image in Venezuela* (Austin: University of Texas Press, 1990).

45. Ministerio de Ultramar to President of the Council of State, April 15, 1879, enclosing letter, dated July 1876, Ultramar, 102, exp. 38, AHN.

46. Testimonio del expediente general sobre introducción de colonos yucatecos en la isla de Cuba, April 24, 1867, Ultramar, 91, exp. 1, AHN.

47. Report, Gobernador General to Ministro de Ultramar, September 11, 1879, Ultramar, 102, exp. 39, AHN.

48. Dirección General de Administración y Fomento, Ministerio de Ultramar, to Presidente del Consejo de Estado, November 13, 1879, Ultramar, 102, exp. 39, AHN.

49. Report from Dirección General de Administración y Fomento, Ministerio de Ultramar, May 20, 1880, Ultramar, 102, exp. 39, AHN.

50. Ibid.

51. Louis A. Pérez Jr., *Cuba and the United States: Ties of Singular Intimacy* (Athens: University of Georgia Press, 1989), 56.

52. A number of ministry and colonial government reports make this point; see González Navarro, *Raza y tierra*, 148–49.

53. Corbitt, "Immigration in Cuba," 304–5.

54. Knight, "Migration and Culture," 26.

55. Bergad, *Cuban Rural Society*, 259.

56. R. Scott, *Slave Emancipation in Cuba*, 102–3, 172–81.

57. Ibid.

58. Cuello, "Persistence of Indian Slavery."

59. Deeds, "Rural Work in Nueva Vizcaya," 427–28.

60. Ibid.

61. See Larson, *Trials of Nation Making*, and Mark Van Arken, "The Lingering Death of Indian Tribute in Ecuador," *Hispanic American Historical Review* 61, no. 3 (1981): 429–59.

62. Larson, *Trials of Nation Making*, 106.

63. Ibid., 107.

64. Rugeley, *Rebellion Now and Forever*, 18.

65. Ibid., 22–25.

66. González Navarro, *Raza y tierra*, 54–61.

67. See R. Scott, *Slave Emancipation in Cuba*; Bergad, *Cuban Rural Society*; and Bergad, Iglesias Garcia, and Barcia, *Cuban Slave Market*.

68. See Emeterio S. Santovenia and Raul M. Shelton, *Cuba y su historia*, vol. 1, 2nd ed. (Miami: Cuba Corporation, 1966), 135; Lyle N. McAlister, *Spain and Portugal in the New World, 1492–1700* (Minneapolis: University of Minnesota Press, 1984), 157–65; and David A. Brading, *The First America: The Spanish Monarchy, Creole Patriots, and the Liberal State, 1492–1867* (Cambridge: Cambridge University Press, 1991), 67–72.

69. R. Scott, *Slave Emancipation in Cuba*, 102–3.

70. Patch, *Maya Revolt*, 177–78. See also Allen Wells, "From Hacienda to Plantation: The Transformation of Santo Domingo Xcuyum," in *Land, Labour, and Capital in Modern Yucatan: Essays in Regional History and Political Economy*, edited by Jeffrey T. Brannon and Gilbert M. Joseph, 112–42 (Tuscaloosa: University of Alabama Press, 1991).

71. "Noticia de Repartimiento de Mecos y Mecas . . . en el Navio de Guerra San Roman," February [1802], Cuba, leg. 1716, AGI.

72. See discussions in González Navarro, *Raza y tierra*; Rugeley, *Rebellion Now and Forever*; and Yaremko, "Colonial Wars and Indigenous Geopolitics."

73. See chapter 5 of this volume.

74. Bergad, *Cuban Rural Society*, 259. Importantly, Bergad refers here to the late nineteenth century; conditions during the mid-nineteenth century were even more pronounced than in this reference to slave society.

75. Ibid.

76. "Expediente sobre la introducción de indios," December 13, 1849, fols. 161–62, BNE.

77. Ibid., December 15, 1849, fols. 162, 165–66. See also Ojeda, "Los indigenas Mayas del servicio doméstico," 335–65. For an elaboration of conditions for orphaned children in colonial Cuba, see Ondina E. González, "Consuming Interests: The Response to Abandoned Children in Colonial Havana," 137–62, and Ann Twinam, "The Church, the State, and the Abandoned: Expósitos in Late Eighteenth-Century Havana," 163–86, both in *Raising an Empire: Children in Early Modern Iberia and Colonial Latin America*, edited by Ondina E. González and Bianca Premo (Albuquerque: University of New Mexico Press, 2007).

78. "Expediente sobre la introducción de indios," December 15, 1849, fols. 162, 165–66, BNE.

79. Regarding the motivations of elites requesting domestic servants, see correspondence in Cuba, leg. 1716, AGI.

80. "Expediente sobre la introducción de indios," December 1849, fols. 162–66, BNE.

81. González, "Consuming Interests," 139.

82. "Expediente sobre la introducción de indios," December 1849, fols. 162–66, BNE.

83. González, "Consuming Interests," 155.

84. Examples are found in "Expediente sobre la introducción de indios," fols. 149–59, BNE.

85. Ibid., fols. 16–17.

86. Ibid.

87. Ibid.

88. Ibid., April 25, 1849, fols. 18–20.

89. Ibid., May 15, 1849, fols. 20–21.

90. See ibid., fols. 20–26, 48–53.

91. Ibid., fol. 151.

92. Ibid.

93. Ibid., fol. 152.

94. See ibid., fols. 27–32.

95. Ibid., fol. 29.

96. Ibid., fols. 29–30.

97. Ibid., fols. 153–59.

98. Ibid., fols. 28–29.

99. Probably the best-known existing community of Maya descendants is the town of Madruga, near Havana.

Conclusion: Diaspora and the Enduring (and Diverse) Indigenous Presence in Cuba

1. Immigration records, Ministerio de Ultramar, January 1, 1889–December 31, 1893, Torrelaguna, 297, Sección Nobleza del Archivo Histórico Nacional, AHN.

2. Ship passenger lists, 1900, "Passengers Data Base," CubaGenWeb, http://www.cubagenweb.org/ships/index.htm; accessed 2014.

3. Cited in Julio Le Riverend Brusone, "Relaciones entre Nueva España y Cuba (1518–1820)," *Revista de Historia de América*, nos. 37–38 (1954): 97–98.

4. Cabildo de 14 de febrero 1575, Actas Capitulares del Ayuntamiento de La Habana, February 14, 1575, 93, AMCH.

5. MacLeod, *Spanish Central America*, 52.

6. Cabildo de 14 de febrero 1575, Actas Capitulares del Ayuntamiento de La Habana, February 14, 1575, 93, AMCH.

7. I. Wright, *Early History of Cuba*, 185–86.

8. Cited in Antonio J. Valdés, *Historia de la isla de Cuba y en especial de la Habana*, vol. 1 (Havana: Oficina de a Cena, 1813), 342.

9. Bojórquez Urzaiz, "El barrio de Campeche," 31.

10. Pérez de la Riva, "Cuban Palenques," 57.

11. "Declaración de Da. María Lucia Camara," July 13, 1861, Gobierno Superior Civil, leg. 640, no. 20224, ANC.

12. Reinaldo Funes Monzote, *De bosque a sabana: Azúcar, deforestación y medio ambiente en Cuba, 1492–1926* (Mexico City: Siglo Veintiuno Editores, 2004), 36–45.

13. See the map in Ramón Dacal Moure and Manuel Rivero de la Calle, *Art and Archaeology of Pre-Columbian Cuba* (Pittsburgh, PA: University of Pittsburgh Press, 1996), 26.

14. Juan A. Cosculluela, *Cuatro años en la ciénaga Zapata* (Havana: Imprenta La Universal, 1918), 239–40.

15. Ibid., 239.

16. Ibid., 238. For more on this encounter, see Jason Yaremko, "'Obvious Indian'—Missionaries, Anthropologists, and the 'Wild Indians' of Cuba: Representations of the Amerindian Presence in Cuba," *Ethnohistory* 56, no. 3 (2009): 449–77.

17. See Milan Pospisil, *Indian Remnants from the Oriente Province, Cuba* (Bratislava, Slovakia: Univerzita Komenskeho, 1976), 32, and Karen Mahé Lugo Romera and Sonia Menéndez Castro, "Yucatán en La Habana: Migraciones, encuentros y desarraigos," *La Jiribilla: Revista de Cultura Cubana*, September 22–28, 2007, http://www.lajiribilla.co.cu/2007/n333_09/333_04.html.

18. The extent to which these other sites represent communities of Yucatec Maya descendants from the nineteenth century is unclear. The late distinguished

Cuban anthropologist Manuel Rivero de la Calle suggested that those resident in Madruga and Nueva Paz, to name two, may be descended from the nineteenth-century generation; *Las culturas aborígenes de Cuba*, 60. A recent study by Mexican anthropologist Victoria Novelo on Yucatecans in Cuba also mentions these and other communities; *Yucatecos en Cuba* (Merida, Mexico: Casa Chata, Centro de Investigaciones y Estudios Superiores en Antropología Social, Instituto Cultura de Yucatán, 2009), 117.

19. Novelo, *Yucatecos en Cuba*, 112–13.

20. Interview cited in ibid., 113–14.

21. Ibid.

22. Ibid.

23. Ibid.

24. Ibid., 117.

25. Lugo Romera and Menéndez Castro, "Yucatán en La Habana."

26. See Lisandra Díaz, "Los últimos mayas en Cuba," *Mayabeque*, June 3, 2014, http://diariomayabeque.cu/2014/06/los-ultimos-mayas-en-cuba/.

27. Ibid.

28. Beatriz Marcheco-Teruel, Esteban J. Parra, Evelyn Fuentes-Smith, et al., "Cuba: Exploring the History of Admixture and Genetic Basis of Pigmentation Using Autosomal and Uniparental Markers," *PloS Genet* 10, no. 7 (2014): 1–13.

REFERENCES

Archives

ARCHIVO DEL MUSEO DE LA CIUDAD DE LA HABANA, HAVANA (AMCH)
Actas Capitulares del Ayuntamiento de La Habana

ARCHIVO GENERAL DE LA NACIÓN, MEXICO CITY (AGN)
Gobierno Virreinal, Correspondencia de Diversas Autoridades (GVC)
Gobierno Virreinal, Reales Cédulas Originales y Duplicados (GVRC)
Instituciones Gubernamentales
Provincias Internas (PI)
Real Hacienda, Archivo Histórico de Hacienda (RHA)
Relaciones Exteriores

ARCHIVO GENERAL DE INDIAS, SEVILLE (AGI)
Cuba
Mexico
Santo Domingo

ARCHIVO GENERAL DE SIMANCAS, SPAIN (AGS)

ARCHIVO HISTÓRICO NACIONAL, MADRID (AHN)
Ultramar

ARCHIVO HISTÓRICO PROVINCIAL DE MATANZAS, CUBA (AHPM)
Actas Capitulares de Matanzas

ARCHIVO NACIONAL DE LA REPÚBLICA DE CUBA, HAVANA (ANC)

Fondo Escribanías
Fondos Gobierno Superior Civil
Gobierno Civil
Gobierno General
Gobierno Superior Civil
Junta de Fomento
Reales Cédulas y Órdenes

BIBLIOTECA NACIONAL DE ESPAÑA, MADRID (BNE)

BIBLIOTECA NACIONAL JOSÉ MARTÍ, HAVANA

IGLESIA DEL ESPIRITU SANTO, HAVANA

IGLESIA DEL SANTO CRISTO DEL BUEN VIAJE, HAVANA

Parish records accessed through Ecclesiastical and Secular Sources for Slave Societies [ESSSS]. www.vanderbilt.edu/esss.

INSTITUTO DE LITERATURA Y LINGÜÍSTICA, HAVANA

WILLIAM L. CLEMENTS LIBRARY, UNIVERSITY OF MICHIGAN, ANN ARBOR

Thomas Gage Papers, American Series

Published Sources

Alegre, Francisco Javier. *Historia de la provincia de Jesús de Nueva España.* 4 vols. Edited by Ernest Burrus and Félix Zubillaga. Rome: Institutum Historicum S.J., 1956–1960.

Alfonso, Pedro A. *Memorias de un matancero. Apuntes para la historia de la isla de Cuba conrrelación de la ciudad de San Carlos y San Severino de Matanzas.* Matanzas, Cuba: Ediciones de la Imprenta de Marsal, adjunta a la de la Aurora, 1854.

Álvarez Cuartero, Izaskun. "De Tihosuco a la Habana: La venta de indios yucatecos a Cuba durante la guerra de castas." *Studia Historica. Historia Antigua* 25 (2007): 559–76.

Archer, Christon. "The Deportation of Barbarian Indians from the Internal Provinces of New Spain, 1789–1810." *The Americas* 29, no. 3 (1973): 376–85.

Arriaga Mesa, Marcos. *La Habana, 1550–1600: Tierra, hombres y mercado.* Madrid: Silex Ediciones, 2014.

Barcia, Manuel. *Seeds of Insurrection: Domination and Slave Resistance on Cuban Plantations.* Baton Rouge: Louisiana State University Press, 2008.

Barr, Julianna. *Peace Came in the Form of a Woman: Indians and Spaniards in the Texas Borderlands*. Chapel Hill: University of North Carolina Press, 2007.

Bartram, William. *Travels Through North & South Carolina, Georgia, East & West Florida, the Cherokee Country, the Extensive Territories of the Muscolges, or Creek Confederacy, and the Country of the Choctaws*. Philadelphia: James and Johnson, 1791.

Bergad, Laird. *Cuban Rural Society in the Nineteenth Century: The Social and Economic History of Monoculture in Matanzas*. Princeton, NJ: Princeton University Press, 1990.

Bergad, Laird, Fe Iglesias García, and María del Carmen Barcia. *The Cuban Slave Market, 1790–1880*. Cambridge: Cambridge University Press, 1995.

Berman, Mary Jane. "Good as Gold: The Aesthetic Brilliance of the Lucayans." In *Islands at the Crossroads: Migration, Seafaring, and Interaction in the Caribbean*, edited by L. Antonio Curet and Mark W. Hauser, 104–136. Tuscaloosa: University of Alabama Press, 2011.

Blackburn, Robin. *The Making of New World Slavery: From the Baroque to the Modern, 1492–1800*. London: Verso, 1998.

Blanton, Justin. "The Role of Cattle Ranching in the 1656 Timucuan Rebellion: A Struggle for Land, Labor, and Chiefly Power." *Florida Historical Quarterly* 92, no. 4 (2014): 667–84.

Bojórquez Urzaiz, Carlos E. "El barrio de Campeche en La Habana." *Cuadernos Culturales* 5 (1994): 18–30.

Bojórquez Urzaiz, Carlos E., Enrique Sosa Rodríguez, and Luis Millet Camara. *Habanero campechano*. Merida, Mexico: Ediciones de la Universidad Autónoma de Yucatán, 1991.

Boyd, Mark F. "From a Remote Frontier: Letters and Documents Pertaining to San Marcos de Apalache, 1763–1769," *Florida Historical Quarterly* 19, no. 3 (January 1941): 179–212.

Boyd, Mark F., and Jose N. Latorre. "Spanish Interest in British Florida." *Florida Historical Quarterly* 32, no. 2 (1953): 92–130.

Brading, David A. *The First America: The Spanish Monarchy, Creole Patriots, and the Liberal State, 1492–1867*. Cambridge: Cambridge University Press, 1991.

Braniff, Beatriz, ed. *La Gran Chichimeca: El lugar de las rocas secas*. Mexico City: Conaculta, Editorial Jaca, 2001.

Brannon, Jeffrey T., and Gilbert M. Joseph. "The Erosion of Traditional Society: The Early Expansion of Commercial Agriculture and the Mayan Response." In Brannon and Joseph, *Land, Labor, and Capital in Modern Yucatán*, 13–17.

Brannon, Jeffrey T., and Gilbert M. Joseph, eds. *Land, Labor, and Capital in Modern Yucatán: Essays in Regional History and Political Economy*. Tuscaloosa: University of Alabama Press, 1991.

Bricker, Victoria Reifler. *The Indian Christ, the Indian King: The Historical Substrate of Maya Myth and Ritual.* Austin: University of Texas Press, 1981.

Britain. *Correspondence with the British Commissioners at Sierra Leone, Havana, the Cape of Good Hope, and Loanda, and Reports from British Admiralty Courts and from British Naval Officers Relating to the Slave Trade, from April 1, 1859, to March 31, 1860.* London: Harrison and Sons, 1860.

Brooks, James F. *Captives and Cousins: Slavery, Kinship, and Community in the Southwest Borderlands.* Chapel Hill: University of North Carolina Press, 2002.

Bushnell, Amy Turner. *Situado and Sabana: Spain's Support System for the Presidio and Mission Provinces of Florida.* Anthropological Papers, No. 74. Athens, GA: American Museum of Natural History, September 21, 1994.

Callaghan, Richard T. "Comments on the Mainland Origins of the Preceramic Cultures of the Greater Antilles." *Latin American Antiquity* 14, no. 3 (2003): 323–38.

———. "Patterns of Contact between the Islands of the Caribbean and the Surrounding Mainland as a Navigational Problem." In *Islands at the Crossroads: Migration, Seafaring, and Interaction in the Caribbean,* edited by L. Antonio Curet and Mark W. Hauser, 59-72. Tuscaloosa: University of Alabama Press, 2011.

Caplan, Karen. *Indigenous Citizens: Local Liberalism in Early National Oaxaca and Yucatán.* Stanford, CA: Stanford University Press, 2010.

Carpentier, Alejo. *Obras completas de Alejo Carpentier XII: Ese músico que llevo dentro.* Mexico City: Siglo Ventiuno Editores, 1987.

Carrillo Cazares, Alberto. *El debate sobre la guerra Chichimeca, 1531–1585.* 2 vols. Zamora, Mexico: Colegio de Michoacán, 2000.

Casanovas, Joan. *Bread or Bullets! Urban Labor and Spanish Colonialism in Cuba, 1850–1898.* Pittsburgh, PA: University of Pittsburgh Press, 1998.

Castro, Inés de. *Cantones y comandantes: Una visión diferente de la Guerra de Castas desde la región de los Pacíficos del Sur.* Campeche, Mexico City: Universidad Autónoma de Campeche, 2007.

Chávez-Gómez, José Manuel A. "Waterways, Legal Ways, and Ethnic Interactions: The Rios District of Tabasco during the Seventeenth and Eighteenth Centuries," in *Negotiation within Domination,* Ruiz Medrano and Kellogg, 205–28.

Chipman, Donald. "The Traffic in Indian Slaves in the Province of Panuco, New Spain, 1523–1533," *The Americas* 23, no. 2 (1966): 142–55.

Clifford, James. "Diasporas." *Cultural Anthropology* 9, no. 3 (August 1994): 302–338.

Corbitt, Duvon C. "Immigration in Cuba." *Hispanic American Historical Review* 22, no. 2 (1942): 280–308.

———. "Los colonos yucatecos." *Revista Bimestre Cubana* 39, no. 1 (1937): 64–70.

Cosculluela, Juan A. *Cuatro años en la ciénaga Zapata*. Havana: Imprenta La Universal, 1918.

Covington, James W., ed. "A Petition from Some Latin American Fishermen, 1838." *Tequesta* 14 (1954): 61–65.

———. "Trade Relations between Southwestern Florida and Cuba, 1600–1840." *Florida Historical Quarterly* 38, no. 2 (1959): 114–28.

Cuello, José. "The Persistence of Indian Slavery and Encomienda in the Northeast of Colonial Mexico, 1577–1723." *Journal of Social History* 21, no. 4 (1988): 683–700.

Cutter, Charles. *The Legal Culture of Northern New Spain*. Albuquerque: University of New Mexico Press, 1995.

Dacal Moure, Ramón, and Manuel Rivero de la Calle. *Art and Archaeology of Pre-Columbian Cuba*. Pittsburgh, PA: University of Pittsburgh Press, 1996.

Deeds, Susan. "Rural Work in Nueva Vizcaya: Forms of Labor Coercion on the Periphery." *Hispanic American Historical Review* 69, no. 3 (1989): 425–49.

de la Torre Curiel, José Refugio. "'Enemigos encubiertos': Bandas pluriétnicas y estado de alerta en la frontera sonorense a finales del siglo XVIII." *Takwá*, no. 14 (2008): 11–31.

de la Pezuela y Lobo, Jacobo. *Diccionario geográfico, estadístico e histórico de la isla de Cuba*. Vol. 4. Madrid: Mellado, 1866.

———. *Historia de la isla de Cuba*. Vol. 2. Madrid: Bally-Bailliere, 1868.

de la Torre, José María. *Lo que fuimos y lo que somos: La Habana antigua y moderna*. Havana: Imprenta Spencer, 1857.

Díaz, Lisandra. "Los últimos mayas en Cuba." *Mayabeque*, June 3, 2014. http:// diariomayabeque.cu/2014/06/los-ultimos-mayas-en-cuba/.

Dorsey, Joseph C. "Identity, Rebellion, and Social Justice among Chinese Contract Workers in Nineteenth-Century Cuba." *Latin American Perspectives* 31, no. 3 (2004): 18–47.

Dumond, Don E. *The Machete and the Cross: Campesino Rebellion in Yucatan*. Lincoln: University of Nebraska Press, 1996.

DuVal, Kathleen. "Choosing Enemies: The Prospects for an Anti-American Alliance in the Louisiana Territory." *Arkansas Historical Quarterly* 62, no. 3 (2003): 233–52.

———. *The Native Ground: Indians and Colonists in the Heart of the Continent*. Philadelphia: University of Pennsylvania Press, 2006.

Fairbanks, Charles. *Florida Indians III: Ethnohistorical Report on the Florida Indians*. New York: Garland, 1974.

Farriss, Nancy M. "Persistent Maya Resistance and Cultural Retention in Yucatan."

The Indian in Latin American History: Resistance, Resilience, and Acculturation, edited by John E. Kicza, 51–68. Wilmington, DE: Scholarly Resources, 1993.

Fernández de Oviedo, Gonzalo. *Historia general y natural de las Indias*. Part 1. Edited by José Amador de los Rios. Madrid: Imprenta de la Real Academia de la Historia, 1851.

Forte, Maximilian C., ed. *Indigenous Resurgence in the Contemporary Caribbean: Amerindian Survival and Revival*. New York: Peter Lang, 2006.

———. "Introduction: The Dual Absences of Extinction and Marginality—What Difference Does an Indigenous Presence Make?" In *Indigenous Resurgence*, edited by Forte, 1–17.

Franco, José Luciano. *Comercio clandestino de esclavos*. Havana: Editorial de Ciencias Sociales, 1985.

Fuente, Alejandro de la. "Slaves and the Creation of Legal Rights in Cuba: Coartación and Papel." *Hispanic American Historical Review* 87, no. 4 (2007): 659–92.

Funes Monzotes, Reinaldo. *De bosque a sabana: Azúcar, deforestación y medio ambiente en Cuba, 1492–1926*. Mexico City: Siglo Veintiuno Editores, 2004.

Gabbert, Wolfgang. *Becoming Maya: Ethnicity and Social Inequality in Yucatan since 1500*. Tucson: University of Arizona Press, 2004.

Galgano, Robert C. *Feast of Souls: Indians and Spaniards in the Seventeenth-Century Missions of Florida and New Mexico*. Albuquerque: University of New Mexico Press, 2005.

Gallay, Alan. *The Indian Slave Trade*. New Haven, CT: Yale University Press, 2002.

Gallay, Alan, ed. *Indian Slavery in Colonial America*. Lincoln: University of Nebraska Press, 2009.

García Alvarez, Alejandro. "Traficante en el golfo," *Revista Historia Social* 17 (1994): 33–46.

García Díaz, Bernardo, and Sergio Guerra Vilaboy, eds. *La Habana/Veracruz, Veracruz/La Habana: Las dos orillas*. Veracruz, Mexico: Universidad Veracruzana, 2002.

García Icazbalceta, Joaquin. *Don Fray Juan de Zumárraga, primer obispo y arzobispo de México: Estudio biográfico y bibliográfico*. Mexico City: Antigua Libreria de Andrade y Morales, 1881.

Gold, Robert L. "The East Florida Indians under Spanish and English Control: 1763–1765." *Florida Historical Quarterly* 44, nos. 1–2 (1965): 105–20.

González, Ondina E. "Consuming Interests: The Response to Abandoned Children in Colonial Havana." In *Raising an Empire*, edited by González and Premo, 137–62.

González, Ondina E., and Bianca Premo. *Raising an Empire: Children in Early Modern Iberia and Colonial Latin America*. Edited by Ondina E. González and Bianca Premo. Albuquerque: University of New Mexico Press, 2007.

González de la Vara, Martín. "Amigos, enemigos o socios? El comercio con los 'indios bárbaros' en Nuevo México, siglo XVIII." *Relaciones* 23, no. 92 (2002): 109–34.

González Navarro, Moisés. "La guerra de castas en Yucatán y la venta de mayas a Cuba," *Historia Mexicana* 18, no. 1 (1968): 11–34.

———. *Raza y tierra: La guerra de castas y el henequén.* Nueva serie 10. Mexico City: Centro de Estudios Históricos, Colegio de México, 1970.

Gott, Richard. "Latin America as a White Settler Society." *Bulletin of Latin American Research* 26, no. 2 (2007): 269–89.

Gould, Jeffrey. *To Die in This Way: Nicaraguan Indians and the Myth of Mestizaje.* Durham, NC: Duke University Press, 2007.

Griffen, William. *Apaches at War and Peace: The Janos Presidio, 1750–1858.* Norman: University of Oklahoma Press, 1998.

Grijalva, Juan de. *The Discovery of New Spain in 1518.* Edited and translated by Henry Wagner. New York: Cortes Society, Kraus Reprint, 1942.

Güémez Pineda, Arturo. "Everyday Forms of Maya Resistance: Cattle Rustling in Northwestern Yucatan." In Brannon and Joseph, *Land, Labor, and Capital in Modern Yucatán*, 18–50.

———. *Mayas: Gobierno y tierras frente a la acometida liberal en Yucatán, 1812–1847.* Merida, Mexico: Universidad Autónoma de Yucatán, 2005.

Gutiérrez Calvache, Divaldo, Racso Fernández Ortega, and José B. González Tendero. "Notas sobre la presencia de figuras antropomorfas de arqueros en el arte rupestre cubano." *Rupestreweb: Arte Rupestre en América Latina*, 2008. http:// rupestreweb.info/arqueros.html.

Hann, John H. *Indians of Central and South Florida, 1513–1763.* Gainesville: University Press of Florida, 2003.

Hann, John H, ed. *Missions to the Calusa.* Gainesville: University Press of Florida, 1991.

Harrington, Mark. *Cuba before Columbus: Indian Notes and Monographs.* Part 1, vol. 1. New York: Museum of the American Indian, Heye Foundation, 1921.

Hers, Marie-Areti, and José Luis Mirafuente, eds. *Nómadas y sedentarios en el Norte de México.* Mexico City: Universidad Nacional Autónoma de México, 2000.

Howard, Rosalyn. *Black Seminoles in the Bahamas.* Gainesville: University Press of Florida, 2002.

Irigoyen, Renán. "El henequén en el época colonial." In *Yucatán: Historia y cultura henequenera; surgimiento, auge, revolución y reforma*, edited by Eric Villanueva Mukul, 1:73–85. Merida, Mexico: Instituto de Cultura de Yucatán, 2010.

Jennings, Evelyn Powell. "'Some Unhappy Indians Trafficked by Force': Race, Status, and Work Discipline in Mid-Nineteenth-Century Cuba." In *Human Bondage in the Cultural Contact Zone*, edited by Raphael Hormann and Gesa Mackenthun, 209–25. Munich: Waxmann, 2010.

———. "State Enslavement in Colonial Havana." In *Slavery without Sugar: Diversity in Caribbean Economy and Society since the 17th Century*, edited by Verene A. Shepherd, 152–82. Gainesville: University Press of Florida, 2002.

Keegan, William F. "West Indian Archaeology. [Part] 3. Ceramic Age." *Journal of Archaeological Research* 8, no. 2 (2000): 135–67.

Klein, Herbert. *African Slavery in Latin America and the Caribbean*. Oxford: Oxford University Press, 1986.

Knight, Franklin. "Migration and Culture: A Case Study of Cuba, 1750–1900." Paper presented at the Historical Society Conference on Migration, Diaspora, Ethnicity, and Nationalism, June 5–7, 2008. Johns Hopkins University, Baltimore.

———. *Slave Society in Cuba during the Nineteenth Century*. Madison: University of Wisconsin Press, 1970.

Kuethe, Allan J. *Cuba, 1753–1815: Crown, Military, and Society*. Knoxville: University of Tennessee Press, 1986.

La Rosa Corzo, Gabino. *Runaway Slave Settlements in Cuba: Resistance and Repression*. Chapel Hill: University of North Carolina Press, 1988.

Landers, Janet. "Africans and Native Americans on the Spanish Florida Frontier." In *Beyond Black and Red: African-Native Relations in Colonial Latin America*, edited by Matthew Restall, 53–80. Albuquerque: University of New Mexico Press, 2005.

Larson, Brooke. *Trials of Nation Making: Liberalism, Race, and Ethnicity in the Andes, 1810–1910*. Cambridge: Cambridge University Press, 2004.

Le Riverend Brusone, Julio. "Relaciones entre Nueva España y Cuba (1518–1820)." *Revista de Historia de América* nos. 37–38 (1954): 45–108.

Lovell, George and William Swezey. "Indian Migration and Community Formation." In *Migration in Colonial Spanish America*, edited by David J. Robinson, 18–40. Cambridge: Cambridge University Press, 1990.

Lugo Romera, Karen Mahé, and Sonia Menéndez Castro. *Barrio de Campeche: Tres estudios arqueológicos*. Havana: Fundación Fernando Ortiz, 2003.

———. "Yucatán en La Habana: Migraciones, encuentros y desarraigos." *La Jiribilla: Revista de Cultura Cubana*, September 2007. http://www.lajiribilla.co.cu/2007/n333_09/333_04.html.

Lutz, Christopher H., and W. George Lovell. "Survivors on the Move: Maya Migration in Time and Space." In *The Maya Diaspora: Guatemalan Roots, New American Lives*, edited by James Loucky and Marilyn M. Moors, 11–34. Philadelphia: Temple University Press, 2000.

Machuca Gallegos, Laura. "Los hacendados y rancheros mayas de Yucatán en al siglo XIX." *Estudios de Cultura Maya* 36 (2010): 173–200.

MacLachlan, Colin M. *Criminal Justice in Eighteenth Century Mexico*. Berkeley: University of California Press, 1974.

MacLeod, Murdo J. *Spanish Central America: A Socioeconomic History, 1520–1720*. Austin: University of Texas Press, 2007.

Marcheco-Teruel, Beatriz, Esteban J. Parra, Evelyn Fuentes-Smith, et al. "Cuba: Exploring the History of Admixture and Genetic Basis of Pigmentation Using Autosomal and Uniparental Markers." *PloS Genet* 10, no. 7 (2014):1–13.

McAlister, Lyle N. *Spain and Portugal in the New World, 1492–1700*. Minneapolis: University of Minnesota Press, 1984.

McEnroe, Sean F. "Sites of Diplomacy, Violence, and Refuge: Topography and Negotiation in the Mountains of New Spain." *The Americas* 69, no. 2 (2012): 179–202.

McNally, Michael J. *Catholicism in South Florida*. Gainesville: University Presses of Florida, 1985.

Menéndez, Carlos R. *Historia del infame y vergonzoso comercio de indios vendidos a los esclavistas de Cuba por los políticos yucatecos desde 1848 hasta 1861, justificación de la revolución de 1847, documentos irrefutables que lo comprueban*. Merida, Mexico: Talleres Gráficos de la Revista de Mérida, 1923.

Milanich, Jerald T. *Laboring in the Fields of the Lord: Spanish Missions and Southeastern Indians*. Washington, DC: Smithsonian Institution Press, 1999.

Moorhead, Max L. *The Apache Frontier: Jacobo Ugarte and Spanish-Indian Relations in Northern New Spain, 1769–1791*. Norman: University of Oklahoma Press, 1968.

———. "Spanish Deportation of Hostile Apaches: The Policy and the Practice." *Arizona and the West* 17, no. 3 (1975): 205–20.

Moreno Fraginals, Manuel. *The Sugarmill: The Socioeconomic Complex of Sugar in Cuba, 1760-1860*. New York: Monthly Review Press, 1976.

Murray, David R. *Odious Commerce: Britain, Spain, and the Abolition of the Cuban Slave Trade*. Cambridge: University of Cambridge Press, 1980.

Novelo, Victoria. "Migraciones mayas y yucatecas a Cuba." *Dimensión Antropológica* 59 (2013): 127–46.

———. *Yucatecos en Cuba: Etnografía de una migración*. Mexico City: Casa Chata, Centro de Investigaciones y Estudios Superiores en Antropología Social, Instituto Cultura de Yucatán 2009.

Ortelli, Sara. "Enemigos internos y súbditos disleales: La infidencia en Nueva Vizcaya en tiempos de los Borbones." *Anuario de Estudios Americanos* 61, no. 2 (2004): 467–89.

———. *Trama de una guerra conveniente: Nueva Vizcaya y la sombra de los apaches, 1748-1790*. Mexico City: Colegio de México, 2009.

Ortiz, Fernando. *Nuevo Catauro de cubanismo*. Havana: Ciencias Sociales, 1985.

Owensby, Brian P. *Empire of Law and Indian Justice in Colonial Mexico*. Stanford, CA: Stanford University Press, 2008.

Pagán-Jiménez, Jaime R. "Early Phytocultural Processes in the Pre-Colonial Antilles." In *Communities in Contact: Essays in Archaeology, Ethnohistory, and Ethnography of the Amerindian Circum-Caribbean*, edited by Corinne L. Hofman and Anne van Duijvenbode, 87–116. Leiden, Netherlands: Sidestone Press, 2010.

Patch, Robert W. "Decolonization, the Agrarian Problem, and the Origins of the Caste War, 1812–1847." In Brannon and Joseph, *Land, Labor, and Capital in Modern Yucatán*, 51–82.

———. *Maya Revolt and Revolution in the Eighteenth Century*. New York: M. E. Sharpe, 2002.

Pérez, Louis A. Jr. *Cuba: Between Reform and Revolution*. 2nd ed. New York: Oxford University Press, 1995.

———. *Cuba and the United States: Ties of Singular Intimacy*. Athens: University of Georgia Press, 1989.

Pérez de la Riva, Francisco. "Cuban Palenques." In *Maroon Societies: Rebel Slave Communities in the Americas*, edited by Richard Price, 50–57. 2nd ed. Baltimore, MD: Johns Hopkins University Press, 1979.

Pezuela. *See* de la Pezuela y Lobo, Jacobo.

Pichardo Moya, Felipe. *Los Indios de Cuba en sus tiempos históricos*. Havana: El Siglo XX, A. Muniz y Hno., 1945.

Pichardo y Tapia, Esteban. *Diccionario provincial casi razonado de vozes y frases cubanas*. Havana: Imprenta el Trabajo, 1875.

Pospisil, Milan. *Indian Remnants from the Oriente Province, Cuba*. Bratislava, Slovakia: Univerzita Komenskeho, 1976.

Price, Richard, ed. *Maroon Societies: Rebel Slave Communities in the Americas*. 2nd ed. Baltimore, MD: Johns Hopkins University Press, 1979.

Radding, Cynthia. *Wandering Peoples: Colonialism, Ethnic Spaces, and Ecological Frontiers in Northwestern Mexico, 1700–1850*. Durham: Duke University Press, 1997.

Reddock, Rhoda, ed. *Ethnic Minorities in Caribbean Society*. St. Augustine, Trinidad: University of the West Indies Press, 1996.

Reed, Nelson. *The Caste War of Yucatan*. Stanford, CA: Stanford University Press, 1964.

Reid-Vazquez, Michele. *The Year of the Lash: Free People of Color in Cuba and the Nineteenth-Century Atlantic World*. Athens: University of Georgia Press, 2011.

Restall, Matthew. "'He Wished It in Vein': Subordination and Resistance among Maya Women in Post-Conquest Yucatan." *Ethnohistory* 42, no. 4 (1995): 577–94.

———. "Interculturation and Indigenous Testament in Colonial Yucatan." In *Dead Giveaways: Indigenous Testaments of Colonial Mesoamerica and the Andes*, edited by Matthew Restall and Susan Kellogg, 141–62. Salt Lake City: University of Utah Press, 1998.

———. *The Maya World: Yucatec Culture and Society, 1550–1850*. Stanford, CA: Stanford University Press, 1997.

Rivaya Martínez, Joaquín, "Diplomacia interétnica en la frontera norte de Nueva España: Un análisis de los tratados hispano-comanches de 1785 y 1786 y sus consecuencias desde una perspectiva etnohistórica." Débats. *Nuevo Mundo Mundos Nuevos*. November 30, 2011. http://nuevomundo.revues.org/62228.

Rivero de la Calle, Manuel. *Las culturas aborígenes de Cuba*. Havana: Editora Universitoria, 1966.

Robinson, David J. Introduction to *Migration in Spanish America*. Edited by David J. Robinson, 1–17. Cambridge: Cambridge University Press, 1990.

Rodríguez, José Baltar. *Los Chinos en Cuba: Apuntes etnográficos*. Havana: Fundación Ortiz, 1997.

Rodríguez Piña, Javier. *Guerra de castas: La venta de los indios mayas a Cuba, 1848–1861*. Mexico City: Consejo Nacional para la Cultura y las Artes, Dirección General de Publicaciones, 1990.

Rodríguez Ramos, Reniel. "Close Encounters of the Caribbean Kind." In *Islands at the Crossroads: Migration, Seafaring, and Interaction in the Caribbean*, edited by L. Antonio Curet and Mark Hauser, 164–92. Tuscaloosa: University of Alabama Press, 2011.

Rodríguez Villamil, Marcos A. *Indios al este de La Habana*. Havana: Ediciones Extramuros, 2002.

Romans, Bernard. *A Concise Natural History of East and West Florida*. New York: Printed for the author, 1775.

Rugeley, Terry. *Rebellion Now and Forever: Maya, Hispanics, and Caste War Violence in Yucatan, 1800–1880*. Stanford, CA: Stanford University Press, 2009.

———. "Rural Political Violence and the Origins of the Caste War." *The Americas*, 53, no. 4 (1997): 479–80.

———. *Yucatan's Maya Peasantry and the Origins of the Caste War*. Austin: University of Texas Press, 1996.

Ruíz Medrano, Ethelia. *Mexico's Indigenous Communities: Their Lands and Histories, 1500–2010*. Boulder: University of Colorado Press, 2010.

Ruíz Medrano, Ethelia, and Susan Kellogg, eds. *Negotiation within Domination: New Spain's Indian Pueblos Confront the Spanish State*. Boulder: University Press of Colorado, 2010.

Rushforth, Brett. *Bonds of Alliance: Indigenous and Atlantic Slaveries in New France*. Chapel Hill: University of North Carolina Press, 2012.

Ruz Menéndez, Rodolfo. "Yucatán y Cuba. Dos pueblos hermanos. *Revista de la Biblioteca Nacional José Martí* 3 (1988): 97–108.

Sánchez Moreno, Francisco Javier. "Los indios bárbaros en la frontera noreste de Nueva España entre 1810 y 1821," *Temas Americanistas,* no. 26 (2011): 20–47.

Santamaría García, Antonio, and Sigfrido Vázquez. "Indios foráneos en Cuba a principios del siglo XIX: Historia de un suceso en el contexto de la movilidad poblacional y la geoestrategia del imperio español." *Colonial Latin American Historical Review* 1 (2013):1–34.

Santiago, Mark. *The Jar of Severed Hands: Spanish Deportation of Apache Prisoners of War, 1770–1810.* Norman: University of Oklahoma Press, 2011.

Santovenia, Emeterio S. and Raul M. Shelton, *Cuba y su historia.* Vol. 1. 2nd ed. Miami: Cuba Corporation, 1966.

Saunt, Claudio. *A New Order of Things: Property, Power, and the Transformation of the Creek Indians, 1733–1816.* Cambridge: Cambridge University Press, 1999.

Scott, James C. *Domination and the Arts of Resistance: Hidden Transcripts.* New Haven, CT: Yale University Press, 1990.

———. *Weapons of the Weak: Everyday Forms of Peasant Resistance.* New Haven, CT: Yale University Press, 1985.

Scott, Rebecca. *Slave Emancipation in Cuba: The Transition to Free Labor, 1860–1899.* Princeton, NJ: Princeton University Press, 1985.

Sheridan Prieto, Cecilia. "Reflexiones en torno: A las identidades nativas en el noreste colonial." *Relaciones. Estudios de Historia y Sociedad* 23, no. 92 (2002): 77–106.

Sosa Rodríguez, Enrique. "Aproximadamente al studio de la presencia yucateca en La Habana a partir de algunos libros en archivos parroquiales." In *Habanero campechano.* By Carlos E. Bojorquez Urzaiz, Enrique Sosa Rodríguez, and Luis Millet Camara, 27–62. Merida, Mexico: Ediciones de la Universidad Autónoma de Yucatán, 1991.

Spicer, Edward H. *Cycles of Conquest: The Impact of Spain, Mexico, and the United States on the Indians of the Southwest, 1533–1960.* Tucson: University of Arizona Press, 2006.

Stack, Margaret. "An Archaeological and Archival Appraisal of 'Spanish Indians' on the West Coast of Florida in the Eighteenth and Nineteenth Centuries." Master's thesis, Department of Applied Anthropology, University of South Florida, 2011.

Sturtevant, William C. "Last of the South Florida Aborigines." In *Tacachale: Essays on the Indians of Florida and Southeastern Georgia during the Historic Period,* edited by Jerald Milanich and Samuel Proctor, 141–62. Gainesville: University Presses of Florida, 1978.

———. "Spanish-Indian Relations in Southeastern North America." *Ethnohistory* 9, no. 1 (1962): 41–94.

Suárez y Navarro, Juan. *Informe de Yucatán.* Mexico City: Publicación Oficial, 1861.

Swanton, John R. *The Indians of the Southeastern United States.* Washington, DC: Smithsonian Institution Press, 1979.

Sweeney, Lean. *La supervivencia de los bandidos: Los mayas icaichés y la política fronteriza del sureste de la península de Yucatán, 1847–1904.* Merida, Mexico: Universidad Nacional Autónoma de México, 2006.

Thompson, Victor D., and John E. Worth. "Dwellers by the Sea: Native American Adaptations Along the Southern Coasts of Eastern North America." *Journal of Archaeological Research* 19, no. 1 (March 2011): 51–111.

Tilley, Virginia. *Seeing Indians: Race, Nation, and Power in El Salvador.* Albuquerque: University of New Mexico Press, 2005.

Torres Lasqueti, Juan. *Colección de datos históricos-geográficos y estadísticas de Puerto del Príncipe y su jurisdicción.* Havana: El Retiro, 1888.

Twinam, Ann. "The Church, the State, and the Abandoned: Expósitos in Late Eighteenth-Century Havana." In *Raising an Empire,* edited by González and Premo, 163–86.

U.S. Government. Papers Relating to Foreign Affairs Accompanying the Annual Message of the President to the First Session Thirty-Ninth Congress. Part 1. Washington, DC: GPO, 1866.

———. Report on the Census of Cuba, 1899. Washington, DC: GPO, 1900.

Valcarcel Rojas, Roberto, Darlene A. Weston, Hayley L. Mickleburgh, Jason E. Laffoon, and Anne van Duijvenbode. "El Chorro de Maíta: A Diverse Approach to a Context of Diversity." In *Communities in Contact: Essays in Archaeology, Ethnohistory, and Ethnography of the Amerindian circum-Caribbean,* edited by Corinne Hofman and Anne van Duijvenbode, 236–42. Leiden, Netherlands: Sidestone Press, 2011.

Valdés, Antonio J. *Historia de la isla de Cuba y en especial de la Habana.* Vol. I. Havana: Oficina de a Cena, 1813.

Valdés Bernal, Sergio. "Las inquietudes lingüísticas de Antonio Bachiller y Morales." Paper presented at the conference "Tres lunes, tres bicentenarios: Antonio Bachiller y Morales, Ramon de Palma y Cirilo Villaverde," May 21, 2012, Aula Magna del Colegio Universitario San Gerónimo de la Habana, Havana.

Valdés Bernal, Sergio, and Yohanis Balga Rodríguez. "El legado indoamericano en el español del Caribe insular hispánico." *Convergencia* 32 (2003): 57–84.

Van Arken, Mark. "The Lingering Death of Indian Tribute in Ecuador." *Hispanic American Historical Review* 61, no. 3 (1981): 429–59.

Velasco Ávila, Cuauhtémoc. "Peace Agreements and War Signals: Negotiations with the Apaches and Comanches in the Interior Provinces of New Spain." In *Negotiation within Domination: New Spain's Indian Pueblos Confront the Spanish State*, edited by Ethelia Ruíz Medrano and Susan Kellogg, 173–204. Boulder: University Press of Colorado, 2010.

Venegas Delgado, Hernan Maximiliano, Carlos Manuel Valdes Davila, and Paloma Amanda Alvarado Cardenas. "Emigración forzosa de los indios de la frontera norte imperial española en América y su envío a la Habana, Cuba, en calidad de esclavos (1763–1821)." Paper presented at the 28th Simpósio Nacional de História, Associação Nacional dos Professores Universitários de História (ANPUH), Natal, Brazil, July 22–26, 2013.

Victoria Ojeda, Jorge. "Los indígenas mayas del servicio doméstico en Cuba, 1847–1853." *Chacmool: Cuadernos de Trabajo Cubano-Mexicanos* 1 (2003): 335–65.

Villalobos González, Martha Herminia. *El bosque sitiado: Asaltos armados, concesiones forestales y estrategias de resistencia durante la guerra de castas.* Mexico City: Miguel Angel Porrua, 2006.

Villanueva Mukul, Eric, ed. *Yucatán: Historia y cultura henequenera; surgimiento, auge, revolución y reforma.* 2 vols. Merida, Mexico: Instituto de Cultura de Yucatán, 2010.

Vivó, Buenaventura. *Las memorias de D. Buenaventura Vivó y la venta de indios yucatecos en Cuba.* Edited by Carlos Menéndez. Merida, Mexico: Talleres de la Compañia Tipográfica Yucateca, 1932.

Weber, David J. *Bárbaros: Spaniards and Their Savages in the Age of Enlightenment.* New Haven, CT: Yale University Press, 2005.

Wells, Allen. "Forgotten Chapters of Yucatan's Past: Nineteenth-Century Politics in Historiographical Perspective." *Mexican Studies/Estudios Mexicanos* 12, no. 2 (1996): 205–6.

———. "From Hacienda to Plantation: The Transformation of Santo Domingo Xcuyum." In Brannon and Joseph, *Land, Labor, and Capital in Modern Yucatán*, 112–42.

White, Richard. *The Middle Ground: Indians, Empires, and Republics in the Great Lakes Region, 1650–1815.* Cambridge: Cambridge University Press, 1999.

Wilson, Samuel, Harry B. Iceland, and Thomas R. Hester. "Preceramic Connections between Yucatan and the Caribbean." *Latin American Antiquity* 9, no. 4 (1998): 342–52.

Worth, John E. "A History of Southeastern Indians in Cuba, 1513–1823." Paper presented at the 61st Annual Meeting of the Southeastern Archaeological Conference, St. Louis, MO, October 22, 2004.

———. "Pineland during the Spanish Period." In *The Archaeology of Pineland: A Coastal Southwest Florida Village Complex, AD 50–1700*, edited by Karen J.

Walker and William H. Marquardt, 767–92. Monograph No. 4. Gainesville, FL: Institute of Archaeology and Paleoenvironmental Studies, 2013.

———. "Timucua and the Colonial System in Florida: The Rebellion of 1656." Paper presented in the symposium "New Perspective on the Spanish Colonial Experience" at the 25th Conference of the Society for Historical Archaeology, Kingston, Jamaica, January 9, 1992.

Wright, I. A. *The Early History of Cuba: 1492–1586*. New York: Macmillan, 1916.

Wright, J. Leitch Jr. *Creeks and Seminoles: Destruction and Regeneration of the Muscogulge People*. Lincoln: University of Nebraska Press, 1986.

Wright, Winthrop R. *Café con leche: Race, Class, and National Image in Venezuela*. Austin: University of Texas Press, 1990.

Yannakakis, Yanna. *The Art of Being In-Between: Native Intermediaries, Indian Identity, and Local Rule in Colonial Oaxaca*. Durham, NC: Duke University Press, 2008.

Yaremko, Jason M. "Colonial Wars and Indigenous Geopolitics: Aboriginal Agency, the Cuba-Florida-Mexico Nexus, and the Other Diaspora." *Canadian Journal of Latin American and Caribbean Studies* 35, no. 70 (2011): 165–95.

———. "De Campeche a la Guerra de Castas: La presencia maya en Cuba, siglos XVI al XIX." *Chacmool: Cuadernos de Trabajo Cubano-Mexicanos* 6 (2010): 85–114.

———. "'Obvious Indian'—Missionaries, Anthropologists, and the 'Wild Indians' of Cuba: Representations of the Amerindian Presence in Cuba." *Ethnohistory* 56, no. 3 (2009): 449–77.

———. "'Frontier Indians': 'Indios Mansos,' 'Indios Bravos,' and the Layers of Indigenous Existence in the Caribbean Borderlands." In *Borderlands in World History, 1700–1914*. Edited by Paul Readman, Cynthia Radding, and Chad Bryant, 217–36. London: Palgrave Macmillan, 2014.

Yun, Lisa. *The Coolie Speaks: Chinese Indentured Laborers and African Slaves in Cuba*. Philadelphia: Temple University Press, 2008.

Zubillaga, Félix, ed. *Monumenta antiquae Floridae, 1566–1572*. Rome: Monumenta Historica Societatus Iesu, 1946.

INDEX

JASON YAREMKO is professor with the Department of History and Faculty of Education at the University of Winnipeg. His teaching and research interests focus on comparative colonization, borderlands, indigenous, and cultural history in the Americas. His current research interests focus on indigenous diaspora, land claims, transculturation, identity, extinction tropes and indigenous survivance, and indigenous and non-indigenous representations of indigenous identity. He is author of a number of publications on colonization and indigenous peoples in North America, Cuba, and the Circum-Caribbean..

CPSIA information can be obtained
at www.ICGtesting.com
Printed in the USA
JSHW040206260822
29667JS00001B/42